Christian–Jewish Relations, 1000–1300

The Medieval World

Series editor: Julia Smith, The University of Glasgow

Christian–Jewish Relations, 1000–1300

Jews in the service of medieval Christendom

Anna Sapir Abulafia

Routledge
Taylor & Francis Group

LONDON AND NEW YORK

First published 2011 by Pearson Education Limited

Published 2014 by Routledge
2 Park Square, Milton Park, Abingdon, Oxon OX14 4RN
711 Third Avenue, New York, NY 10017, USA

Routledge is an imprint of the Taylor & Francis Group, an informa business

Copyright © 2011, Taylor & Francis.

The right of Anna Sapir Abulafia to be identified as author
of this work has been asserted by her in accordance
with the Copyright, Designs and Patents Act 1988.

ISBN 13: 978-0-582-82296-2 (pbk)

British Library Cataloguing in Publication Data
A CIP catalogue record for this book can be obtained from the British Library

Library of Congress Cataloging in Publication Data
Sapir Abulafia, Anna.
   Christian–Jewish relations, 1000–1300 : Jews in the service of Medieval
Christendom / Anna Sapir Abulafia. – 1st ed.
      p. cm. – (Medieval world series list)
   Includes index.
   ISBN 978-0-582-82296-2 (pbk.)
   1. Judaism–Relations–Christianity.   2. Christianity and other religions–Judaism.
3. Christianity and antisemitism–History.   4. Jews–History–70-1789.   5. Judaism
(Christian theology)–History of doctrines–Middle Ages, 600–1500.   6. Europe–
Church history–600–1500.   I. Title.
   BM535.S244 2011
   261.2′60940902–dc22

                                                                              2010032842

Set by 35 in 10/14 pt Galliard

TO BIANCA AND ROSA

'Many daughters have done virtuously,
but you excel them all' (cf. Proverbs 31:29)

Contents

Series editor's preface

Relations between Jews and Christians are one of the most fraught issues in European history. Yet conventional histories of medieval Christendom have rarely paid more than superficial, passing attention to the Jews who lived amongst the Christians. By the same token, Jewish history has conventionally been a separate one, whose divergent priorities and self-contained debates reflect a separate body of Hebrew source material. As Dr Anna Sapir Abulafia demonstrates in this remarkable book, the stories of Jews and Christians in the Middle Ages were inextricably intertwined. Using her mastery of both Latin and Hebrew sources, she tells us a new story in which both dimensions, Christian and Jewish, are enriched by, explained by, and complicated by the other. Her even-handed stance epitomises a recent strand in the study of Jewish history, one ready to confront issues of acculturation and interaction as well as of segregation and hostility, and her book represents a major new addition to Longman's *Medieval World* series.

As Abulafia shows, relations between Christians and Jews in the centuries from 1000 to 1300 did not fall into any straightforward or predictable pattern. Instead, they oscillated between protection and exploitation, co-operation and hostility, knowledge and prejudice. As Abulafia repeatedly demonstrates, 'ambiguity' is their most notable feature. This ambiguity reflects a dominant Christian worldview which Jews, as a minority, had to negotiate, even though they did not share or accept it: the notion that the Jews' place in the Christian scheme of things was one of service to Christians. In her skilled analysis 'service' has two strands of meaning. One is theological, reflecting the relationship of Hebrew scripture to Christian revelation and of 'unbelievers' to 'believers'. The other is political, reflecting the delicate balance between lordly protection and fiscal exploitation which framed the existence of many Jewish communities in the

Middle Ages. Here, the intimate link between serving and pre-serving – between subordination and sustaining – lies at the heart of that ambiguity.

Abulafia prefaces her account with a succinct explanation of the late antique patristic legacy of ideas about the place of Jews in Christian society and thought. There follows a country-by-country study of the central three centuries of the Middle Ages, in which she makes clear that the fate of each Jewish community was integrally bound up with specific, local configurations of power among the Christians that varied widely across place and time. Kings, counts, bishops, popes and towns squabbled, fought, or supported one another – and Jewish communities were often caught in the interstices. The third part of the book explores how each religion responded to the other in poetry, prayer, polemic, treatise or tract. Many of those images were violent ones, indeed sometimes vituperative, and Abulafia's humane and dispassionate analysis of this deeply emotive subject helps readers distinguish cruel rhetoric from messy reality. Whilst not shunning the brutality and slaughter which undoubtedly marked some episodes of Jewish–Christian relations, she nevertheless makes us realise that words can be as much an instrument of violence as weapons. All those interested in the history of Europe's medieval past have much to learn from her, and I warmly welcome this newest addition to Longman's *Medieval World*.

Julia M.H. Smith

Preface

This book attempts to make sense of the myriad of ambiguities and paradoxes underlying Christian–Jewish relations by arguing that Jewish service to Christendom is the key to gaining a better understanding of the changing political, socio-economic, cultural and religious positions of Jews in the different areas of Latin Christendom between 1000 and 1300. The fact that Jews in practice were meant to serve their Christian lords through paying taxes was intrinsically bound up with the concept that Jews were thought to perform a theoretical service to Christendom, by preserving the prophecies concerning Christ in the Hebrew Bible and by reminding Christians of the penalties of rejecting Christ through their dispersion. The nature of that service ranged from the positive to the negative at different times in different places. Our twenty-first-century ideals of religious tolerance must not blind us to the fact that it was, in fact, remarkable that Jews were allowed to continue to exist at all in medieval Christendom. Pagans were steadily rooted out; heretics did not have the right to practise their 'deviant' beliefs. The position of Muslims in Southern Europe was connected to wider issues governing centuries of confrontation between Christianity and Islam in the Latin Mediterranean and the Middle East.

Part 1 examines the place assigned to Jews in Christian society by exploring the antecedents of Jewish service in the ideas of Augustine and Gregory the Great and in Roman and canon law. References will be made to heretics and Muslims throughout the book, because on a practical level especially Muslims were treated in similar ways to Jews; but limitation of space precluded extensive discussion of either group. Having said that, relations between Christians and Jews were far more ambiguous and tortured than Christian relations with heretics and Muslims. Judaism could not be excised from the Christian agenda because of the special role Jews had been assigned in Christian salvational history. Not only were Jews meant to remind Christians of events in the past; they were supposed to embody the expectation of their conversion in the future, heralding the end of time. At the same time, the figure of the crucified Messiah loomed ever menacingly in the background. The ever-present challenge to princes was how to cope with these theoretical ambiguities in relationship to the practical role real living Jews played in their different polities. As far as Jews were concerned, they constantly had to negotiate their position within the complex political and socio-economic nexus of competing authorities in the places they lived.

The advantage of using Jewish service as the key to medieval Christian–Jewish relations is that it encourages a balanced assessment of the several positions Jews could play in their host communities and guards against the pitfalls of overemphasising the positive or the negative aspects of their interactions with Christians. It also takes the interface between Jewish history and the history of Latin Christendom for granted. This is important. Too many histories of Latin Christendom treat the Jews as an optional extra, if at all, rather than an integral part of the medieval Christian experience. Too many histories of the Jews engage all too superficially with the intricacies of medieval Christian Europe. Part 2 examines the changing nature of Jewish service by exploring the political and socio-economic realities of Jewish service in Germany, France, England and the lands of the Latin Mediterranean. Discussion of Jewish cultural activities gives a sense of what Jews achieved for themselves in these areas; for however aware Jews were of the practical realities of their role in the lands they inhabited in the service of their lords, they did not, of course, subscribe to the role assigned to them in Christian salvational history. Using the lens of Jewish service in all of its different manifestations ensures that theological theories governing Christian–Jewish relations are constantly juxtaposed with pragmatic actions. The concept of Jewish service also helps explain why Jewish life could be so very different from region to region. Limitations of space made it necessary to concentrate on Latin Christendom. Part 3 concentrates on important religious and cultural developments within Latin Christendom between 1000 and 1300 in order to gain greater understanding of the ambiguities of Jewish service. The impact of the crusades on Christian–Jewish relations is analysed; the meanings of the anti-Jewish libels, which developed from the twelfth century, are scrutinised in order to uncover the effects they had on Christian perceptions of Jews. Encounters between Jews and Christians are explored through an examination of narrative sources, biblical exegesis and liturgy, polemics, theological and legal tracts. It is hoped that a dispassionate analysis of Christian and Jewish sources will yield a real sense of what medieval Jews and Christians thought about each other and, even more crucially, how those thoughts were put into practice. For only an honest approach to the past can hope to contribute anything to the much-needed *rapprochement* between different faiths and cultures in the modern world.

I owe many debts to friends and colleagues for their support while I was writing this book. My colleagues at Lucy Cavendish College gave me their fellowship and encouragement. My friend Liba Taub gave me the right advice at exactly the right time on how to carve out writing time from a frantic schedule. Feedback from audiences at lectures and conferences in Cambridge, London, New York, Notre Dame, IN, New Haven, Jerusalem and Aalborg to papers in which I explored material for this book assisted me in developing my thinking on Jewish service. Haym Soloveitchik was particularly generous in helping me gain more insight in the Jewish involvement in the wine trade. Lively discussions with the undergraduates following the course on 'The Jewish Presence in Medieval Society' and stimulating conversations with my PhD and MPhil students over many years have taught me a very great deal. I am particularly grateful to Hannah Meyer for her comments on my chapter on England. Finally, I want to thank the fellow historian of the Abulafia household, my husband David, for his support and encouragement throughout this project. He joined me in setting the first Part II course on Jewish history in the History Faculty in Cambridge. He was my expert travel agent and congenial travel companion in Germany and Spain where I gained so many insights for the book. He was also the first to read the finished manuscript and provide me with useful feedback. I dedicate the book to our two daughters, Bianca and Rosa, from whose love and wisdom I have gained so very much. To paraphrase the words of Proverbs: 'Many daughters have done virtuously, but you excel them all.'

Anna Sapir Abulafia
Lucy Cavendish College
April 2009

Publisher's acknowledgements

We are grateful to the following for permission to reproduce copyright material:

Text

Epigraph Part 2 Asher ben Yehiel, commentary on *Baba Bathra* 1.29 in the Babylonian Talmud. Reprinted by permission of the publisher from *Hispano-Jewish Culture in Transition: The Career and Controversies of Ramah* by Bernard Septimus, p. 13, Cambridge, Mass.: Harvard University Press, Copyright © 1982 by the President and Fellows of Harvard College; Epigraph Part 3 Hostiensis, *Apparatus, ad* 5.6.9, adapted from John A. Watt, 'Jews and Christians in the Gregorian Decretals' in Diana Wood (ed.), *Christianity and Judaism* Studies in Church History, 29 (Oxford, 1992), 105, reprinted with permission from The Ecclesiastical History Society.

In some instances we have been unable to trace the owners of copyright material, and we would appreciate any information that would enable us to do so.

Abbreviations

CCCM	Corpus Christianorum Continuatio Mediaevalis
CCSL	Corpus Christianorum Series Latina
Cluse	Christoph Cluse (ed.), *The Jews of Europe in the Middle Ages (Tenth to Fifteenth Centuries). Proceedings of the International Symposium Held at Speyer, 20–25 October 2002*, Turnhout, 2004.
CSJMA	Robert Chazan, *Church, State and Jew in the Middle Ages*, New York, 1980.
EJ	Robert Chazan, *European Jewry and the First Crusade*, Berkeley, CA, 1987.
Grayzel I	Solomon Grayzel, *The Church and the Jews in the XIIIth Century. A Study of Their Relations During the Years 1198–1254, Based on the Papal Letters and the Conciliar Decrees of the Period*, rev. edn, New York, 1966.
Grayzel II	Solomon Grayzel, *The Church and the Jews in the XIIIth Century. Volume 2: 1254–1314*, ed. Kenneth R. Stow, Detroit, MI, 1989.
HB	*Hebräische Berichte über die Judenverfolgungen während des Ersten Kreuzzugs*, ed. Eva Haverkamp. Monumenta Germaniae Historica, Hebräische Texte aus dem Mittelalterlichen Deutschland, 1, Hanover, 2005.
HC	*The Jews and the Crusaders. The Hebrew Chronicles of the First and Second Crusades*, ed. and trans. S. Eidelberg, Madison, WI, 1977.
JQR	*Jewish Quarterly Review*
JLSEMA	Amnon Linder, *The Jews in the Legal Sources of the Early Middle Ages*, Detroit, MI, 1997.
JMH	*Journal of Medieval History*

JRIL	Amnon Linder, *The Jews in Roman Imperial Legislation*, Detroit, MI, 1987.
MGH	Monumenta Germaniae Historica
PL	J.P. Migne, *Patrologiae Cursus Completus Series Latina*
RS	Rolls Series
Schreckenberg	Heinz Schreckenberg, *Die christlichen Adversus-Judaeos-Texte und ihr literarisches und historisches Umfeld (1.-11.Jh)*, 4th rev. edn, Frankfurt am Main, 1999.
Simonsohn	Shlomo Simonsohn, *The Apostolic See and the Jews: Documents, 492–1404*. Pontifical Institute of Mediaeval Studies: Studies and Texts, 94, Toronto, 1988.

Maps

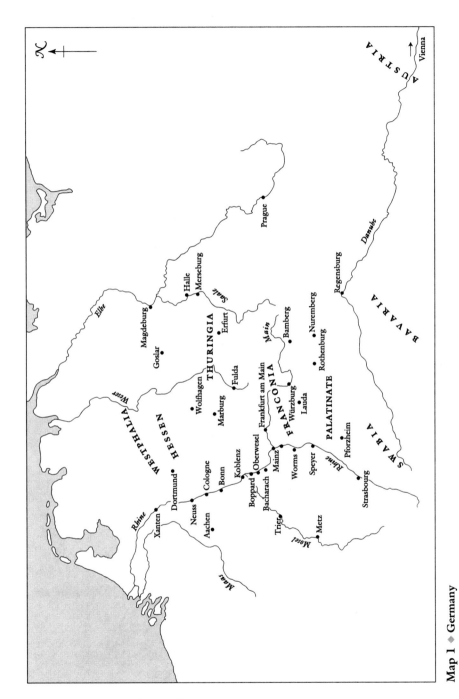

Map 1 ◆ **Germany**

Source: Adapted from I. S. Robinson, *Henry IV of Germany, 1056–1106* (Cambridge, 1999), viii.

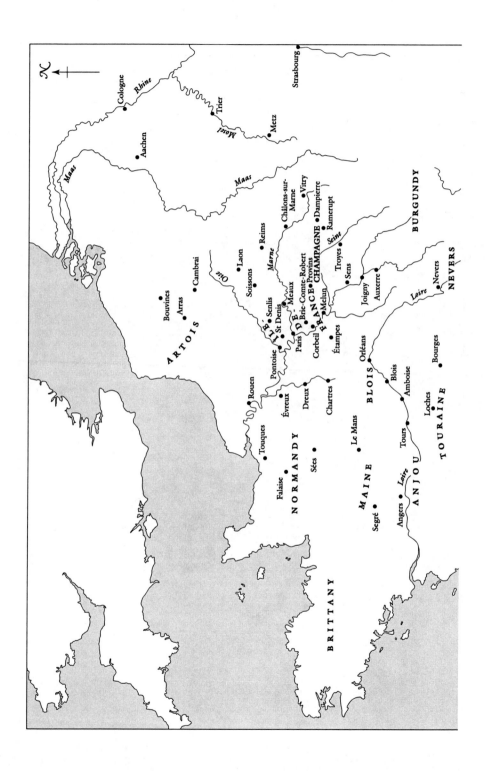

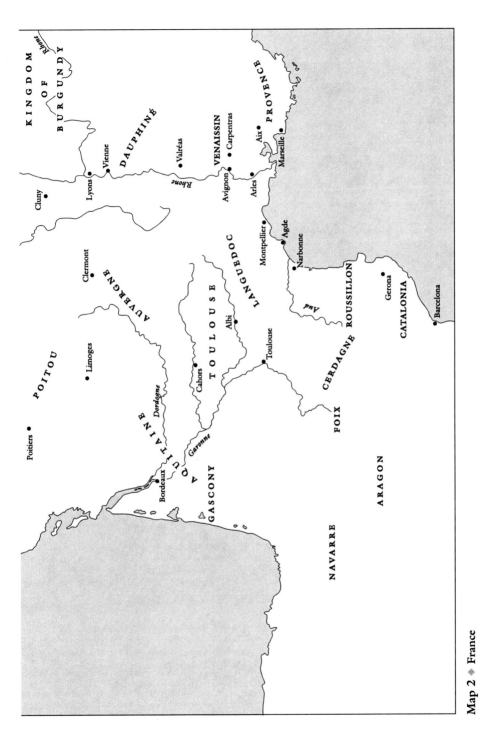

Map 2 ◆ France

Source: Adapted from Grosser Historischer Weltatlas, herausgegeben vom Bayerischen Schulbuch-Verlag, II. Teil, Mittelalter, Redaktion Josef Engel (Munchen, 1970), 77.

Map 3 ◆ **England**
Source: Adapted from Robin R. Mundill, *England: The Island's Jews and Their Economic Pursuits*, in Cluse, 229.

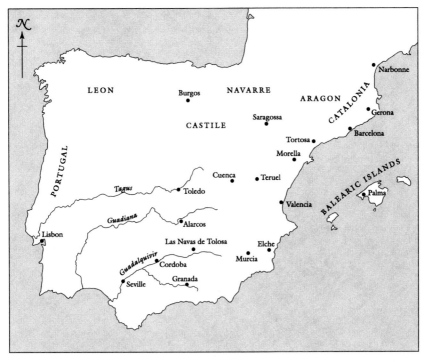

Map 4 ◆ Iberia

Source: Adapted from Lucy K. Pick, *Conflict and Coexistence: Archbishop Rodrigo and the Muslims and Jews of Medieval Spain* (Ann Arbor, MI, 2004), 31.

Map 5 ◆ **Italy and Sicily**
Source: Adapted from David Abulafia, *The Western Mediterranean Kingdoms, 1200–1500: The Struggle for Dominion* (London, 1997), 284.

part 1

The antecedents of Jewish service

'*Hear in what the Jews serve us, and not without cause.*'
(Augustine, *Enarrationes in Psalmos* 40.14,
ed. Eligius Dekkers and Iohannes Fraipont, CCSL 38, 459)

c h a p t e r   1

Augustine and Roman law

Our story starts in the tumultuous events of the first century of the Common Era in the land of Israel which was ruled by the Romans as the province of Judaea. Among the many preachers of the period Jesus gathered a loyal following, which continued to grow after his death around 29 CE. This was the birth of Christianity. In the meantime, Jewish disaffection with Roman rule led to war in 66 CE. Roman victory was coupled with the destruction of the Jewish Temple in 70 CE. The absence of the Temple after that meant that gradually Jews had to adapt their day-to-day religious practices to make up for the fact that they, at least for the time being, could not look to Temple rituals to fulfil their religious obligations. To be sure, many Jews were not working from scratch in this respect. Even while the Temple existed, there were large Jewish communities in places such as Babylon and Alexandria, which had developed religious customs alongside the cultic practices taking place in Jerusalem. Be that as it may, it is fair to say that in the early centuries of the Common Era Jews, as well as Christians, were coming to terms with what one might, very loosely, call biblical Judaism according to their very different perceptions of the meaning of the Hebrew Bible and their new circumstances. Following Israel Yuval, it might well be apposite to describe Jews and Christians engaged in these endeavours at that time as two jealous siblings trying to steal each other's limelight. The oft-cited biblical imagery of the rivalry between Jacob and Esau would support this. For Jews, Esau represented enemy domination, which from the fourth century included Christian Roman rule; they and only they were Jacob. For Christians, Jews had ceased to be Jacob when they refused to recognise Jesus Christ. They were now Esau, serving his younger brother Jacob, i.e. Christians. Yuval has argued that from this very early period rabbinic thought developed within the framework of a continuous engagement with developing Christianity. For in these early centuries of the Common Era neither Jews nor early Christians lived in hermetically closed communities. They mingled with their Gentile neighbours; many might not have been sure whether they were Jews, Jewish Christians, Christian Jews or Christians. People of different ethnic backgrounds married and it was not always clear to which group their offspring belonged. Rabbinic material of this period might have produced only a few direct and overt polemical references to Christianity, but careful examination of many late antique Jewish customs and legends would seem to indicate a lively response to Christian ideas.[1] But for all of this sibling-type rivalry, Christian theologians used biblical Judaism, rather than nascent rabbinic Judaism, as their point of reference. It was from the Hebrew Bible that they consistently drew proof texts to prove the validity of Christian teachings. In this sense Judaism played more the role of a mother than a sister. Indeed, a major aspect of Christian–Jewish relations in the twelfth and thirteenth centuries was the complicated response of Christians when they realised just how much post-biblical Jewish material had been produced and how important it was to contemporary Jewish life and thought. For centuries Christian theologians had been so intent on proving that Christianity had superseded Judaism that they had assumed Judaism had ceased to develop after 70 CE. They were strengthened in this view by the Augustinian concept of Jewish witness. And this takes us to the leading theologian to provide Christianity with definitive concepts concerning the relationship between Christianity and Judaism.

Augustine

Augustine (354–430) was, of course, preoccupied with much more than just Christian–Jewish relations. The vicissitudes of Rome sustaining attacks by the Visigoths made it necessary for him to think hard about the *raison d'être* of a Christian Roman empire. To make matters worse, the Visigoths were Arian heretics, who did not accept the teachings of the Church about the relationship between the three persons of the Trinity. Did the lack of safety of Christian Rome cast doubt on the truth of Christianity and the power of its God, as its pagan detractors claimed? Should Christians like himself be involved in the trappings of temporal society? What did Christian participation in politics entail, what was its purpose and how could Christian integrity be preserved? The responses that Augustine gave to these questions in *The City of God*, which he wrote between 413 and 426, centred on his conception that the whole of mankind was divided into two peoples, the City of God and the earthly City. These cities existed metaphorically in the sense that human beings were destined for one or the other city as they co-existed with each other in the polities where they lived while they were alive. Those who performed all their civic, domestic and religious functions infused with love for God over and above anything else at all times and in all circumstance were pilgrims on their way to the City of God. Those who put anything at all before their love of God were doomed to the earthly City which set what was terrestrial above what was heavenly. Because, according to Augustine, all mankind had been mired in sin ever since the introduction of Original Sin through the fall of Adam, most humans did not truly love God and were members of the earthly City. The main function of polities on earth was to control the wickedness of the majority, who were members of the earthly City, and to institute at least a semblance of order, which would be of benefit to those few who did love God and were en route to the heavenly City. As part of the exercise of curbing evil, polities should help the Church in its fight against heresy. The changing fortunes of political structures mattered little; what mattered was love for God by the elect. But even the elect needed to be tested and purified as they lived their lives surrounded by misery and depravity. They were few in number; within the organisation of the Church, too, many Christians did not really love God and were thus destined for damnation in the earthly City. It was within the context of ideas like these that Augustine thought about the meaning of the Hebrew Bible and the fact that Jews continued to exist as Jews. What could God's plan be?[2]

Augustine referred to Jews and Judaism repeatedly throughout his vast oeuvre which included a *Treatise against the Jews*, which he composed in the final year of his life. His singular contribution to Christian–Jewish relations was the way he assigned to Jews the role of *Testimonium veritatis*, i.e. of being the witnesses to the truth of Christianity. Augustine worked out most of the elements of his witness theory during the period that he was Bishop of Hippo, in north Africa (396–430). Augustine explained the continuing existence of Jews in terms of the service Jews performed to Christians by carrying the books of the Hebrew Bible which, in his view, contained the prophecies concerning Jesus Christ. In so doing, they counteracted pagan claims that Christians had forged the Old Testament in order to establish the validity of their religion. Jews carried their law as the mark of Cain; as Cain they should not be killed. As Augustine said in his commentary on Psalm 40(1):

> 'The elder will serve the younger' has now been fulfilled, brothers, the Jews serve us now, they are, as it were, our book carriers, they carry the books for us as we study. Hear in what the Jews serve us, and not without cause. Cain, that elder brother, who killed the younger brother, received a sign so that he would not be killed, in the same way that people should survive. They have the prophets and the law in which law and in which prophets Christ has been prophesied. When we argue with the pagans and we show that what before was predicted about the name of Christ, the head and body of Christ is now fulfilled in the Church of Christ, we bring out the books of the Jews so that they do not think that we made up those prophecies and wrote up the things which happened as if they were in the future. To be sure, the Jews are our enemies, [and so] by the writings of the enemy the adversary is beaten.[3]

Augustine continued this theme in his exegesis of verse 12 of Psalm 58(9), which in the Vulgate reads as 'God shall let me see over my enemies: slay them not, lest at any time my people forget. Scatter them by thy power; and bring them down, O Lord, my protector.' The version of the Bible Augustine was using seems to have rendered the passage as '. . . slay them not, lest at any time they forget your law . . .'.[4] He wrote:

> What of the Jews 'slay them not, lest they forget your law'? Do not kill those enemies of mine, who killed me. Let the Jewish people survive: certainly they were defeated by the Romans, certainly their city was destroyed and they were not admitted to their city, and yet there are Jews. For all those provinces were subjected to the Romans. Who knows the peoples who have made up the Roman Empire, when all were made Romans and are called Romans? But the Jews survive with a sign and they have not been conquered in such a way that they were absorbed by the conquerors. It is

not without cause that they are like Cain, in whom God placed a sign
when he had killed his brother, so that no one would kill him. This is the
sign which the Jews have: everywhere they take with them the remnants of
their law; they are circumcised, they observe the Sabbath, keep Passover,
and eat unleavened bread. Therefore there are Jews, they have not been
killed, they are necessary for the peoples who believe. Why? . . . He shows his
mercy by way of the engrafted olive tree from which branches have been
pruned through pride. Behold, the place where those who were proud lie
rejected, behold the place where you, who lay rejected, have been engrafted;
and do not be proud so that you do not merit to be cut off yourself
(cf. Romans 11: 17ff). . . . 'Scatter them by your power'. This has already
happened: the Jews are dispersed among all the peoples, as witnesses of
their iniquity and of our truth. For they have the writings in which
Christ was prophesied and we have Christ.[5]

In *The City of God*, Augustine explained that Psalm 58(9) says 'disperse'
them because the Church needs the Jews to witness to its truth everywhere
and not just in Judaea. The dispersion of the Jews and their subjugation
to others was the consequence of their repudiation of Christ and his
Crucifixion. In his earlier treatise against the Manichean dualist heretic
Faustus he had posited that Jewish survival showed believers the just
punishment of those who killed Christ.[6]

Augustine's idea of Jewish witness was premised on his view that the
Hebrew Bible or Old Testament prefigured the New. Even Jewish blindness
to the truth of Christ's teachings accorded with what was prophesied in
the Hebrew Bible. His views on Jews were thus, apart from anything else,
an integral part of his continuing fight against Manicheans like Faustus who
rejected the validity of the Old Testament. The importance of revisiting the
prophecies concerning Christ in the Old Testament is demonstrated by
Augustine's feeling that Christians should continue to engage in polemics
against Jews, even if their words fell on deaf ears. Their conversion at
the end of time as prophesied by St Paul remained a given.[7] To sum up,
Augustine's witness theory postulated that there was space, even a need for
Jews in Christian society. But that need was predicated on the concept of
Jewish service which transformed Jews into a Christian mnemonic device
and unwitting witnesses for Christianity. In this way of thinking even
Jewish lack of belief served to corroborate Christianity. Jews did not exist in

their own right as active agents of their own Jewish destiny. They existed in a kind of limbo, frozen in their role as passive book carriers, reminding Christians of what had gone by, while at the same time held on hold in the expectation of their eventual conversion in the future. Or to use Augustine's own words: the Jews 'have been turned into milestones for them: they have shown something to travellers on their way but they themselves have remained senseless and unmoving'.[8]

The idea that Jews, however wrong-minded Christians thought them to be, should be safeguarded was, of course, embedded in Paul's prophecy that at the end of time the remnant of the Jews would convert to Christ. It goes without saying that this conversion, which would marshal in the end, could not happen if there were no 'professing' Jews left. Paul's conviction that eventually Jews would become Christians was based on his idea that although Jews were wrong not to have recognised Christ as their Messiah, they had not altogether lost God's love. They had been justly cast aside for the moment, but Paul admonished Gentile followers of Christ not to gloat over the misfortune of the Jews. Jewish disbelief was part of God's plan because it served to bring in the non-Jews to Christ. Using the image of a mature cultivated olive tree in his *Letter to the Romans*, which he wrote around the middle of the first century, Paul described how the non-believing Jewish branches of the tree had been pruned and the pagan believing branches had been grafted in their place. But the root of the tree retained its Jewish nature and the hope was nurtured for an eventual return of the pruned branches to the root that bore them (Romans 11). We have seen an example of how Augustine used Pauline imagery in his ideas of Jewish survival and his assessment of the necessary nature of Jewish service to Christianity.

Rome and the destruction of the Temple

But Augustine was also a Roman in touch with Roman ideas about Jews and experiencing Roman laws concerning the Jews. For all its misgivings about Jewish customs such as observing the Sabbath and refraining from the consumption of pork and for all its revulsion at the practice of circumcision, pagan Rome had recognised Judaism as a licit religion. This entailed Jews being allowed to live their lives according to their own traditions. Crucially this meant that, as far as their role in Roman society was concerned,

Jews were exempt from activities which would offend their monotheistic principles. So, although they were required to pray for the safety of the emperor, they were not required to partake in the imperial cult. A well-established Jewish community existed in Rome by the middle of the first century BCE, and, notwithstanding occasional expulsions, Jews were tolerated there as elsewhere as one of the many different types of peoples making up the empire. The regard Jews had for the Temple in Jerusalem and the importance the grandeur of its sacrificial cult had for Jewish identity was well understood by the Romans in whose religious lives magnificent temple buildings and sacrifices played such a prominent role.[9]

Following Martin Goodman we can appreciate the far-reaching consequences of what occurred in 70 CE for Roman–Jewish relations. In many ways it was not so much the destruction of the Sanctuary that rankled, it was the fact that the Romans persisted in their refusal to countenance its rebuilding. After all, reconstruction of the Second Temple was already under way in 535 BCE after the First Temple was destroyed by Nebuchadnezzar in 586 BCE. First-century Jews, smarting under the blow of the vicious repression of the Jewish revolt in 70 CE, would have expected the Romans to allow them, like any other of the peoples of the empire, to regain a sacrificial focal point after a suitable lapse of time. But this was not to be. What had started as a rebellion against the incompetence of the Roman governor of Judaea in 66 had been allowed to escalate into a brutal war. It took Rome four years to overcome the revolt and their retribution was ferocious. Those who were taken captive and who were not able-bodied were brutally murdered; strong men were shipped off to Egypt to quarry stone and labour in the mines or consigned to amuse spectators by their deaths in provincial arenas; youngsters were sold off as slaves. It is not for nothing that the surviving insurrectionists in the stronghold of Masada chose to martyr themselves and their families in 74 rather than surrender themselves into Roman hands. For all of Rome's punitive actions against defeated Judaea, it seems, however, that the burning down of the Temple had not been planned as part of Judaea's punishment for her revolt. Notwithstanding reports to the contrary, Josephus (37 to after 100), the contemporary Jewish historian whose extensive histories provide us with so much of our knowledge of the period, was probably correct when he wrote that Titus had not intended for the Sanctuary to be destroyed. But once it had happened it was important for Titus to make it seem as if this had been his intention all along. For it would not serve his reputation to imply that he had lost control of his forces. Titus had to present his victory in the most positive light. The political need for him to bring the Jewish War to a successful conclusion as quickly as possible after his father Vespasian became emperor in 69 had caused many Roman casualties. Haste rather than caution had governed Titus in his running of the campaign. This, according to Goodman, is why in the aftermath of the war Jews were depicted so negatively as the enemies of Rome and why the destruction of the Temple featured so prominently in the celebration of the victory of Titus and Vespasian. Their triumph was hailed as a victory over Judaea and Judaism: the golden seven-branched candelabrum of the Temple and other Temple treasures were carried in their celebratory procession together with a Torah scroll. The commemorative arch of Titus in Rome sported symbols of the Temple. This kind of imagery was hardly conducive to hopes of reconstructing the Sanctuary. This situation was exacerbated by the fact that Jews throughout the empire were thenceforth required to pay an annual tax of two *denarii* to rebuild, not their own sanctuary, but the temple of Jupiter on the Capitoline Hill in Rome, which had recently burnt down. This is the money they had been accustomed to contribute to the upkeep of the Temple. Many of the coins with which it was paid would have been struck with the legend *JUDAEA CAPTA*. Insult had been added to injury.

It would seem that the politics of Rome, rather than any deep-rooted ideology, perpetuated this situation. The Flavians, Vespasian and his sons Titus and Domitian, who ruled one after the other from 70 to 96, looked to the suppression of the Jewish revolt as proof of their family's military acumen. After a brief let-up under Nerva (r. 96–8), Emperor Trajan (r. 98–117) reinforced the Flavian interpretation of the Jewish War. His father had worked his way up the social ladder through his military exploits in the Jewish War. The tax on the Jews continued to be collected and Judaea remained under the direct military rule of Rome. It was Hadrian (r. 117–38) who took things a step further in 130 by resolving to build a Roman temple on the remains of the Jewish one in Jerusalem. By this time various violent Jewish revolts had been put down in the eastern Mediterranean between 115 and 117. In Judaea Hadrian's plans led to the Bar Kokhba revolt, 132–5, which the Romans eventually succeeded in suppressing with great ferocity after suffering surprisingly heavy losses themselves. Jerusalem was rebuilt as the Roman city of Aelia Capitolina and Jews were forbidden to enter it. As we shall see later, Jewish rabbinic sources of the period accorded much attention to the revolt and to the Jewish martyrs who lost their lives in it. At some period Hadrian seems to have outlawed circumcision, a vital marker of Jewish identity. His successor, Antoninus Pius (r. 138–61) seems to have adapted the edict so that the prohibition applied to non-Jews only. It remains unclear to what extent this edict had any effect. It does not seem to have prevented Jews from continuing to make proselytes.[10]

Early Christian historians such as Eusebius (c. 260–339), who made much use of Josephus, celebrated the victory of Vespasian and Titus over the Jews as just retribution for their spurning of Christ. Eusebius claimed that God, in his mercy, had given the Jews 40 years to repent of their sin. When they did not their Temple was destroyed. In Eusebius's writings Roman enslavement of Jews featured prominently.[11] As far as Roman law was concerned, the suppression of the revolts in Judaea did not make Judaism any less of a legal religion than it had been. By 212 all Jews together with all other free people in the empire had been made Roman citizens. Having said that, it is clear that their lack of a Temple and their lack of a homeland had eroded their status. Apart from that, Jews were conceived in the minds of many as a potentially seditious people. After Hadrian's victory of 135 Judaea was renamed Palestina. This was a Roman attempt to sever Jewish claims over the land. Christian theologians began to call themselves Israel, a term not used by Rome for Jews, harking back to the biblical past they felt Christians were perpetuating, while bypassing contemporary Jews. All these strands were reinforced when Christianity became the official religion of the Roman empire under Theodosius the Great (347–395).[12]

An illustration of the new order of things was the confrontation between Ambrose, Bishop of Milan (c. 338–397), the mentor of Augustine, and Emperor Theodosius I, who made Christianity the official religion of the empire. In 388 Ambrose insisted that Theodosius revoke his demand that the Bishop of Callinicum in Mesopotamia rebuild the synagogue which had been destroyed in the anti-Jewish rioting. To Ambrose's mind, Theodosius's Christian duty outweighed his duty as law enforcer.[13] Another example of how Christian dominance could be detrimental to Jewish interests comes from Minorca, where in 418 riots broke out after relics of St Stephen, the first New Testament martyr, in whose death Jews had been assigned an unflattering role, were brought to the island. In Minorca there seems to have been an especially strong Jewish presence in the harbour town of Mahón; Ciudadela was the seat of the bishop. The arrival of the evocative relics seems to have provoked hostilities between the two communities which had hitherto co-existed comfortably enough, although the institutional Christian authorities bemoaned what they saw as excessive Jewish influence. In his letter recording the event, which has recently regained its reputation as being genuine, Bishop Severus claimed that more than 500 Jews had been pressed to convert. This example of religious coercion which was, of course, illegal accords with many other examples of Christian activities against pagans and those deemed to be heretics, which went beyond what was permitted in law. The ambiguities governing the positions of pagans, Jews and heretics are clearly visible in the law codes of Theodosius II, who was Eastern Roman emperor from 408 to 450, and Justinian who ruled in Byzantium from 527 to 565. These laws forbade excesses against these groups but at the same time the activities of these groups were increasingly circumscribed in the interests of 'orthodox' Christianity. The many regulations concerning indemnification for burnt-down temples and synagogues must indicate that excesses took place on a regular basis.[14]

Roman Law

According to Eusebius, Constantine, the first Christian emperor,

> *made a law that no Christian was to be a slave to Jews, on the ground that it was not right that those redeemed by the Saviour should be subjected by the yoke of bondage to the slayers of the prophets and the murderers of the Lord.*[15]

Constantine promulgated a law in 335 freeing any slave, Christian or 'of any other sect', who had been circumcised by his Jewish master; his son, Constantine II, promulgated that Jews should not hold Christian slaves or slaves 'of another sect or nation' in 339. These laws together with similar ones concerning Jewish ownership of slaves found their way into the Theodosian Code, which collected laws which had been promulgated after 312, and the Justinian Code, which was an attempt to update and substantially improve the process of legal codification a century later. Law

16.9.2 of the Theodosian Code stipulated that if a Jew circumcised a non-Jewish slave, he would not only be deprived of the slave, he himself would be liable to capital punishment. Similar stipulations are found in Law 1:10:1 of the Justinian Code, but in this area, as in so many others, it is well to remember that legal theory was not always put into practice. Apart from the question of Jewish possession of slaves, these laws touched on the vexed problem of circumcision. Circumcising non-Jewish slaves was important for Jews because according to Jewish law a range of household duties could only be performed by males who were circumcised. Circumcising slaves was, in fact, one of the most common ways in which Jews increased their numbers.[16] The Theodosian and Justinian Codes upheld Antoninus Pius's rule that, although Jews were allowed to practise circumcision amongst themselves, they were forbidden to circumcise non-Jewish males.[17] As members of a licit religion, Jews were allowed to engage in their religious practices.[18] Even so, Justinian interfered in Jewish ritual in 553. He ruled that the Greek of the Septuagint should be used for the readings of the Prophets in Synagogue. The Septuagint version supported Christian interpretations of these texts. Also he forbade Jews to study the Mishna, the codification of the Oral Law, which Jews revered alongside the written law of the Law of Moses. Mishnaic material was seen as militating against Christian teaching.[19]

Synagogues were legally protected as places where Jews gathered for religious and other purposes. Theodosius I may have bowed to pressure from Ambrose in the Callinicum affair of 388, but in 393 he ruled that 'the sect of the Jews is prohibited by no law'. He ordered repression of 'the excess of those who presume to commit illegal deeds under the name of the Christian religion and attempt to destroy and despoil synagogues'.[20] The multiple occurrence of similar rulings in the codes would imply, however, that these laws were perhaps less effective than they might be. The hardening of Christian imperial attitudes towards synagogues is, however, evident from 415, when rules started appearing against the building of *new* synagogues. Law 1:9:18 of the Justinian Code, for example, ruled 'that no Jewish synagogue shall be erected in a new building, while granting leave to prop up the old ones which threaten to fall down'.[21] The underlying rationale of this was that, however licit legal tradition considered Judaism to be, Judaism should not be encouraged to spread; nor should Jews become too self-assertive. A good example of increasingly ambiguous attitudes towards Jews is the law, which Theodosius II promulgated in 420 and which was included in both codes, which states:

> *No one shall be destroyed for being a Jew, though innocent of crime. . . .*
> *Their synagogues and habitations shall not be indiscriminately burnt up,*
> *nor wrongfully damaged without any reason. For even if someone is*
> *entangled by his crimes, the vigour of the courts and the protection of*
> *public law appear to have been instituted in our midst for that very*
> *reason, that no one shall have the power to permit himself to take*
> *vengeance. But, just as we wish to provide in this law for all the Jews, we*
> *order that this warning too should be given, lest the Jews grow perchance*
> *insolent, and elated by their security commit something rash against the*
> *reverence of the Christian cult.*[22]

The idea that Jews might be militating against Christians and their religion grew steadily as the Roman empire became increasingly Christian. In a law of 409 Emperor Honorius said in so many words that 'Jewish perversity' was 'alien to the Roman empire'.[23] Indeed, from the early fifth century Jews were gradually prohibited from holding high office in imperial administration or from playing important roles in municipal government. Law 1:9:18 of the Justinian Code stipulated

> *that no Jew, to which all administration and dignities are prohibited,*
> *shall perform even the office of City Protector [municipal official with*
> *legal and administrative responsibilities], nor do we grant that he shall*
> *seize the honour of Father [financial municipal official], lest, armed with*
> *the authority of an ill-gotten office, they shall have the power to judge and*
> *pronounce sentence against Christians, very often even against priests of*
> *the sacred religion, to the insult of our faith.*

This law went back to regulations imposed by Theodosius II in 438, in which he had stated that Jews were 'enemies of the Supreme Majesty and of the Roman laws'.[24] The fact that in 527 Justinian felt compelled to reiterate and reinforce these rules would seem to indicate that prescriptive laws of this nature were not consistently enforced.[25] Nevertheless, the existence of these laws points not only to the legal disadvantages Jews were suffering by the early sixth century. The laws also highlight the increasingly uncomfortable position of Jews in a Christian polity.

Conclusion

And this brings us back to Augustine. Augustine could speak about Jews as ambiguously as he did because in his eyes the vast majority of mankind was mired in sin and deserving damnation. Augustine could not and did not explain how it was that only a few were the elect. This was all part of God's impenetrable ways. As far as Jews were concerned, the only thing that mattered was that they bore witness to Christ's teaching. Their observance of the Law of Moses before the coming of Christ had been invaluable because they observed the letter of the laws which carried in it the spirit of the sacrament of Christ. Once Christ had come, their observance continued to serve a purpose, however wrong-minded it was. Just as Jews had held a privileged position in pagan Rome, insofar as they were excused from engaging in ceremonies which were unacceptable to their religious norms, Jews in Augustine's worldview were privileged over other non-Christians, insofar as their survival was deemed to be necessary for Christians.[26] Or to put it differently, Jews were preserved in order to serve Christians. We have noted how Augustine's views on the Jews and the Hebrew Bible echoed many of St Paul's ideas which could be interpreted as accommodating the continuing existence of Jews. Embedded in these accommodating ideas was the concept of Jewish service. In Romans 9:10–12, Paul wrote: 'when Rebecca . . . had conceived . . . it was said to her "the elder shall serve the younger [Genesis 25:23]"'. Jewish Esau had been overtaken by Christian Jacob. The language is much harsher in Paul's letter to the Galatians, in which he polemicised against judaising Gentiles, that is to say Gentiles who felt the need to adopt Jewish customs. Paul stated:

> *Abraham had two sons: the one by a bondwoman [Hagar], and the other by a free woman [Sarah]. But he who was of the bondwoman [Ishmael], was born according to the flesh: but he of the free woman [Isaac], was by promise (4:22–3).*

In other words, Christians are the descendants of Sarah; Jews of the slave Hagar. Hagar was expelled from the house of Abraham because her son Ishmael persecuted Isaac the son of Sarah (4:28–31). Implicit in this language is the concept that Jews and Judaism posed a threat to Christianity. This kind of imagery went hand in hand with acerbic language against Jewish observance of the Law of Moses, as for example, in 2

Corinthians 3:6 where Paul talked about the letter that kills and the spirit that gives life. In the context of his attack on judaising Gentiles Paul described the Law of Moses as a curse in Galatians 3:13. In 1 Corinthians 5:6–8 he urged Christians to keep themselves from evil-doers:

> purge out the old leaven, that you may be a new paste, as you are unleavened. For Christ our [Passover] is sacrificed. Therefore, let us feast, not with the old leaven, nor with the leaven of malice and wickedness; but with the unleavened bread of sincerity and truth.

Whether or not Paul's concerns lay more with judaising Gentiles than with Jews, language like this promoted ideas that for all the service Jews might perform, they could also be a source of contamination in Christian society.[27] We have noted how the Jewish War and its aftermath spread ideas about Jewish sedition and we have just seen how Christian Roman legislation increasingly attempted to circumscribe Jewish participation in the body politic in order to accommodate the Christian nature of that society. This takes us to our next important churchman, Gregory the Great, whose primary concern was to lay down the correct parameters for Jewish existence in and service to Christian society in line with Christian Roman legislation.

Notes and references

1 Israel J. Yuval, Two Nations in Your Womb. Perceptions of Jews and Christians in Late Antiquity and the Middle Ages, trans. Barbara Harshav and Jonathan Chipman (Berkeley, CA, 2006), 1–91.

2 Augustine, The City of God against the Pagans, ed. and trans. R.W. Dyson. Cambridge Texts in the History of Political Thought (Cambridge, 1998).

3 Enarrationes in Psalmos, 40.14, ed. Eligius Dekkers and Iohannes Fraipont, CCSL 38 (Turnhout, 1956), 459; John Watt, 'Parisian Theologians and the Jews: Peter Lombard and Peter Cantor', in P. Biller and B. Dobson (eds), The Medieval Church: Universities, Heresy, and the Religious Life. Essays in Honour of Gordon Leff (Woodbridge, 1999), 69. Biblical references are to the Vulgate, brackets indicate the numbering in the Hebrew Bible.

4 Jeremy Cohen, Living Letters of the Law. Ideas of the Jew in Medieval Christianity (Berkeley, CA, 1999), 33.

5 *Enarrationes in Psalmos*, 58. 21, CCSL 39 (Turnhout, 1956), 744; Watt, 'Parisian Theologians', 69–71. Biblical translations are based on the Douay Rheims Version of the Vulgate.

6 Augustine, *City of God*, XVIII, 46, trans. Dyson, 891–2; *Contra Faustum*, XII. 12, trans. Richard Stothert in Philip Schaff (ed.), *A Select Library of the Nicene and Post-Nicene Fathers of the Christian Church*, vol. 4: *St. Augustin: The Writings against the Manichaeans and against the Donatists* (Grand Rapids, MI, repr. 1974), 187–8.

7 Cohen, *Living Letters*, 23–71; Paula Fredriksen, 'Divine Justice and Human Freedom: Augustine on Jews and Judaism, 392–398', in J. Cohen (ed.), *From Witness to Witchcraft. Jews and Judaism in Medieval Christian Thought* (Wiesbaden, 1996), 29–54. See also her *Augustine and the Jews. A Christian Defense of Jews and Judaism* (New York, 2008).

8 Sermon 199, PL 38, 1027.

9 Martin Goodman, *Rome and Jerusalem. The Clash of Ancient Civilizations* (London, 2007), 383–422; see also Marcel Simon, *Verus Israel. A Study of the Relations between Christians and Jews in the Roman Empire (AD 135–425)*, trans. H. McKeating from the French [first published in 1948] (Oxford, 1986).

10 Goodman, *Rome and Jerusalem*, 397–511.

11 Schreckenberg, 262–8.

12 Goodman, *Rome and Jerusalem*, 445–548, 578–84.

13 Henry Chadwick, 'Christian Doctrine', in J.H. Burns (ed.), *The Cambridge History of Political Thought, c. 350–c. 1450* (Cambridge, 1988), 96–7.

14 Severus of Minorca, 'Letter on the Conversion of the Jews', ed. and trans. Scott Bradbury (Oxford, 1996), 1–72.

15 Eusebius, *Life of Constantine*, trans. Averil Cameron and Stuart G. Hall (Oxford, 1999), 163.

16 *JRIL*, nos 10 and 11, quotations: pp. 140 and 147–8 and pp. 54–89 for a comprehensive overview of the position of Jews in Roman imperial legislation.

17 *JRIL*, no. 1.

18 *JRIL*, no. 40.

19 *JRIL*, no. 66.

20 *JRIL*, no. 22, quotation: p. 190.

21 *JRIL*, no. 54, quotation: p. 333.

22 *JRIL*, no. 46, quotation: p. 285.

23 *JRIL*, p. 65 and no. 39, quotation: p. 258.

24 *JRIL*, no. 54, quotation: pp. 332–3 and 329; see also p. 65.

25 *JRIL*, no. 56.

26 Fredriksen, 'Divine Justice', 29–54.

27 Kenneth Stow, *Jewish Dogs. An Image and Its Interpreters* (Stanford, CA, 2006), 3–5.

chapter 2

Gregory the Great
and canon law

Pope Gregory reigned from 590 to 604. Gregory's world was quite different from that of Augustine. By the end of the sixth century the Roman emperor in the West had been replaced by numerous German kings. In Gregory's day power in Italy was contested between distant Byzantium, the Lombards and the papacy. In the city of Rome, as in many other cities of the empire, civic affairs had been taken over by ecclesiastical structures. In Rome itself the papacy had to deal with everything from repairing aqueducts, regulating food supplies, looking after the poor to settling property disputes and keeping the peace from outside attacks and internal disturbances. Thus Gregory did not share Augustine's view of temporal society as a temporary and neutral shared space between the damned and the elect; his society was a Christian one, in desperate need of purification as it approached the end of time. Whereas Augustine found the solution to his perplexity about the course of events in the newly Christianised Roman empire by divorcing the goings-on in cities on earth from God's work, Gregory sought to locate God's work in those Christian cities. For him the Church was the community of believers in Christ which had merged with the rest of society. The godliness in man was something to be actively pursued. This is the pope who actively promoted the contemplative life of monasticism and who advocated the pastoral role of those in power like himself. Conversion of non-believers was an important part of his agenda. This is the pope who sent Augustine of Canterbury to convert the English. As far as Gregory was concerned, Christ's second coming was nigh and elements in society which seemed to militate against the speedy and successful fruition of the end of time were harbingers of the Antichrist who would unleash a final period of mayhem before Christ's ultimate redeeming victory at the end.[1]

The legal framework in which Gregory functioned was that of Roman law. Following the tradition of Roman law, Gregory did not question the legality of Jews continuing to exist as Jews. As an administrator he insisted that Jews should retain their traditional position which protected them within a restrictive framework which served the theological interests of Christians. We see this clearly in five of his decretals which John Gilchrist has identified among the 10 Christian rulings concerning Jews which were most widely disseminated between 906 and 1141.[2] These are *Hortamur* ('we admonish'), *Fraternitatem vestram* ('your Fraternity'), *Sicut Iudeis* ('Just as the Jews'), *Ioseph* ('Joseph') and *Plurimi Iudaice* ('many men of the Jewish [religion]'), which protected Jews from forced conversion and synagogues from wanton destruction or confiscation, but at the same time insisted that no Jew should hold Christian slaves and forbade the circumcision of non-Jews. Let us examine these rulings in more detail.

Gregory's decretals

Gregory sent *Hortamur* to the bishop of a city in Etruria in 594 to admonish him to put into practice the traditional Roman law that forbade Jews from owning a Christian slave. For Jews to possess Christians was not just illegal; the implication of Gregory's words seems to be that the situation was an inversion of the correct relationship between the 'right' Christian religion and the wrong 'superstition' of Jews, which would put simple Christians into a defenceless position vis-à-vis Jews. Those who were legally free but 'belonged' to the land were allowed to continue to cultivate the land and pay rent to Jewish landlords and fulfil their customary obligations.[3] These people were evidently not considered at risk. *Fraternitatem vestram*, which Gregory addressed to the Bishop of Naples in 596, contains further stipulations with regard to Jewish ownership of slaves. If a Jewish or a pagan slave of a Jew announced that he wanted to convert to Christianity, he must be freed. His Jewish owner was not allowed to sell him. The only possible exception concerned slaves bought by Jews for resale rather than for their personal use. If such a slave declared his wish to convert before the Jew had had the opportunity to sell him, then the Jew might sell him to a Christian owner.[4] Once again, a fine balance was struck between restricting Jewish activity and protecting the livelihood of Jews as landowners and merchants, whose commodities included slaves.

Sicut Iudeis is, of course, the most celebrated Gregorian decretal concerning Jews because from the early 1120s popes issued decretals in protection of Jews throughout Christendom, which incorporated the first sentence of Gregory's text: 'Just as the Jews should not have the freedom to presume anything in their synagogues beyond what is permitted by law, in the same way, they should not suffer any prejudice in those matters that were granted them.' Gregory's original letter was addressed to the Bishop of Palermo in June 598 and concerned a local affair. Using the Jews of Rome as their intermediaries, the Jews of Palermo had complained that Bishop Victor had seized their synagogues in order to turn them into churches. Gregory reminded Victor to observe the laws concerning synagogues. As we have seen, Roman law safeguarded existing synagogues while forbidding the construction of new ones. As long as the case was *sub iudice*, the seized buildings should not be consecrated. In a following letter of October 598 to Fantinus, rector of Palermo, Gregory requested him to ensure that Bishop Victor compensated the Jews for their loss of property. For in the meantime Victor had consecrated the seized buildings as churches. Although this had been illegal, the buildings could not now be restored to the Jews as synagogues.[5] Gregory's working principle is clear: as long as Jews did not overstep the boundaries that had been set for them by Christians and in the interest of Christians, they should not be molested. This is straightforward Roman law in its Christian guise. Although no mention is made of Augustinian ideas of witness, one could interpret this ruling as a legal expression of the theological concept of allowing Jews a place in Christian society. *Ioseph* and *Plurimi Iudaice* work on much the same principles.

Ioseph was addressed to the Bishop of Terracina, a city not far from Rome, in 591. In response to a petition from a Jew called Joseph, Gregory admonished the bishop to cease expelling Jews from the places he had granted them in order to celebrate their holidays. Gregory stressed the importance of wooing those who were opposed to the Christian religion to the unity of faith through 'gentleness, friendliness, exhortation, and persuasion'. He was concerned that potential converts would be scared off by the bishop's excessive harshness. *Plurimi Iudaice* was addressed to the Archbishop of Arles and the Bishop of Marseilles in June 591 in response to complaints Gregory had received from Jews who had travelled to Marseilles on business about Jews being forced to convert there. Gregory's response betrays his pastoral mindset. He desperately wanted the 'souls of the deviants' to be saved and he praised the intention lying behind the forced conversions and was sure the perpetrators were acting out of love for God. What concerned him was that unless their methods complied with Holy Scripture, true conversions would not be achieved. His particular concern was that Jews would return to their 'vomit' (cf. Proverbs 26:11, 2 Peter 2:22). Jews should be converted through the sweetness of preaching, not force.[6] These rulings can leave us with no doubt as to how vital the issue of Jewish conversion was to Gregory who, as we have noted, expected the end of time sooner rather than later. In a letter of July 592, for example, he asked that Jews, who lived on a certain Sicilian church estate and who wanted to convert, should be given a rent discount to encourage other Jews to join them in developing a desire for conversion. Less subtly, he suggested in 594 that Jews who refused to convert should be offered a rent discount if they became Christians. 'For even if they themselves come with but little faith, their children after them shall be baptized with greater faith.'[7] For all the urgency of the matter of Jewish conversion, Gregory did not stray beyond what was acceptable within the broad parameters of Christian Roman law: force was forbidden, though bribery seemingly not. Gregory's desire for Jewish converts did not abrogate the place Jews had been allotted in Christian society by Paul and Augustine.

Gregory's outlook on Jews

Gregory's intense concern about Jewish ownership of Christian slaves betrays the theological concerns underlying the Christian Roman law ordinances against the practice. In 597, for example, Gregory wrote that it was oppressive and detestable for Jews to enslave Christians; in a letter to Queen Brunhild of the Franks of 599 he wrote:

We are utterly amazed that in your kingdom you permit the Jews to possess Christian slaves. For what are all Christians but members of Christ? We all know their head, for you honour it faithfully. But what a difference let your Excellence judge, between honouring the head and permitting his enemies to tread down his members.[8]

This form of words not only excluded Jews from the Christian body politic, it portrayed Jews as enemies of Christians. As 'deviants' whose ways were equated to 'vomit', Jews were seen as a threat to the Christianising society for which Gregory was working. Indeed, Jews together with others, whom Gregory deemed wicked, were accomplices of the devil and minions of the Antichrist. In his monumental exposition on the trials of Job, the *Moralia in Job*, he depicted Jews as the limbs of the devil militating against the Christian servants of Christ. At the same time, the plight of the Jews lacking a land of their own served as straightforward proof of how God punished disbelief in Christ. Their continuing inability to read beyond the letter of the Hebrew Bible (the literal and historical meanings for which Gregory had so little time) and to recognise Christ in the figurative and moral meanings of the text constituted part of God's judgement against them for their crime against Christ.[9] The historical destruction of Jerusalem played an important role in this. Gregory earmarked one of the Sundays after Pentecost at the end of July or beginning of August as the day to celebrate Titus's burning of the city. At the core of the commemoration lay the passage from Luke 19:41–7 in which Jesus foretold the defeat of the Jews at the hands of their enemies. As Linder has observed, the timing of this Christian feast must have been chosen to coincide as far as possible with the ninth of Av, the day upon which Jews mourned the loss of Jerusalem by fasting and reciting the Book of Lamentations, the book which provided Christians with readings for their celebrations of Easter. In the fourth century Jerome (d. 420) had already contrasted the Jewish defeat, which was marked on the ninth of Av, with Christian victory. After falling into disuse, the celebration of the destruction of Jerusalem resurfaced around 740, becoming a fixed moment in the calendar on which in the later Middle Ages vernacular plays were put on to re-enact the 'Vengeance of the Lord'.[10]

These vengeance plays developed over the centuries out of the legends which had crystallised by the seventh or eighth century concerning Vespasian and Titus's campaign against the Jews. In these legends the Roman father and son performed God's work in wreaking vengeance on the Jews for their role in the Crucifixion. Both had been inspired to do this by Titus's cure of an illness through his belief in the healing powers of Christ. A striking detail of the legend concerns the enslavement of the Jews by the Romans. In the versions presented by the legends Jewish betrayal of Christ for 30 pieces of silver was fittingly repaid by the fact that 30 Jewish slaves were sold for only one denarius. The strong emphasis on Jewish slavery in these legends reinforced Christian theological views of the service Jews owed to Christians, even though it was at odds with the true nature of the status of Jews in the Roman empire. The Jews developed their own legends concerning Vespasian and Titus. In the Babylonian Talmud, for example, a tale is told how Titus was punished for his violation of the Temple by being tortured for seven years by violent headaches caused by a gnat which had entered his head through his nostril. Vespasian on the other hand was cured by the leading scholar of the period, Rabbi Yochanan ben Zakkai. His reward was imperial permission to establish his academy of learning in Yavneh. Israel Yuval interprets these and similar Jewish tales as a response to the Christian 'Vengeance of the Lord' tradition, whose ideological origins he seeks in the second half of the fourth century.[11]

To return to Gregory, in his commentary on Job he posits that Jews deserved to lose their land and bend their necks to Christians because they refused to submit themselves to God.[12] Jewish punishment witnessing to the supremacy of Christianity seemed to have mattered much more to Gregory than Jews witnessing to the truth of Christianity by carrying the books of the Hebrew Bible. From Gregory's decretals it is hard to conclude that Jews were as necessary a part of reality for him as for Augustine. But Gregory was not just a theologian and a churchman. He carried massive temporal responsibilities as the effective governor over Italy and Gaul. His statements concerning Jews were more than anything else his reactions to situations that were brought to his attention, often by Jews. His responses did not belie his theological outlook; Jews who were being punished by subjection for disregarding the message of the Apostles should on no account rule over Christian slaves. Gregory's rulings consisted of a practical application of existing laws to concrete circumstances. However it is noteworthy that the laws he used tended to be those of the Theodosian code, avoiding some of the sharper edges of the Justinian code. Nor did he manipulate the laws to increase the restrictions they contained; his rulings sought to be fair within the dictates of law. The fact that so many of his letters had to deal with the problem of Jewish slaveholding, of course, only serves to prove that Jews continued to hold Christian slaves as they carried out their daily business, whatever the law said. On the other hand the fact that so many others dealt with endangered synagogues prove that these buildings were threatened on a regular basis, again, whatever the law said. These opposites point to the unresolved tension in Gregory's thinking about Jews. What was the nature of their position in the Christian body politic, which according to Gregory was edging towards the end of time? As Jews they were deemed by Gregory to be the enemies of Christ and working against Christianity in the prelude to the final struggle. Their existence in the diaspora proved how badly disbelievers in Christ fared, yet they continued to disbelieve. This was an additional punishment from God. At the very end the Pauline prophecy concerning their conversion would be fulfilled. But before that happened Jews were, as it were, suspended in time, cocooned in the shell of traditional laws that offered them protection within the restrictive parameters which served Christian interests.[13]

Service and conversion in canon law

As we have seen, five of the ten most popular canonical rulings concerning Jews in circulation between 906 and 1141 derived from the decretals of Gregory I. The longevity of rulings concerning Jewish slaveholding kept the issue of service within Christian–Jewish relations firmly on the agenda. Anxieties concerning Jewish authority seemed to go hand in hand with the question of who should be serving whom. Gregory VII's synodial ruling of 1078 that Jews 'should not be set over Christians' followed in the footsteps of countless temporal and ecclesiastical decrees from the early fifth century onwards. We have already seen some of these rulings in their Theodosian and Justinian guise. The Visigothic Third Council of Toledo of 589 combined in one canon the prohibition of Jews having Christian slaves with the ruling 'that they should not act in any public office that would provide them with the opportunity to inflict punishment on Christians'.[14] The *Ne Iudei administratorio* ruling in the seventh-century *Law of the Visigoths* stipulated: 'that the Jews shall not dare to manage Christian households in an administrative function'. Severe penalties were decreed against ecclesiastics who gave them these functions over church property so they would learn 'how impious it is to set unfaithful over faithful Christians'. This ruling passed into a number of later canonical collections, including two of the most influential collections of the eleventh century: the *Decretum* of about 1012 of Burchard of Worms and that of Ivo of Chartres of around 1094–5. Both of these collections together with Ivo's other collection, the *Panormia*, which was completed around the same time as the *Decretum* – the exact relationship between the two remains mysterious – but much more widely disseminated, impacted on the work undertaken in Bologna in the middle of the twelfth century to collect and systematise all available canonical material. That work resulted in what is known as Gratian's *Decretum*, which was probably completed by 1158.[15] The frequent issuing of rulings concerning Jewish authority ironically betrays the fact that Jews continued to have power over Christians in all the ways these canons found so objectionable.

The other issue covered by the most popular Gregorian decretals was the complicated question of conversion. The problem was how to strike the right balance between encouraging Jews to the font in such a way that, if they converted, they did so sincerely, and forcing conversion on unwilling people and in so doing creating a weak link within the Christian body politic, consisting of nominal Christians whose religious loyalties lay elsewhere. Pauline theology clearly condemned the use of force, and we have seen how even a missionary as fervent as Pope Gregory toed this line. The *Iudei quorum perfidia* ruling of the Council of Agde, in the Visigothic south of France, of 506, was another one of Gilchrist's most popular ten rulings concerning Jews. It tried to guarantee the sincerity of prospective Jewish converts by making them wait eight months before receiving baptism. Only if they were on their deathbeds should they be baptised any earlier.[16]

Visigothic canons

Anxieties concerning the contamination insincere converts might generate come to the fore in the remaining four canons on Gilchrist's list of 'bestsellers'. All of these derive from the Fourth Council of Toledo. This Council was convened in December 633 under the auspices of King Sisenand (r. 631–6). The council was attended by an array of archbishops and bishops under the lead of Archbishop Isidore of Seville (*c.* 560–636), the leading scholar of this period. The aim of the Council was to promote political and religious unity throughout the disparate kingdom of the

Visigoths which spanned most of Iberia and areas of southern Gaul. As far as Jews were concerned, the Council had to make sense of the confusion which had come about through the actions of Sisebut (r. 612–21), who had forced the Jews of his kingdom to convert in 615–16. To understand what might have impelled Sisebut to have taken this extraordinary decision we need to recall that some 25 years earlier Reccared had converted from Arian Christianity to Catholicism in 587. The Third Council of Toledo in 589 had formalised the conversion of the Visigoths and celebrated their newfound Catholic dedication to God under the leadership of their Christian king. Their conversion had been orchestrated by the king. As Drews and Bronisch point out, we know from a letter that Sisebut wrote to the Lombard king admonishing him to convert from Arianism to Catholicism that Sisebut modelled himself on Reccared. Conversion to Catholicism is recommended to the Lombards as a way to revitalise one's kingdom. Bronisch's work suggests that Sisebut took ecclesiastical enthusiasm for Catholic conversion to extremes; Drews sets Sisebut's decision in the framework of his attempt to forge a greater sense of unity among his disparate subjects. In the light of these ideas I would seek the explanation of Sisebut's astonishing decision within the tensions and ambiguities we have studied so far. How should a lay ruler deal with Jews whose conversion was eagerly sought by churchmen using derogatory servile language about Jews and Judaism? How could Jews fit into a Christian kingdom which had adopted the many Theodosian restrictions on Jews in its Visigothic version of Roman law? It would seem that Sisebut decided to get rid of all of these persistent incongruities by eradicating Judaism once and for all. However strong Sisebut's Christian religiosity, he did not appear to have sought ecclesiastical permission to convert Jews forcibly. As we shall see in a moment, canon 57 of the Fourth Council of Toledo makes it clear that Isidore of Seville and others had not, in fact, agreed with Sisebut's policy. They seem to have co-operated because they saw him as acting in God's stead. Once forced baptisms had taken place, it was their task to work out the many complications which had arisen from actions which ran counter to theological norms.[17]

The supreme irony is that Sisebut created more problems than he had thought to solve. From the moment Jews were forced to convert the Visigothic kings became obsessed by the thought of insincere conversions. The *Law of the Visigoths*, which was codified by Kings Reccesvinth

(r. 653–72) and Erviga (r. 680–7) bewailed 'the pollution of the land under our rule by the iniquity of the Jews alone'. Another article states that 'the deadly dominion of Jews over Christians should be abhorred . . .'. The *Law of the Visigoths* survived the Muslim conquest of the kingdom in 711; it acquired a new lease of life in the Christian kingdoms of Reconquest Spain.[18]

Let us return to the four canons of the Fourth Council of Toledo which proved to be so very popular among Christian–Jewish legal texts. Canon 57, *De Iudeis autem* ('On the Jews however'), dealt with the problem of forced baptism. The canon starts by reiterating the Pauline view that 'God hath mercy on whom he will and whom he will he hardeneth' (Romans 9:18) and stating that 'no one should henceforth be forced to believe'. Jews 'should be persuaded to convert'. But crucially the canon goes on to say:

> *Those, however, who were formerly forced to come to Christianity (as was done in the days of the most religious prince Sisebut), since it is clear that they have been associated in the divine sacraments, received the grace of baptism . . . should be forced to keep the faith even though they had undertaken it under duress, lest the name of the Lord be blasphemed and the faith they had undertaken be treated as vile and contemptible.*

In other words Jews, who had unlawfully been forced to become Christians, were now to be forced to *remain* Christians. The fate of the children of forced converts was considered in *Iudeorum filios et filias* ('Sons and daughters of the Jews'), which stipulated that the children of forced converts should be removed from their parents' sinister influence and entrusted to monasteries or pious Christian laypeople for a solid Christian upbringing. *Plerique qui ex Iudeis* ('Many who [were formerly elevated] from being Jews') stipulated that Jewish converts should be prevented from practising Judaism. If they circumcised their sons, these should be removed from their care. *Saepe malorum consortia . . .* ('Even the good are frequently corrupted from associating with the evil, how much more so people who are prone to sin') ruled that converts should have no contact with their former co-religionists. Ideas about the corrupting forces of Judaism emerge from other canons which speak about Jews/Jewish converts as 'members of Antichrist's body' or 'ministers of Antichrist'.[19] This would conform to Isidore of Seville's identification of anyone who deviated from Catholic orthodoxy with Antichrist. Cohen has stressed Isidore's negativity towards Jews. Although he did use Augustinian ideas of Jewish witness to the truth of Christianity in his commentaries on the Old Testament, he stressed how inimical Jews had been to Christ. Drews has taken this a step further. He argues that Isidore thought that Jews should ideally be converted, but **not** forcibly baptised. According to Drews, Isidore used his influential *De Fide Catholica contra Judaeos* ('On the Catholic faith against the Jews') to present Jews as 'negative foils' in the service of Catholic unity. Isidore's negative typology of Jews could have helped promote the harsh canons dwelling on Jewish treachery in the ensuing Toledan Councils, culminating in the seventeenth Council's ruling of 694 that recalcitrant Jewish converts should be 'stripped of all their properties . . . and subjected to perpetual servitude'. Jews serving Christians by functioning as the archetypal 'outsider' provides us with another interesting twist to the idea of Jewish service.[20]

Studies of Christian–Jewish relations often treat the Visigothic episode as a blip. The Visigothic kings' treatment of the Jews stood in sharp contrast to much milder treatment by their contemporaries, such as Queen Brunhild of the Franks, whose tolerance for Jewish slave-ownership had provoked Gregory's complaint in 599. Apart from that, we lack concrete evidence for the widespread presence of Jews in Iberia to whom Visigothic laws and canons would seem to refer. Nor do we have any real idea how the Visigothic measures actually affected Iberian Jewry. Historians such as Michael Toch have concluded from this that Iberian Jews were more the product of febrile ecclesiastical and royal brains than flesh-and-blood human beings. Others, such as Friedrich Lotter, have hotly contested this. Bronisch's conclusions that these rulings concerned unwilling Jewish converts and their offspring and that they were meant to ensure Catholic orthodoxy and to protect it from any corrupting forces seem compelling. Although we know next to nothing about Jewish life in Visigothic Spain and although it is more than likely that many of these laws and canons were not, in fact, applied as rigorously as their lawgivers would have liked, what matters in the context of this book is that the Toledan canons often conflated Jewish converts with Jews and, crucially, that four of their number proved to be so very, very popular.[21]

All four passed into Burchard's, Ivo's and Gratian's *Decretum*; of the four only *Plerique* was not included in Ivo's *Panormia*. Canon 57 played a crucial role in determining the Church's position vis-à-vis forced conversions at the time of the crusades. To appreciate how influential the Visigothic measures were it is worth mentioning that for all their popularity in a variety of canonical collections between 906 and 1141 none of the 'bestselling' Gregorian decretals had this kind of presence in the collections. The most popular of Gilchrist's canons was the Toledan canon 57 on forced conversion, second place went to Gregory's *Hortamur* on slaves; tied third place was held by Gregory's *Fraternitatem* on slaves, the Agde canon on conversion, the Toledan canon on the children of forced converts and Gregory's *Sicut Iudeis*. The Toledan canon on contact between converts from Judaism and Jews and Gregory's *Ioseph* on conversion shared fourth place. The Toledan canon on backsliding Jewish converts, *Plerique* and Gregory's *Plurimi Iudaice* brought up the rear.[22]

Conclusion

These introductory chapters have explored the uneasy position of Jews in the early centuries of the Common Era. Augustine tried to make sense of continuing Jewish presence in society through his idea of Jewish service. His particular approach to Jewish service was the witness Jews provided to Christian truth by carrying the books of the Old Testament on behalf of Christians. But he and others also spoke of the service Jews provided by demonstrating through their dispersion how God punished disbelief in Christ, or even worse, his Crucifixion. This introduced a punitive aspect to Jewish service. We have seen how Christian Roman laws protected Jews while incorporating restrictions on them which served the interests of Christendom. Gregory's decretals followed in this mould but his concerns and those of others about Jews working in the service of Antichrist added another element to the equation. Pauline ideas about the dangers of corruption of Christian society co-existed with the fundamental Pauline principle concerning the conversion of Jews at the end of time. Many a regional council in Gaul attempted to prevent Christians from joining Jews for meals, and Jews were required by some to stay indoors at Easter time.[23] Once again the frequency of these canons and others must indicate that contacts between Christians and Jews remained more frequent and, indeed more cordial, than many churchmen would have wished.

The conflicting categories of protection, service, conversion and pollution made it hard to form a consistent view about the correct role real, live

Jews should play within a Christian polity in the present. The conundrum princes faced was how to rhyme theological views, which had so much to do with what lay in the past and what was supposed to happen in the future, with their present, practical political and economic needs. The Visigoths attempted to solve the conundrum by forcing their Jews to convert. This was not the path chosen by other princes, as we shall see in the following chapters. Jewish service, rather than Jewish conversion, was how princes sought to make sense of the presence of Jews in their lands.

We shall start by exploring this in the areas of Latin Christendom where Christianity had become the dominant religion. From imperial Germany we shall move westwards to France and then northwards to England before we enter the lands of the Latin Mediterranean where Christendom was confronted by the powerful presence of Islam. Our focus on Jewish service will ensure that the political and socio-economic issues of these separate regions will be considered in tandem with crucial theological concerns. The relationship between the princes of Latin Christendom and the Pope and local ecclesiastical functionaries will be a constant backdrop to our discussion. Reference to Jewish cultural activities will evoke a sense of the realities of Jewish life in the lands of Latin Christendom. Specific ecclesiastical, theological and intellectual developments within Christendom will provide the context of the final section of the book which will start by exploring the Jewish experience of the crusades and the emergence of anti-Jewish libels. The final and concluding chapter will address the evolution of Christian views on Jewish service through an investigation of religious and cultural encounters between Christians and Jews between 1000 and 1300.

Notes and references

1 Robert A. Markus, 'The Sacred and the Secular: From Augustine to Gregory the Great', *Journal of Theological Studies*, n.s. 36 (1985), 84–96; Carole Shaw, *Gregory the Great. Perfection in Imperfection* (Berkeley, CA, 1988); Jeremy Cohen, *Living Letters of the Law. Ideas of the Jew in Medieval Christianity* (Berkeley, CA, 1999), 73–94.

2 John Gilchrist, 'The Canonistic Treatment of Jews in the Latin West in the Eleventh and Early Twelfth Centuries', *Zeitschrift der Savigny-Stiftung für Rechtsgeschichte Kanonistische Abteilung* 106 (1989), 74–5; John Gilchrist,

'The Perception of Jews in the Canon Law in the Period of the First Two Crusades', *Jewish History* 3 (1988), 12–13.

3 *JLSEMA*, 426–7; John A. Watt, 'Jews and Christians in the Gregorian Decretals', in Diana Wood (ed.), *Christianity and Judaism*, Studies in Church History, 29 (Oxford, 1992), 95–6.

4 *JLSEMA*, 429–31.

5 *JLSEMA*, 433–6, quotation: p. 434.

6 *JLSEMA*, 417–19, quotations: pp. 418, 419.

7 *JLSEMA*, 423–4, 428–9, quotation: p. 429.

8 *JLSEMA*, 431, 440–1, quotation: p. 440.

9 Cohen, *Living Letters*, 79–85.

10 Amnon Linder, 'Jews and Judaism in the Eyes of Christian Thinkers', in J. Cohen (ed.), *From Witness to Witchcraft. Jews and Judaism in Medieval Christian Thought* (Wiesbaden, 1996), 115–17 and Amnon Linder, 'The Destruction of Jerusalem Sunday', *Sacris Erudiri* 30 (187–8), 253–92.

11 Schreckenberg, 463–5; Israel J. Yuval, *Two Nations in Your Womb. Perceptions of Jews and Christians in Late Antiquity and the Middle Ages*, trans. Barbara Harshav and Jonathan Chipman (Berkeley, CA, 2006), 38–56.

12 Schreckenberg, 426; *Moralia in Iob*, IX.VII. 7 in *Moralia in Iob, libri I-X*, ed. Marcus Adriaen. CCSL, 143 (Turnhout, 1979), 460.

13 On Gregory see *JLSEMA*, 417–43; Cohen, *Living Letters*, 73–94; Schreckenberg, 424–35; Solomon Katz, 'Pope Gregory the Great and the Jews', *Jewish Quarterly Review* 24 (1933–4), 113–36; and also the to-my-mind excessively positive assessment by Bernard S. Bachrach, *Early Medieval Jewish Policy in Western Europe* (Minneapolis, MN, 1977), 35–9.

14 *JLSEMA*, 558–9, 484–5, quotation: p. 485.

15 *JLSEMA*, 320–1, 633, 637, 649–50, 674, quotation: p. 321; Gilchrist, 'The Canonistic Treatment', 70–4; Anders Winroth, *The Making of Gratian's Decretum* (Cambridge, 2000).

16 *JLSEMA*, 466–7.

17 Wolfram Drews, *The Unknown Neighbour. The Jew in the Thought of Isidore of Seville* (Leiden, 2006), 7–32 and the illuminating online review by Rachel Stocking, The Medieval Review – TMR 06.10.35; Alexander P. Bronisch, *Die Judengesetzgebung im katholischen West-gotenreich von Toledo* (Hanover, 2005), 33–60.

18 *JLSEMA*, 257–332, quotations: pp. 261, 273.

19 *JLSEMA*, 485–91, quotations: pp. 486–7, 488, 489, 487, 491.

20 Drews, *The Unknown Neighbour*, 169, 186, 222–3, 288, 307–22; Cohen, *Living Letters*, 95–122; Linder, *JLSEMA*, 491–538, quotation on p. 537.

21 Drews, *The Unknown Neighbour*; Bronisch, *Die Judengesetzgebung*; see Bronisch, pp. 12–13 for the dispute between Toch and Lotter; Michael Toch, 'The Jews in Europe, 500–1050', in Paul Fouracre (ed.), *The New Cambridge Medieval History*, vol. 1 (Cambridge, 2005), 550–1.

22 Gilchrist, 'The Canonistic Treatment of Jews', 73–4; 101–5.

23 Linder, *JLSEMA*, 465–82, e.g. on pp. 467, 471, 474–5.

part 2

The political and socio-economic realities of Jewish service

*'It seems to me that all types of taxes must be considered defence
expenditures. For it is they that preserve us among the Gentiles. For what
purpose do some of the Gentile nations find in preserving us and allowing
us to live among them if not the benefit that they derive from Israel in
their collection of taxes and extortions from them.'*

(Asher ben Yehiel, commentary on *Baba Bathra* 1.29 in the Babylonian Talmud, translation
from B. Septimus, *Hispano–Jewish Culture in Transition* [Cambridge, MA, 1982], 13)

c h a p t e r   3

The Jews of Germany

The history of Christian–Jewish relations in medieval Germany between 1000 and 1300 is full of contradictions. A sombre picture is projected by the pogroms of the First Crusade and wholesale massacres connected with thirteenth-century blood libels and host-desecration accusations. A different picture emerges from the fact that unlike England and France (and fifteenth-century Spain) German Jews did not suffer universal expulsion from German lands. Worms, for example, retained a Jewish community until the takeover by the Nazis in the 1930s. A grim image is offered by traditional interpretations of German royal/imperial stipulations concerning Jewish chamber serfdom; a more positive impression is gathered from details of Jewish socio-economic activity within the budding German cities of the eleventh, twelfth and thirteenth centuries. Ever present are the dark shadows of the Shoa which continue to make it difficult to analyse objectively the true circumstances of medieval German Jewry. At the same time German centres of Jewish Studies, as for example in Trier, are providing us with a much better understanding of medieval *Ashkenaz* (the Hebrew term for Germany).

The fact of the matter is, of course, that there was no 'Germany' in its modern sense in this period. In order to examine the political and socio-economic realities of Jewish service in medieval Germany, we need to take into account the vagaries of the German empire after the German king Otto I was crowned emperor by the Pope in 962.[1] Not only were the

German kings invariably drawn into confrontations with the papacy on account of their imperial claims in Italy and the fact that their imperial title depended on papal acquiescence; they were nominally in charge of vast lands in which their writ existed alongside the rule of territorial lay and ecclesiastical princes. Germany was a loose conglomeration of lands governed by many different levels of authority. As imperial fortunes waned after the death of Frederick II in 1250, the power of the territorial princes and towns grew even stronger than it had been before. It was not only the emperors who needed to make sense of the presence of Jews in their lands; local lords and urban centres needed to do so as well. In the following pages it will therefore be important to examine not just imperial charters concerning Jews and their relationship to papal and canonical pronouncements; it will also be important to examine a number of Jewish communities to get a better feel for the realities of Jewish life and the daily interaction between Christians and Jews.

Settlement and economic activities

First of all, when did Jews arrive in medieval Germany, where did they live and what were they doing? Following Michael Toch we can confidently trace the development of Jewish settlement in German lands by Jews stemming from Italy and France. The first Jewish community emerged in the late ninth century in Metz and the next in Mainz around 950; within 30 years communities were established in Magdeburg, Merseburg, Worms and Regensburg. An additional seven settlements came into being before the First Crusade in 1096: Trier, Cologne, Speyer, Halle, Prague, Xanten and Bonn. Bamberg might bring the number to eight. The community in Prague might have existed even earlier. Although Toch accepts that before 900 there were travelling Jewish merchants in places such as Aachen, he insists that there is insufficient evidence to suppose continuity between Jewish settlement of Roman Cologne and Trier and their medieval counterparts. After the violence of the First Crusade the existing communities, with the exception of Metz, were rebuilt; only five new settlements were set up before 1150. These included Würzburg, Koblenz and Bacharach. The rate doubled after 1150 to 11. New settlements included Strasbourg, Frankfurt am Main, Vienna and Neuss. After 1200 the rate accelerated dramatically with more than 300 new settlements coming into being in the thirteenth century. Expansion continued apace till around 1350; many of these new thirteenth- and fourteenth-century settlements came into being as a direct result of attacks on existing communities such as the Good Werner persecutions after 1287 and the Rintfleisch pogroms of 1298, which will be discussed in Chapter 8. Or to put it more sharply, the establishment of new communities from the second half of the thirteenth century was often accompanied by the temporary or permanent dissolution of older communities. Jewish existence in Ashkenaz, even in the best of times, remained precarious. This was greatly exacerbated in the fourteenth and fifteenth centuries. Many new Jewish settlements lasted for hardly any time at all.

The names of the towns in which Jews settled in the eleventh and twelfth centuries reveal the intimate connections between Jewish and Christian endeavours. All these towns were focal points of important political, ecclesiastical and economic developments. The position of Regensburg on the Danube allowed Christian and Jewish merchants to access the goods of south-eastern Europe; Magdeburg and Prague offered them the exciting opportunities of the north-east. The Rhineland lay at the heart of the development of Germany under the Salian emperors (1024–1125) and the Hohenstaufen (1138–1254), and it was here that Jewish communities especially thrived both economically and culturally. As further economic opportunities were sought in north-eastern and central areas in the course of the twelfth and thirteenth centuries, Jews established numerous communities in Westphalia, Hessen, Thuringia, Franconia, the Palatinate and Swabia. Communities along the Danube led the way into Austria. Jews would settle in towns which had need of the services they could render through their activities in trade and the credit market.[2]

As Toch and others have demonstrated the precise nature of Jewish business activities in Germany in the tenth, eleventh and twelfth centuries has to be deduced from the available Hebrew sources in conjunction with what can be gleaned from sparser Latin material. Much of the Hebrew material consists of so-called *responsa*. These are rabbinical responses to questions put to them by fellow Jews about the application of Jewish law. Many of the matters raised concerned business affairs. The material also includes the Hebrew crusade chronicles which will feature in Chapter 7. Unsurprisingly, these sources reveal the activities of Jewish doctors, bakers, butchers and smiths. Jewish viticulturists produced wine which they sold to

Jews and Christians. Other goods in which Jews traded were medicines, spices, dyes, salted fish, cattle, pelts, furs, clothes and cloth, precious metals and vessels. Toch argues strenuously that slaves mentioned in the sources would usually be house slaves belonging to Jews and not a major commodity in which they traded. Jewish merchants sold their goods to Christians and Jews. Merchandise was transported along the Rhine between Mainz, Worms and Cologne. The fair at Cologne was an important centre of business. By 1074 goods were also taken eastwards to places such as Frankfurt, Dortmund and Goslar, by 1112 to Nuremberg. Ships were used together with wagons and pack horses. Christian lay and ecclesiastical lords would have been the clients of 'better-off' Jews. Less affluent Christians would be employed by Jewish merchants and viticulturists. The wine trade offers us particularly useful insights into the interface between trade and moneylending. Wine was one of the staple goods in the Rhineland and much more wine was produced by Christians than Jews. This presented Jewish traders with a problem because German Jews stringently observed the maxim in Jewish law (*halachah*), forbidding Jewish use of Gentile wine, which went back to ancient times when wine was an integral part of pagan idol worship. This was applied in Ashkenaz to mean that Jews were not allowed to derive any benefit from Christian wine, including engaging in its trade. From the middle of the tenth century, however, it was reluctantly deemed permissible for Jews to accept payment in wine produced by Christians. Haym Soloveitchik has argued convincingly that this loophole allowed Jews to play a vital role in the wine trade. For Jews provided Christian viticulturists with credit with the stipulation that payment was to be in kind. The wine which they received as repayment for the loans which they had extended could then be traded. This is an excellent example of how before 1100 Jewish moneylending came into being as a sideline of trade rather than as a business in its own right. In the course of the twelfth century moneylending came to equal trade in importance. From the available source material it seems that Christian debtors belonged to the higher echelons of society. But it is likely that many loans to 'lesser' people were verbal and remained unrecorded. It appears that moneylending became ever more dominant after 1200. Having said that, we know of Jews in late fourteenth-century Germany who traded in wine and cloth and made their living from binding books, working leather, silver and gold, making glass and tailoring.[3]

The German emperor and the Jews

What was the relationship between the German emperors and the Jews who began to settle in their lands from the tenth century? In July 965 Otto I (r. 936–73) entrusted the church of St Maurice in Magdeburg with his imperial *bannum* (public authority) over the city, which included authority over 'the Jews and the other merchants living there'. St Maurice was revered by Otto as the saint to whom he owed his victory over the Magyars in 955. His charter was confirmed by Otto II (r. 961–83) in June 973 immediately after Otto I had been buried in St Maurice's, which by then was a cathedral, much enriched by Otto I as the place where he chose to be entombed. Otto II reiterated the archiepiscopal church's possession of his *bannum* when he visited Magdeburg in 979. It is clear that Jews were identified as merchants and that they functioned alongside non-Jewish ones.[4] The charters which Henry IV (r. 1056–1106) granted the Jews of Speyer and Worms in 1090 are much more informative. As far as Speyer is concerned, the royal charter elaborated on what Bishop Rüdiger Huozman had already granted in 1084 to the Jews whom he had invited to settle in his city. Henry's charters have much in common with the privileges which had been given by Louis the Pious (781–840) some 250 years earlier to Jewish merchants in his empire.

Louis's privileges have been transmitted in so-called formulary books in which the bare bones of imperial charters were recorded. The presence of Jewish privileges in these books means that they were not a rarity; this would seem to reflect increased Jewish presence in the southern and central regions of France, including Lyons from the middle of the eighth century. Unlike the Visigothic kings before him, Louis seemed happy to allow these Jews to get on with their business without worrying whether this meant that they were overstepping canonical rulings about Jewish service. What mattered was that he had taken them under his protection so that they could serve his palace faithfully. Jews were exempted from all kinds of taxes and tolls and were permitted to live according to their law; they were allowed to employ Christians as long as their employees were not compelled to work on Sundays and festivals. They were allowed to bring foreign slaves into the empire to sell them and Christians were forbidden to baptise them in order to emancipate them from Jewish ownership. As we have seen, Toch argues that the slaves in question would have been for the most part

Jewish house slaves. If these Jews had a legal case against a Christian they had to produce Christian witnesses; if a Christian had a case against them he had to bring along three Christian and three Jewish witnesses. Anyone who plotted against the protected Jews or murdered them would have to pay a huge fine to the imperial palace.[5]

Henry IV's privileges for Speyer and Worms

Henry IV went even further than Louis the Pious in disregarding ecclesiastical concerns. Not only were Jews allowed to employ Christians; the Worms privilege permitted them to have Christian wet-nurses. This is remarkable because Jewish use of Christian wet-nursing would seem to be an especially poignant way for Jews to wield authority over Christians. Interesting too is that Henry IV's charters ruled that the children of the Jews were not to be taken away to be baptised; startling is his provision that Jewish converts would lose their inheritance. The stipulation would hardly encourage Jews to seek the font. And Jews coming forward to be baptised had to wait three days to make sure they were doing so out of their own volition. Beyond these provisions the king safeguarded Jewish property and exempted them from tolls and taxes. Jews were granted the freedom to travel and engage in trade throughout the empire and freely sell wine, dyes and medicines, all crucial benefits for Jewish merchants negotiating the Rhine and other transport routes for business. If a Jew was found in possession of a stolen object, he had the right to claim back the money he had paid for it before returning it to its rightful owner. Jews were not allowed to buy Christian slaves but no one was allowed to baptise pagan slaves owned by Jews in order to free them. In the event of legal proceedings arising between Christians and Jews both parties were to have access to their own law and witnesses of their own faith. Jews were not to be subjected to trial by ordeal; they were to swear an oath according to their law after 40 days. Legal cases between Jews were to be settled within the Jewish community, with recourse to the bishop (in the case of Speyer). In Worms Jews could refer to the emperor if a serious accusation arose against them. The penalties for infringing any of these privileges were hefty fines to the imperial or episcopal treasury. Henry underlined his relationship with the Jews of Worms by stating that they 'pertain to his chamber'. There had been a gap in episcopal authority in Worms since 1074.[6]

Speyer

Henry's Jewry privileges exude a positive outlook on the role of Jews in Christian society on which negative ecclesiastical views on the nature of Jewish service had little bearing. This impression is confirmed by the fact that he defied anti-Pope Clement III, whom he had elevated as a rival to his enemy Pope Gregory VII, in allowing Jews, who had been forcibly baptised by crusaders in 1096, to return to Judaism in 1097. Clement had crowned Henry emperor in 1084 (see Chapter 7). As we have seen, the Toledan ruling that baptism could not be undone was widely disseminated in the tenth and eleventh centuries. And in reaction to the bloodshed of the First Crusade, he included the Jews of his imperial lands in the Imperial Land Peace of 1103 as a group in special need of protection alongside merchants, women, monks and clerics. But the charter Bishop Rüdiger gave to the Jews whom he brought to Speyer in 1084 show us that churchmen too could act against ecclesiastical precedent. It is vital to remember that within the Church too there were always different ways of interpreting Christian ambiguities vis-à-vis Jews. Apart from that Rüdiger was a staunch supporter of Henry against Pope Gregory VII. Rüdiger had, for example, given the Jews of Speyer permission to have Christian servants, including wet-nurses. And he allowed them to sell meat which was ritually unsuitable for Jewish consumption to Christians. Legal cases between Jews and against Jews would be settled by the Jewish court; matters could be referred to the bishop if necessary. The Jewish settlers were to guard their part of town and share guard duty with the sergeants of the city. To his mind Speyer would benefit 'a thousand fold' if Jews settled there and to this end Rüdiger seemed willing to forget ecclesiastical norms about Jews not wielding any authority over Christians. But the fact that he deemed it necessary to situate the new Jewry outside the city and enclose it within a wall must indicate that he was unsure whether the citizens of Speyer would be as enthusiastic about the influx of Jews as their bishop. In any case, it seems that Jews were soon settling in the centre of Speyer too. This pattern increased after the First Crusade from which the Jews of Speyer emerged more or less unscathed owing to the effective protection of the reigning bishop. Only eleven Jews lost their lives; the rest of the community was evacuated by Bishop John to safe havens. Citizens who had taken part in the violence were severely punished. By 1104 a new synagogue was consecrated. Some of the walls have been uncovered and part of the structure excavated. The beautiful ritual bath (*mikva*), which was built at the same time, can still be visited. The synagogue was extended in the thirteenth and fourteenth centuries. Visible is the room which was built onto the south wall in the late thirteenth century to accommodate women. Six windows would have enabled women to follow what was happening in the main building. A chamber which might have served as a school (*yeshiva*) was also added at some stage to the north-east corner of the synagogue.

The synagogue and the *mikva* help us to gain a real sense of the ambiguities of the existence of Jews in Speyer. On the one hand, the need for the new synagogue arose from the fact that Jews living in the centre were too concerned for their safety to make their way to the synagogue in the original Jewry. It appears time was needed for the traumas of 1096 to settle. On the other hand, only a flourishing community would have had the wherewithal to finance such fine new buildings. And only a well-protected community would have been allowed to buy such a central site which was already in domestic and commercial use. Even more telling is that the Jews were allowed to do this less than 200 metres to the south-west of Speyer Cathedral, the imperial church of Henry IV's dynasty, founded by his grandfather, Conrad II, and consecrated in 1061. It contained the imperial crypt for the kings and their wives. It was Henry's pride and joy: to him it embodied his imperial dignity. Henry visited Speyer seven times between 1100 and 1106, lavishing benefaction on the cathedral which was remodelled between *c.* 1080 and 1111. Only a very well-disposed emperor could have countenanced the building of a synagogue practically around the corner from 'his' cathedral. Finally, a comparison between the materials used for the Jewish buildings and the cathedral reveal that the same workshops must have provided labour for both projects. In other words, what we see in Speyer is how a Jewish community was able to secure for itself an advantageous position in trade and banking as it negotiated its way between its imperial and episcopal protectors and its Christian neighbours. The relationship between emperor, bishop and town would always impinge on Jewish fortunes. As royal/imperial power diminished in the second half of the thirteenth century together with episcopal power in Speyer, civic authority in the city increased. The ties between the city and its Jews were so strong that Jews could even obtain a form of citizenship of the town. Jewish citizenship was not quite the same as Christian citizenship. Jews could own land and hold on to land until the loan covered by it had been repaid. They could serve as officials in the Jewish council but could not participate in town councils or practise a number of occupations. Apart from anything else Jewish citizenship underlined the mutual understanding between Jews and Christians that effective protection against anti-Jewish riots could only come from local authorities. This had been particularly apparent during the so-called Good Werner and Rintfleisch blood-libel and host-desecration pogroms at the close of the thirteenth century which swept through Germany. In the bloody pogroms in the wake of the Black Death in 1349 the synagogue was destroyed and many Jews of Speyer perished. By the time Jews had resettled in the city in 1352, Speyer had managed to acquire imperial and episcopal rights over them.[7]

Worms

Jews settled in Worms at the end of the tenth century in the northern corner of the city adjacent to a docking area on the Pfrimm tributary of the Rhine. One of the many ways in which Jews served the city was the role they played in defending this vital part of town from attack. Together with Christian merchants they provided Henry IV with much-needed economic and political support in his struggles against the Pope and his allies. Henry's gratitude is vividly expressed in his privilege for Worms of 1074: 'when every single city seemed to have been virtually closed against our approach . . . only Worms, in the common goodwill of its citizens, preserved itself for our coming . . .' The inhabitants of Worms were rewarded by exemption from tolls along the Rhine and elsewhere. The original charter is extant and includes the Jews of Worms by saying *Iudei et coeteri Uvormatienses* (Jews and others inhabitants of Worms), but it would seem that the words *Iudei et coeteri* were added in the thirteenth century. Whatever the case may be, in 1090 the Jews of Worms were not only given far reaching privileges to engage in their merchant activities, they were also allowed to exchange silver throughout the city as long as they did not get in the way of the mint masters. It is clear that both they and the citizens of Worms benefited from imperial largesse. The vacuum in episcopal power between 1074 and 1125 allowed the citizens of Worms to flex their muscles and develop municipal structures; as far as the Jews were concerned it meant that they lacked the protection they needed in 1096 once their fellow townsmen had joined forces with the crusaders. Although the Jewish community suffered grievous losses it managed to recover during the twelfth century, benefiting from the confirmation by Emperor Frederick Barbarossa (r. 1152–1190) of Henry's privileges in 1157, which included the right of Jews being judged by Jewish courts. Remodelling of the synagogue took place in 1174–5; as had happened in Speyer, inspiration was taken from work done for the cathedral. The *mikva*, which was built in 1185–6, copied the one in Speyer. A women's chamber was added to the synagogue in 1212. The Jewish cemetery dated from the previous century. It has survived the ravages of time together with the *mikva*. The present synagogue is a modern reconstruction of the medieval synagogue destroyed by the Nazis in 1938. By 1200 a flourishing Jewish community worked alongside a strong citizenry in close partnership with the emperor and re-established episcopal authority. But as imperial power diminished from the second half of the thirteenth century, the position of the Jews depended ever more on dealings with civic and episcopal forces within the city. The extent of Jewish integration into the civic fabric of Worms can be measured by a legal text from c. 1300–3 which describes the process by which Jews could become citizens of the city. Jews who had been vetted by the Jewish council would be accepted as worthy of citizenship by the civic council. Jews like Christians would have to swear their citizen oath before the bishop pledging their loyalty and obedience to him as well as to the council and the common well-being of the city. Just before the Black Death the civic authorities were given all rights over the Jews by Emperor Charles IV. This did not mean, however, that the crown ceased to be a factor of importance for the city's Jews; Worms remained one of the imperial cities and its citizens used this to counteract episcopal authority. In a remarkable way the Jewish community managed to negotiate its way alongside opposing forces from within and from outside the city and survive until its demise in the 1930s.[8]

Jewish cultural life

The Jewish communities of Speyer and Worms were closely tied to each other and to the even older Jewish community in the cathedral city of Mainz. The so-called *Shum* (acronym of the first letters of the Hebrew names of the towns) communities were renowned for their scholarship. When Rashi,

Tosafits)

the famous late-eleventh-century French Jewish scholar, went to study in the Rhineland, he sat at the feet of masters in Mainz and Worms. The so-called Rashi chapel adjacent to the synagogue in Worms commemorates this, but it was, in fact, built in the seventeenth century. As we shall see in the next chapter, Rashi returned to Troyes to become the unrivalled expositor of the Bible and the Talmud. His output and that of his followers, the so-called *Tosafists*, overtook all previous work on the Talmud. The methods of Rashi and the French *Tosafists* were adopted by the academies of the Rhineland, Regensburg and elsewhere as they recovered from the traumas of 1096. As Soloveitchik has shown, the intellectual emphasis of the German scholars was not as focused as that of their French colleagues on expounding the meanings of the Talmudic text. They were more interested in providing discussions of topics emerging from the Talmud and engaged creatively in the field of liturgy. They produced an impressive body of *responsa*, the very *responsa* alluded to at the start of this chapter.

Particularly interesting is the Pietist movement which existed in the *Shum* communities and Regensburg from 1150 to 1250. The Pietists (in Hebrew, the *Hasidei Ashkenaz*) were mystics who put together a stringent ethical programme to ensure that its followers would be holier than anyone else, be they ordinary Jews or Christians. The fundamental text of the Pietist was the *Sefer Hasidim* (the Book of the Pious) which is ascribed to R. Judah the Pious (d. 1217) who founded a *yeshiva* in Regensburg in *c.* 1195. His star pupil, R. Eleazar ben Judah of Worms (d. 1230) had an important input too. In its attempt to regulate its followers' actions and thoughts, the Book of the Pious covered every imaginable aspect of daily life. As Peter Schäfer and others have pointed out, this makes the *Sefer Hasidim* an invaluable source for studying the relationship between Jews and Christians in these medieval cities. The vignettes making up the text bring to life the concrete circumstances of Jewish existence far better than even the best analysis of Jewry privileges can offer. Real Jews emerge from the text faced with real decisions as they interacted with their neighbours in good times and bad.

Unsurprisingly, the events of the 1096 pogroms, which we shall discuss at length in Chapter 7, remained an important issue. The *Sefer Hasidim* explores in depth how a 'Pietist' should react to the threat of forced baptism and what rewards lay in store for holy martyrs. While women were allowed to pretend to be men and even nuns to avoid being raped, pious Jewish men were not to hide behind clerical garments or wear crosses. These examples highlight the threats Jews faced from their Christian surroundings but others point to Jews embracing Christian culture. Why else would the *Sefer Hasidim* warn the pious against possessing and studying Christian books, going so far as to forbid transporting and storing Jewish books together with Christian ones? Equally, the Pietists were opposed to the use of Christian melodies in Jewish services; nor did they want Christians to use Jewish tunes in theirs. The sharp separation which they desired between Christians and Jews clearly did not exist. As far as business affairs were concerned, it is interesting to note that the Pietists cautioned Jews to deal as correctly with Christians as they did with Jews. This confirms what we know from so many other sources: not only did Jews and Christians do regular business with each other; they also formed partnerships which were meant to be mutually beneficial.[9]

Regensburg

Research into the Jewish community of Regensburg has benefited even more from recent archaeological finds than in the case of Speyer. In 1995 the repaving of the Neupfarrplatz led to the discovery of the core of the medieval Jewry lying directly under the square. Combined with documentary evidence these findings give us a picture of a small Jewish town of some 1700 square metres nestling in the heart of Christian Regensburg. Jewish houses with plenty of storage cellars for merchant goods were originally constructed from wood before the twelfth century. As elsewhere in the city they were gradually remodelled in stone after that. Among the many alleys and streets crisscrossing the Jewry, a wide street provided easy access to the stone bridge over the Danube. Jewish merchants had their warehouses alongside the street. This was the city's most direct route to the bridge and it seems more than likely that Christians made as much use of it as Jews. Jewish houses on the east, north and west sides of the Jewry abutted onto Christian properties. Houses on the south-eastern side reached a street leading to a parish church. From every side, including the south-western corner of the Jewry where a courtyard surrounded the synagogue, Christians would have had easy access to the Jewry. From the stipulations of a synod held in Vienna in 1267 at which the Bishop of Regensburg was present, it would seem that there were all kinds of interaction between Jews and

Jewish migration

Christians which ecclesiastics were wont to deplore. But in a charter of 1287 Jews and Christians are sharing a privy with episcopal acquiescence. The finds of the synagogue show that it was probably first erected in the late eleventh century and remodelled in the early thirteenth into a fine gothic building with a vaulted hall with two aisles, separated by three columns. As in Speyer and Worms the stonework reveals that Jews employed the same kind of craftsmen to work on their synagogue as Christians their cathedral.

where did they come from?

Jews are firmly attested in Regensburg from 981 onwards. As merchants they contributed to the wealth of the city by trading in furs, wax, metals and horses from Kiev and areas around the Volga. By 1020 there is mention in the written sources of an area of the city where Jews live. In 1096 the Jews of Regensburg escaped death by being forcibly herded into the Danube to receive baptism. When Henry IV stopped in Regensburg on his way back from Italy in 1097 he allowed forced converts to revert to Judaism. It is not impossible that he used the occasion to grant the Jews of Regensburg the kinds of privileges he had given to the Jews of Worms and Speyer. For Frederick Barbarossa's charter of 1182 in favour of the Jews refers back to the

> good customs derived from their predecessors down to our time by the
> grace and favor of our predecessors, namely, that they should be allowed
> to sell and to purchase according to their ancient usage gold, silver,
> and any kind of metal and merchandise; to put their properties and
> merchandise into trade, and to provide for their gain in the ways they
> have been used to.

Buying and selling gold and silver would also have involved the moneylending activities in which the Jews became increasingly involved in the course of the twelfth century. The charter was confirmed by Frederick II in 1216. But as we have seen in the case of Speyer and even more so Worms, the Jews of Regensburg were not just beholden to the emperor. They were enmeshed in the political networks of their city, which besides the emperor involved the Duke of Bavaria, the bishop and the civic authorities. Also important were the powerful religious houses of the city, including the monastery of St Emmeram, from whom the Jews acquired land for their cemetery in 1210. From 1207 Jews were obligated to pay taxes to the city as well as to the emperor. An imperial charter of 1251 states unambiguously that the clergy and the laity, including the Jews, were all responsible for defending the city. It was in the interests of both the Jews and the civic authorities to use their connection to the emperor as leverage against the authority of duke and bishop. Political and economic exigencies prompted the city to safeguard its Jews against the Rintfleisch attacks of 1298 and the pogroms in the wake of the Black Death. The 'magic' formula worked until the expulsion of the Jews in 1519. By this time the city had suffered a decline in its economic and political significance.[10]

Papal rulings

As we have noted, Henry IV responded to the pogroms of the First Crusade by including the Jews in his Land Peace of 1103. Frederick Barbarossa followed suit in 1179. The papacy was much slower in its response to the problems arising from outbursts of violence against Jews. It took till the early 1120s for Pope Calixtus II to promulgate a bull of protection for all the Jews of Christendom. The bull was re-issued five times by twelfth-century popes, including Alexander III (*c.* 1165) and Innocent III (1199) and many times during the thirteenth century as Jews petitioned the papacy for protection. When the popes did spring into action, they did so as if they had the prerogative to protect Jews throughout the lands of Latin Christendom. This was not only in conflict with the realities of the position of the Jews; it also flouted the claims princes made vis-à-vis the Jews of their lands. Papal claim to universal power was certainly not restricted to Jews. As we shall see in Chapter 7, this was an important aspect of the Reform Movement starting in the late eleventh century. One expression of that claim was the summoning of universal councils to legislate on all aspects of Christian life and thought. And part of that was the desire to put into force the existing canonical rules concerning Christian–Jewish relations. The Third Lateran Council of 1179 reiterated the prohibition of Jews employing Christian wet-nurses and insisted that Jews who converted to Christianity should not have to forego their property. In an emotive bull of 1205, known as *Etsi Iudeos*, Innocent III (r. 1198–1216) railed against Jewish use of Christian wet-nurses in France, stipulating that Jews were condemned to 'perpetual servitude' on account of their guilt for Christ's suffering. Lateran IV in 1215 was a showpiece of Innocent's vision of a universal Christian society under strong papal direction. It pulled together and updated

Lateran IV

many previous rulings concerning Jews, including legislation on Jewish moneylending. New was the universal demand that Jews (and Muslims) be required to wear clothing which would distinguish them from Christians in order to avoid illicit sexual encounters between them. These and other canonical rulings concerning Jews were gathered together in Gregory IX's *Decretals*, the definitive canonical collection of 1234. Papal protection of the position of Jews in Christian society evidently carried with it clear notions of the correct parameters of Jewish service. Epitomising this is the menacing additional clause contained in *Sicut Iudeis* by the time of Innocent III, which stipulated that Jews were only protected as long as they did not undermine Christian society. What constituted undermining society was, of course, open to many different interpretations.[11]

The language of Jewish service

The German charters we have looked at so far sing a very different tune. It is indeed ironic that the first years of Jewish settlement in Worms should have coincided with the rule of Bishop Burchard (1000–25) who was so careful to separate Jews from Christians and keep Jews from having authority over Christians in his *Decretum* of canon law. Henry IV's charters for Speyer and Worms, Frederick Barbarossa's and Frederick II's confirmation of the latter all explicitly allowed Jews to do things of which the papacy roundly disapproved. Given the rivalry between Pope and German emperor, the royal position was at least in part motivated by the wish to make plain that they, and not the Pope, or indeed anyone else, had the right to determine the fate of the Jews in Germany.

Of the Jews of Worms Henry had said that they '*pertain to his chamber (ad cameram nostram attineant)*'; Frederick I repeated this phrase in his confirmation of 1157; Frederick II did so too when he extended the privileges to all the Jews of Germany in 1236. In his Land Peace of 1179 Frederick declared that the Jews of Germany *belonged to the emperor's fisc*. In his charter for the Jews of Regensburg Frederick started off by saying that it was his duty to protect 'those who are opposed to our faith and live according to the rite of their ancestral tradition' before he went on to say that all Jews in Germany *belonged to the imperial chamber*. Frederick II introduced his 1236 charter by saying that all the '*servi*' of his chamber had supplicated him to confer the privileges of the Jews of Worms on *all the Jews of*

Germany. The second part of the charter unequivocally condemned the blood libel which had been brought against the Jews of Fulda in 1235 (see Chapter 8) and forbade anyone to use it to harm the Jews of Fulda and the rest of Germany, admonishing everyone that because '*a lord is honoured through his servants, those who deal favourably and kindly with our servants, the Jews, (Iudeis servis nostris), without doubt honour us*'. To an ever-complaining Pope Gregory IX, a few months later Frederick stated emphatically that the Jews of Germany (and Sicily) were *directly* under his authority according to common law and that he had not taken the Jews from any church that could claim special rights over them which could justly be placed ahead of his own common law. In his 1238 charter for the Jews of Vienna Frederick spelt out that he was receiving them in favour and as *servi camere nostre*. He went on to grant them a selection of the Worms' privileges, but crucially omitted the controversial permission to employ Christians or have Christian wet-nurses. For a year earlier he had excluded Jews from presiding over offices in his charter for Vienna, using the standard canonical explanation that this could lead to Jews oppressing Christians, adding that imperial authority from times of yore had imposed perpetual servitude on the Jews in revenge for the crime they had committed against Christ. In 1230 Frederick's son Henry confirmed the privileges of the Jews of Regensburg without using the term *servi camere nostre*; Conrad IV, another one of his sons did so in his charter of 1251, commanding Christians and Jews to work together in the defence of their city. In an unpublished late-fourteenth-century exercise book which contains copies of imperial letters, another charter of Conrad IV explained that the Jews are *servi camere* because 'the disparity of their law and the humility of their condition subjected them to Christians', stipulating that they were to remain under his domain in perpetuity 'so that they could be relieved under the mildness of our dominion'. In Rudolf of Habsburg's confirmation of the privileges of the Jews of Regensburg of 1274 he described the fact that all the Jews of his kingdom belonged to his imperial chamber as a sign of special dignity. A year later he confirmed Pope Gregory X's *Sicut Iudeis* bull of 1272 and his confirmation of July 1274 of Innocent IV's bull of 1247 protecting the Jews of Germany against blood-libel accusations. In 1281 Rudolf went along with canonical rules in ordering the Jews of Regensburg to obey the bishop and stay indoors on Good Friday. In mandates of 1286 Rudolf seized the possessions left behind by Jews of Speyer, Worms and Mainz and

other neighbouring towns who fled Germany to escape increased burdens
of taxation, saying explicitly that Jews were '*camere nostre servi* and that
they belong to him with their persons and all their possessions or to the
princes to whom he had enfiefed them'. Rudolf had been the first generally
accepted king since the death of Conrad IV and it is clear that he was doing
everything he could to redress the steady erosion of royal authority which
had occurred in the so-called interregnum. To this end he attempted to
collect more taxes from cities and, as far as Jews were concerned, decided
that they no longer had the freedom to move from one place to another
without his permission. His protection entailed overall control over their
persons and their possessions.[12]

On the basis of these texts historians have developed elaborate theories
of Jewish chamber serfdom through which Jews were supposed to have
gradually lost their legal liberty to the emperor (or to the lord(s) to whom
he had transferred them) becoming royal/imperial serfs. Too much ink
has been spilt on trying to define the legal nature of this supposed Jewish
serfdom or servitude.[13] After all, how could Jews have been serfs if in
1315 Worms and Speyer were granted the right to have Jewish citizens
by Emperor Louis of Bavaria, who went on to claim control of Jews and
their possessions even more possessively than Rudolf? It would seem to me
much more fruitful to understand the language German emperors used
to describe 'their' Jews in terms of the role Jews were thought to play in
Christian society. As has been shown in previous chapters, the presence of
Jews in Latin Christendom was based on the premise that they *served* the
interests of Christians. Their *raison d'être* lay in the *service* they provided
the Church and their lay protectors. The parameters of this service were
ambiguous and they were under constant discussion as theory clashed
with practice. What we see in the German charters is the way different
German emperors interpreted Jewish service according to the changing
circumstances of their reign. The same words could mean different things
even for the same king. Emphatic statements tying Jews to the imperial
chamber or fisc conveyed the message that it was the right of the emperor
and not the Pope or any of his ecclesiastical representatives or any of his
political rivals closer to home to benefit from Jewish service. What was
at stake was not that Jews owed princes service. That was a given. What
was at stake was the nature of that service. After all, both in Judaism
and Christianity service does not have to be servile. Service to God is

honourable; the Pope is *servus servorum Dei*, 'the servant of the servants of God'. Under Henry IV and his successors a category of unfree men, called *ministeriales*, overcame their servile status by serving the king.[14] The quality of Jewish royal service depended on the protection kings were willing and capable of providing and the level of taxes they demanded in return. Both were directly dependent on the realities of the king's authority; both were negotiated in an intellectual and religious milieu in which ecclesiastics seemed ever more keen to shape Christian–Jewish relations to reflect Jewish supersession. The use of the term *servi* does not, I would argue, in itself point to a deterioration in Jewish status. The Latin word can mean 'servant' as well as 'serf' or 'slave'. Frederick II used it for the first time in Germany to emphasise how an attack on Jews would constitute an attack on himself. If anything, he was elevating Jewish status by drawing Jews even closer to imperial majesty than they had been before. But the ambiguity of the term in conjunction with such a high degree of dependency did invite less positive connotations, especially in the light of papal insistence on perpetual Jewish servitude. In 1237–8 Frederick II gave the concept of perpetual Jewish servitude an imperial twist. Conrad IV too made ecclesiastical concerns about Jews his own. And however positive Rudolf was in 1274 about the special dignity of being a *servus* of his chamber, his 1281 charter saw him following ecclesiastical norms about the correct behaviour of Jews during Holy Week. His 1286 mandates made it plain that at least some Jews had chosen to leave Germany rather than pay the high price Rudolf was exacting for his royal protection.

Frederick II's imperial adoption of the concept of perpetual Jewish servitude reflects the contents of the 'Vengeance of the Lord' legends we touched on in Chapter 2. As we have seen, Vespasian and Titus appeared in these legends as champions of Christ, wreaking vengeance on the Jews and becoming their slave masters. Jewish legends record that Vespasian was medically assisted by Yohanan ben Zakkai and that he rewarded Yohanan by allowing him to open a school in Yavneh. By *c.* 1000 a Christian legend had developed in which Titus was cured by the historian Josephus. In 1221–4 Eike von Repkow made use of this legendary material when he tried to make sense of the position of Jews in Germany in his law book, the *Sachsenspiegel,* which was widely known in the northern and eastern parts of Germany. According to him, Josephus had been granted imperial protection for his co-religionists as his reward for curing Titus. As the successors of

honorable

dishonorable

Roman imperial authority, the German emperors were, therefore, beholden to look after the Jews. That is why Jews fell under their special royal/imperial peace. In Eike's hands there is nothing dishonourable about the relationship between the Jews and their emperor. In the *Schwabenspiegel*, however, which was composed around 1275 in southern Germany, there most certainly is. Its Franciscan compiler made much use of canonical material and belaboured the dishonourable and servile character of Jewish service. The *Schwabenspiegel* was highly influential in southern Germany.[15]

But however important it is to understand better the relationship between the German emperors and the Jews, it is essential to remember that, as our brief case studies of three significant Jewish communities have shown, Jewish status did not just rely on the emperor. Royal/imperial charters expressed only one aspect of their position in Germany and the protection they promised was often not as effective as both emperors and Jews hoped. For good or for ill, the Jews of Germany had to look to many different powers, including the papacy to get the protection they needed. Their success depended on a myriad of factors in which their involvement in local politics and finances played a decisive role. For from the second half of the thirteenth century Jews relied ever more heavily on the protection of the civic authorities of the towns they inhabited with or without the agreement of that city's immediate overlord, be he bishop, duke or other lay lord or emperor or as in Regensburg a combination of all three. The possibility of Jews possessing some kind of 'citizenship' epitomises just how close ties could be between them and their co-citizens. Different types of Jewish 'citizenship' were adopted by various German cities in the course of the fourteenth century. This is what Alfred Haverkamp has dubbed the *concivilitas* ('co-citizenship') of Christians and Jews in many medieval German towns. The complex political and fiscal interface between Jewish communities and the civic authorities of the towns they inhabited is what seems to have protected Jews in German territories longer from wholesale expulsion than in France and England. Although the persecutions of the late thirteenth and especially the fourteenth centuries took a very heavy toll, Jewish life did persist in many Germany cities till the fifteenth century and beyond. But from around 1400 expulsion of Jews from urban centres became a regular feature. Some Jews found refuge in villages surrounding the cities which had excluded them; others had to go further afield to the east or southwards to Italy.[16]

Rabbi Meir of Rothenburg

We conclude this chapter by briefly looking at the career of the great Talmud scholar and prolific writer of *responsa*, Rabbi Meir of Rothenburg, which highlights many of the themes discussed so far. Meir was born in Worms around 1215–20 to a family of scholars. He studied in Würzburg and Mainz before going to Paris, where he studied with R. Samuel of Falaise and R. Yehiel of Paris. He was in Paris during the Talmud Trial of 1240 in which his teachers were unsuccessful in saving the Talmud from condemnation. He witnessed the burning of the Talmud in 1242 and wrote an elegy to memorialise the event. By *c.* 1245 he was back in Germany teaching in Rothenburg. His large house of more than 21 rooms included a study hall and accommodation for his students. His erudition was such that during the following decades legal questions were sent to him by Jews from all over Germany and beyond. His manifold *responsa* touched on everyday matters such as the proper conduct of business, property rights and inheritance. His *responsa* reflect the competition we have discussed between civic authorities and lay and ecclesiastical lords over Jewish taxation. In one of his best-known *responsa* he wrote:

> . . . *Jews are not required to pay taxes to their overlord, unless they actually live in the domain of these overlords. For Jews are not subjugated to their overlords as the Gentiles are, in the sense that they have to pay taxes to a particular overlord even when they do not live in his domain. The status of the Jew, in this land, is that of a free land owner who lost his land but did not lose his personal liberty. This definition of the status of the Jews is followed by the government in its customary relations with the Jews.*

Whatever Meir thought of the matter, in 1286 King Rudolf interpreted Jewish service to entail royal rights over Jewish possessions and freedom of movement. Thus, when Meir was apprehended in Lombardy after he had joined Jews fleeing Germany, he was thrown into prison. Some claim that Meir refused to allow his co-religionists to ransom him to protect them from further extortion. Others claim that it was Rudolf who refused to release him. Whatever the case may be, Meir died in prison in 1293. In 1307 his body was finally retrieved and he was buried in Worms, where his tomb still stands.[17]

Meir of Rothenburg's life embodies the stark ambiguities underlying Jewish existence in eleventh-, twelfth- and thirteenth-century Germany. On the one hand, Jews were embedded in their several localities, conducting their business, engaging in scholarship and governing their own communities. On the other hand, they were exposed to periodic hostility, which increased at the end of the thirteenth century as blood libels and other accusations became more common and more violent. By the turn of the fourteenth century German Jewish scholarship had lost not only Meir; one of his prominent pupils was murdered in 1298, another, R. Asher ben Yehiel, and his son Jacob, who was also to become a famous scholar, moved south to Spain.[18] The survival of the Jews who remained behind continued to depend on the complex interface between weak royal/imperial government and the many conflicting authorities vying for power in the places where they lived. It is now time to move westwards to France to examine the lands where Rashi flourished and the Talmud burned.

Notes and references

1 Not all German kings were crowned emperor, but for ease of reference I shall refer to the rulers of Germany as emperor.

2 Michael Toch, 'The Formation of a Diaspora: the Settlement of Jews in the Medieval German *Reich*', *Aschkenas* 7 (1997), 55–78; Michael Toch, 'The Jews in Europe, 500–1050', in Paul Fouracre (ed.), *The New Cambridge Medieval History*, vol. 1 (Cambridge, 2005), 553–4; Alfred Haverkamp, 'Jews and Urban Life: Bonds and Relationships', in Cluse, 62. See also A. Haverkamp (ed.), *Geschichte der Juden im Mittelalter von der Nordsee bis zu den Südalpen. Kommentiertes Kartenwerk*, 3 volumes, Hanover, 2002.

3 Michael Toch, 'Wirtschaft und Verfolgung: Die Bedeutung der Ökonomie für die Kreuzzugspogrome des 11. und 12. Jahrhunderts. Mit einem Anhang zum Sklavenhandel der Juden', in A. Haverkamp (ed.), *Juden und Christen zur Zeit der Kreuzzüge* (Sigmaringen, 1999), 253–85; Toch, 'The Jews in Europe', 558–9; Haym Soloveitchik, '*Halakhah*, Taboo and the Origin of Jewish Moneylending in Germany', and Alfred Haverkamp, 'The Jews of Europe in the Middle Ages: By Way of Introduction' and 'Jews and Urban Life: Bonds and Relationships', in Cluse, 295–303, 13–4, 55–69 and Soloveitchik, *Principles and Pressures: Jewish Trade in Gentile Wine in the Middle Ages* [Hebrew] (Tel Aviv, 2003); Irving A. Agus, *Urban Civilization in Pre-Crusade Europe. A Study of Organized Town-Life in Northwestern Europe*

During the Tenth and Eleventh Centuries Based on the Responsa *Literature*, two volumes (Leiden, 1965); Hans-Georg von Mutius, *Rechtsentscheide Rheinischer Rabbinen vor dem Ersten Kreuzzug. Quellen über die Sozialen und Wirtschaftlichen Beziehungen zwischen Juden und Christen*, Judentum und Umwelt, 13 i–ii (Frankfurt am Main, 1984–5).

4 *JLSEMA*, 377–83; K.H. Krüger, 'Mauritius', in *Lexikon des Mittelalters*, vol. 6, col. 412.

5 *JLSEMA*, 333–43, 365–7; Toch, 'Jews', 553–4, 566–7.

6 Friedrich Lotter, 'The Scope and Effectiveness of Imperial Jewry Law in the High Middle Ages', *Jewish History* 4 (1989), 31–58; *JLSEMA*, 391–402. Henry's charter for Worms is known only through its confirmation by Frederick Barbarossa in 1157. Alexander Patschovsky ('The Relationship between the Jews of Germany and the King (11th–14th Centuries). A European Comparison', in Alfred Haverkamp and Hanna Vollrath (eds), *England and Germany in the High Middle Ages* (London, 1996), 211–12) argues that the phrase *ad cameram nostram attineant* was an interpolation by Frederick and was not part of Henry's original charter. Lotter ('Geltungsbereich und Wirksamkeit des Rechts der kaiserlichen Judenprivilegien im Hochmittelater', *Aschkenas* 1 (1991), 31) and others disagree; Gerold Bönnen, 'Worms: The Jews between the City, the Bishops and the Crown', Cluse, 450.

7 *JLSEMA*, 351–2, 400–2; Werner Transier, 'Speyer: The Jewish Community in the Middle Ages', Monika Porsche, 'Speyer: The Medieval Synagogue' and Bönnen, 'Worms', in Cluse, 435–45, 421–32 and 453; I.S. Robinson, *Henry IV of Germany, 1056–1106* (Cambridge, 1999), 86, 202–3, 257–8, 308, 329; Michael Toch, *Die Juden im mittelalterichen Reich* (Munich, 1998), 52–3; Ernst Voltmer, 'Zur Geschichte der Juden im spätmittelalterlichen Speyer. Die Judengemeinde im Spannungsfeld zwischen König, Bishof und Stadt', in *Zur Geschichte der Juden im Deutschland des späten Mittelalters und der frühen Neuzeit* (Stuttgart, 1981), 98–9.

8 Bönnen, 'Worms', Cluse, 449–57; idem, 'Jüdische Gemeinde und christliche Stadtgemeinde im spätmittelalterlichen Worms', in C. Cluse, *et al.* (eds), *Jüdische Gemeinden und ihr christlicher Kontext in kulturräumlich vergleichender Betrachtung von der Spätantike bis zum 18. Jahrhundert* (Hanover, 2003), 318–19; *JLSEMA*, 353–5.

9 Haym Soloveitchik, 'Catastrophe and Halakhic Creativity: Ashkenaz – 1096, 1242, 1306 and 1298', *Jewish History* 12 (1998), 71–85; Porsche, 'Speyer', Peter Schäfer, 'Jews and Christians in the High Middle Ages: the *Book of the Pious*' and Rainier Barzen, 'Jewish Regional Organization in the Rhineland: The *Kehillot Shum* around 1300', in Cluse, 428, 29–42, 233–7; see Toch, *Juden*, 93–5 on the vast literature on the *Sefer Hasidim*.

10 Silvia Codreanu-Windauer, 'Regensburg: The Archaeology of the Medieval Jewish Quarter' in Cluse, 391–403; Siegfried Wittmer, *Jüdisches Leben in Regensburg. Vom frühen Mittelalter bis 1519* (Regensburg, 2001), 9–72; *JLSEMA*, 403–4; Toch, *Juden*, 52, 60, 116.

11 Kenneth Stow, *Alienated Minority. The Jews of Medieval Latin Europe* (Cambridge, MA, 1992), 242–51 and 'The Church and the Jews', in David Abulafia (ed.), *The New Cambridge Medieval History*, vol. 5. (Cambridge, 1999), 204–19; Shlomo Simonsohn, *The Apostolic See and the Jews: History.* Pontifical Institute of Mediaeval Studies: Studies and Texts, 109 (Toronto, 1991), 16–21, 44–5; Solomon Grayzel, 'Popes, Jews, and Inquisition. From "Sicut" to "Turbato" ', reprinted in Grayzel II, 4–6; John A. Watt, 'Jews and Christians in the Gregorian Decretals', in Diana Wood (ed.), *Christianity and Judaism.* Studies in Church History, 29 (Oxford, 1992), 93–105.

12 Salo Wittmayer Baron, ' "Plenitude of Apostolic Powers" and Medieval "Jewish Serfdom" ', in *Ancient and Medieval Jewish History* (New Brunswick, NJ, 1972), 296–7; Lotter, 'Scope', 31–58; *JLSEMA*, 353–65, 396–400; MGH, *Diplomata*, 10.4: *Friderici I. Diplomata*, 43–4; MGH, *Constitutiones* II, 274–6; MGH, *Constitutiones*, III, 72–3, 267, 368–9; [J. Widemann (ed.)] *Regensburger Urkundenbuch*, I: Urkunden der Stadt zum Jahre 1350 (Munich, 1912), 12, 19–20, 24, 39, 56–7; J.A. Tomaschek (ed.), *Die Rechte und Freiheiten der Stadt Wien*, vol. 1 (Vienna, 1877), 15–21; Innsbruck Universitätsbibliothek MS 400, no. 131 ff. 163ᵛ–164ʳ (I am very grateful to David Abulafia for showing me his transcription of this document); Guido Kisch, *The Jews of Medieval Germany. A Study of Their legal and Social Status.* 2nd edn (New York, 1970), 135–45; David Abulafia, 'The Servitude of Jews and Muslims in the Medieval Mediterranean: Origins and Diffusion', *Mélanges de l'École Française de Rome* 112 (2000), 687–714; idem, 'The King and the Jews – The Jews in the Ruler's Service', in Cluse, 43–54; Irving A. Agus, *Rabbi Meir of Rothenburg. His Life and His Works as Sources for the Religious, Legal, and Social History of the Jews of Germany in the Thirteenth Century*, 1 (Philadelphia, PA, 1947), 138–44; John A. Watt, 'The Jews, the Law, and the Church: the Concept of Jewish Serfdom in Thirteenth-century England', in Diana Wood (ed.), *The Church and Sovereignty c. 590–1918. Essays in Honour of Michael Wilks.* Studies in Church History, subsidia, 9 (Oxford, 1991), 153–72.

13 For example Kisch, *The Jews*, pp. 145–68, 331–64 and more recently Patschovsky, 'The Relationship', 193–218.

14 Abulafia, 'The King and the Jews', 43–54.

15 Kisch, *The Jews*, 29–41, 153–68.

16 Alfred Haverkamp, ' "Concivilitas" von Christen und Juden im Aschkenaz im Mittelalter', in Robert Jütte and Abraham P. Kustermann (eds), *Jüdische*

Gemeinden und Organisationsformen von der Antike bis zur Gegenwart
(Vienna, 1996), 103–36; Toch, 'The Formation of a Diaspora', 76–7. See also
Gilbert Dahan, 'Le Pouvoir royal, l'église et les Juifs, ou de la condition
politique du Juif en occident médiéval'; in D. Tollet (ed.), *Politique et religion
dans le judaïsme ancien et médiéval* (Paris, 1989), 100–1.

17 Agus, *Rabbi Meir of Rothenburg*, vol. 1 and no. 594 in vol. 2, 551–3,
quotation: 553.

18 Soloveitchik, 'Catastrophe', 78.

chapter 4

The Jews of France

The history of the Jews in medieval France is inexorably linked to the efforts of the Capetian kings of France to expand their royal remit beyond the Île-de-France with Paris at its centre to the other areas which we now call France. The expansion of Capetian power did not just depend on the accretion of royal control over greater stretches of France, as for example when Philip Augustus gained Normandy for his crown from John of England in 1204. It also expressed itself through greater acceptance of the king's overlordship in the course of the thirteenth century by the counts, dukes and princes who ruled the several principalities of France. And even in periods when Capetian authority was minimal in any practical sense of the word, the idea of kingship was kept alive through the existence of royal bishoprics and abbeys throughout France. Control over Jews and the income they delivered through taxation was one of the markers of the extent of royal authority. When Philip Augustus expelled the Jews from his kingdom in 1182, only the Jews of the Île-de-France were affected; when Philip IV did the same in 1306 Jews throughout France had to leave their homes.[1]

These facts point to a number of issues. Both the German emperors and the French kings were jealous of their share of Jewish taxes and did what they could to safeguard their income and to fight off any rival claims to it. But whereas the German kings/emperors seem to have used ecclesiastical rhetoric to tighten their own hold over 'their' Jews, the French kings seem to have internalised the same rhetoric to circumscribe Jewish activities ever more fiercely and ultimately to expel them. The increasing weakness of German royal/imperial power in comparison to the increasing strength of the French played a crucial role in this. As we have seen, the German king/emperor's effective power over the Jews of Germany was severely curtailed by local power structures in urban centres in which Jews played an important part. In France this was different; also different was the role Jews played in the economy. Whereas the Jews of Ashkenaz were engaged in merchant activities well into the thirteenth century alongside money-lending, the Jews of *Zarfat* (the Hebrew term for the 'Langue d'Oïl', i.e. France to the north of the Loire) had become engaged predominantly in moneylending by the middle of the twelfth century, if not earlier. Although there is scholarly disagreement about the nature of Jewish settlement in northern France in the early Middle Ages, there can be no doubt that southern France (Langue d'Oc) remained the place where most French Jews lived throughout the Middle Ages. By the start of the eleventh century we have unequivocal evidence of Jewish communities in areas such as Maine, Anjou, Champagne and Normandy. As we move into the twelfth century a charter of Louis VI (r. 1108–37) of 1119 records his return of properties and income to the abbey of Saint Martin in Tours which had been part of the goods settled on Queen Bertrada by Philip I (r. 1060–1108). Part of this income derived from taxes on Jews in Tours. In 1122 the royal abbey of Saint-Denis was given control over five Jewish houses by King Louis. Guibert of Nogent (d. *c.* 1125) informs us that the Jews of Rouen in Normandy were put to the sword by crusaders in 1096. In striking contrast to Henry IV of Germany, in 1144 Louis VII (r. 1137–80) forbade the return of forced Jewish converts to Judaism on pain of being put to death or mutilated. He did not follow the advice of Peter the Venerable (abbot of Cluny) to make the Jews pay for the ill-fated Second Crusade, but he does seem to have followed Bernard of Clairvaux's advice to make them free any crusader debtors they had from paying interest while on crusade. On the other hand, he seems to have prevented the ritual murder accusation from spreading beyond the borders of Blois in 1171 (see Chapters 7 and 8). On the whole, Louis VII seems to have been quite favourable to the Jews. According to a monastic chronicle from Sens, for example, Louis granted privileges to Jews in the new towns he founded, which included building new synagogues. The chronicler says he did this out of greed. Rigord (d. 1207–9?), the biographer of Philip Augustus, was harshly critical of the way Jews had been allowed to employ Christians servants and to engage in moneylending. Indeed, around 1180 Alexander III complained about Louis's laxity in this respect and for allowing Jews to build new synagogues.[2]

Philip Augustus

By the time the fifteen-year-old Philip Augustus was first crowned as joint king with his father on 1 November 1179 some 1,000 Jews had settled in the heart of Paris on the Île-de-la-Cité, where the royal palace stood and the cathedral of Notre Dame had been under construction since 1163. Other Jews lived elsewhere in Paris and were scattered in towns within the Île-de-France, such as Orléans, Pontoise, Melun, Bourges and Saint-Denis. In Saint-Denis Jews fell under the lordship of the abbey; they were not expelled in 1182. William Chester Jordan believes that there might have been about 5,000 Jews in the royal domain at this stage. Fewer Jews lived there than in Champagne and Jewish communities were often small. Paris had been built up by Louis VI and Louis VII and Jews would have been attracted to the city by its booming economy. By this time many would have been engaged in moneylending as a result of increasing restrictions on Jewish participation in artisanship. Viticulture did not seem to have featured in Jewish life of northern France in the way that it did in Ashkenaz. Somehow royal Jews were prosperous enough for the adolescent king to exact a very high ransom from them to retrieve the goods he had seized from them in 1180 or 1181, just before or just after the death of Louis VII in September 1180. This is the first example we have of a French king attacking 'his' Jews rather than protecting them, though Count Theobald of Blois attacked his own Jews in 1171. In 1182 Philip expelled them from his royal domain. What made Philip reverse his father's policy towards the Jews and what made him act so very differently to his German counterpart, who had confirmed the privileges of the Jews of Regensburg that very year?[3]

Jordan, who has looked at this more carefully than anyone else, has argued that French kings often embarked on new Jewish policies to emphasise their independence from their predecessors' approach.[4] Rigord provides us with a good many details about Philip Augustus's reasons for seizing Jewish goods for a huge ransom in 1180, cancelling Jewish debts and expelling the Jews from his lands in 1182. Rigord claims that Philip thought that Jews were guilty of ritual murder. A certain Richard of Pontoise was supposed to have been killed by the Jews in 1163 and a shrine was constructed in his honour in Paris in the Church of the Holy Innocents. However, if the king really believed Jews ritually murdered Christian children, he would surely have done more than just expel them. This is borne out by the fact that in 1192 Philip burned 80 Jews in retaliation for the death of one of his men who had been executed at their behest. It is important to distinguish between Rigord's interpretation of the king's views and the views themselves. Both Rigord and William the Breton, who reworked and continued Rigord's biography before he composed a poem in honour of Philip, twisted the event of 1192 into a ritual murder story, as we shall see in Chapter 8. The other issues Rigord raises are the employment by Jews of Christian servants, the oppression of Christians by Jews through usury and mistreatment by Jews of Christian religious objects which churchmen had left in their care as pawns. All three of these matters indicate that Rigord clearly felt that the correct balance between Christians and Jews had been upset. Jews were supposed to serve Christians and not have the authority of employers or creditors over them; nor should they be in a position to handle crucifixes and chalices. All of this ran against the principles of canon law. As far as usury was concerned, canon law considered any interest charged beyond the principle as constituting usury. Usury was condemned by theologians such as Peter the Chanter (d. 1197) of Notre Dame and by canonists as a form of theft that endangered the fabric of Christian society. According to Rigord, the young Philip was urged to cancel Jewish loans by the hermit Bernard of Vincennes, one of his advisors at court. Whatever Philip's own thoughts were on these matters, his actions against the Jews, as 'a most Christian king' in Rigord's admiring words, brought him an enormous amount of revenue. The ransom money exacted from the Jews in 1180 alone may well have amounted to more than a year's royal revenue. Philip also retained one-fifth of the Jewish debts he had cancelled for himself, though it is not impossible, as Jordan opines, that this formed part of the ransom sum. And although the Jews were allowed to sell their movable possessions before leaving in 1182, their properties fell to the king without any form of compensation. Synagogues were turned into churches, as for example the synagogue on the Île-de-la-Cité which was turned into the Madeleine by Bishop Maurice de Sully, who was masterminding the construction of Notre Dame. As William the Breton said in his poem some 30 years afterwards:

> *the king could have taken all [of the Jewish debts] if he had wished, nor would he have done anything wrong to them concerning what were just like the things and debts of his servants* (tamquam servorum res et catalla suorum).

The words *tamquam servorum* remind us of Innocent III's bull of 1205 in which he condemned the way Jews employed Christian wet-nurses and declared that Jews had been sentenced to perpetual servitude. '. . . just as *servi* (*tamquam servi*) repudiated by the Lord, in whose death they wickedly plotted . . . they must acknowledge that they are the *servi* of those whom the death of Christ liberated and made them *servi*'.[5] The Jews were the servants of the king whom the king could use as he pleased.

Expelling the Jews from the Île-de-France may have been lucrative in the short run, but Philip seems to have realised that in the long run he had only enriched the lords of, for example, Champagne, Burgundy, Normandy and Maine to whose lands the Jews had fled. That must have been the reason why he recalled them in July 1198, much to Rigord's chagrin. Interesting for our purposes is that Philip had to negotiate with Count Theobald III of Champagne to determine under whose control Jews would now fall. Jews and the financial service they provided were used by king and count to demarcate each other's jurisdiction. It is hardly surprising that Philip was less successful in negotiating such an agreement with his rival King Richard of England who held Normandy, Maine, Anjou, Touraine, Poitou and Aquitaine. Indeed in 1199, King John, Richard's successor ruled that no Jew was allowed to leave his lands. As Jordan has said, all of this must mean that not that many Jews returned to the Île-de-France in 1198, although some Jews who migrated there seem to have been Jews who had been expelled from their domains in the 1190s by minor lords in response to Fulk of Neuilly's preaching against usury. Fulk (d. 1202) had been a pupil of Peter the Chanter. Some of these Jews might originally have been royal Jews. Of the Jews that did return to the royal domain, most went to Paris, but not back to the Île-de-la-Cité; they settled in a new quarter on the right bank of the Seine. It was really only after Philip had managed to secure Normandy, Maine, Anjou and northern Poitou from

John, from 1204 onwards, that he once again gained control over a significant number of Jews.

From the available evidence we can say that there were probably about 2,000 Jews in Normandy in 1204. Although they were less wealthy than their daughter-communities in England, they were prosperous enough to have been a source of revenue for the English kings through taxes, tallages and fines. Using earlier findings of Chazan and Nahon, Jordan points to the existence of some 18 localities in the duchy with some kind of Jewish community; a further 20 are mentioned in the sources in connection with an individual Jew. That the Jewish community of Rouen must have recovered quickly from the 1096 massacre is proved by the archaeological discovery in 1976 of a large twelfth-century Jewish building under the courtyard of the present Palais de Justice. Norman Golb has argued passionately that the building was a major Jewish academy; others following Bernhard Blumenkranz have more modestly recognised it as a synagogue. Synagogues were, of course, also places of study. In John's charter of 1201, which the Jews of Normandy shared with the Jews of England, they were granted protection for themselves and their property. With the conquest of Normandy it was the French king's writ rather than the English one that would govern the Jews. The same applied to the Jews of Maine, Anjou, Touraine and northern Poitou. It is in the latter three areas that the most Jews lived, in cities such as Angers, Saumur, Tours and Poitiers and in towns and villages along the Loire such as Segré, Loches and Amboise.[6]

The French kings did not grant their Jews charters of protection; they promulgated ordinances which regulated Jewish moneylending. And the nature of these ordinances was intimately connected to the way they were trying to assert their royal dignity in their kingdom. Thus in 1206 Philip issued an ordinance concerning the Jews with the agreement of Blanche, the widowed Countess of Champagne, who fell under his guardianship and Guy of Dampierre (a vassal of the Count of Champagne) which clearly sought to address Christian concerns. Following Jordan's reading, the ordinance stipulated that interest rates on Jewish loans were henceforth limited to two pennies a pound per week, i.e. 43 per cent per annum. Jews were not allowed to demand repayment of their loans before a year had passed. Debtors were, however, allowed to arrange to pay back their loans earlier if they so wished without being penalised for doing so. All these debts had to be sealed with the new seals in circulation; Jews were forbidden to accept ecclesiastical objects as pledges or cloth that had blood on it or had been recently washed. Nor were they permitted to accept church lands which fell under the king's or the countess's or other barons' jurisdiction as securities for loans unless they had obtained permission to do so. No extra charges were allowed to be made to creditors who were prevented from repaying their loan at the stipulated time such as pilgrims. In each town two upright Christians would look after the Jewish seals, and a special scribe would produce the contracts. In other words, the king who had in 1182 expelled Jews among other things for engaging in usury was now regulating their moneylending business. Although he was restricting the amount of interest they could charge, he was at the same time endorsing a system which protected Jewish loans, which, of course, ultimately served his own interests as well. Doing all of this in conjunction with his neighbours in Champagne was meant to prevent royal Jews from being tempted to try to avoid the new rules by moving to Champagne. In any case Philip and Blanche renewed the agreement Philip had made with her late husband restricting the movement of Jews from each other's lordship in 1210. Similar agreements were made that year with the Count of Saint-Pol to the north of Philip's lands and with the Count of Nevers to the southeast.[7]

Requiring special seals for Jewish debts and making sure loan agreements were properly drawn up did not offer Philip information about the amount of money Jews had lent and to whom. Particularly worrying for Philip in his guise as 'most Christian king' was the fact that monastic houses often owed considerable sums to Jewish moneylenders. In the autumn of 1209 Philip was obliged to ratify the sale of some of the lands of La Charité-sur-Loire, a religious house which was close to his heart on account of its support for him in his conflict with King Richard. The sale was necessary to repay an enormous debt to a Jewish moneylender. Philip proceeded to command a special audit into all Jewish loans in his now extended domain. When for some reason he came to believe that Jews were being less than frank about their loans, he imprisoned them, requiring a ransom for their release. These Jews had to call in their debts to raise the necessary funds. Many a Christian creditor was caught out in the ensuing scramble to find the cash needed to free the Jews from the king's prisons. Eventually, all were released after eight Jews were selected to guarantee the necessary payments.[8]

Some time in the following years Philip reissued his ordinance concerning Jewish moneylending. The circle of Peter the Chanter was fuelling ecclesiastical condemnation of lending on interest, whether by Christians or Jews. Peter the Chanter had decried the protection given to usurers by princes. As such, they became 'his Jews', whether or not they were in fact Jewish. Besides Fulk of Neuilly, Robert of Courson preached passionately about how the practice of usury was eating away at the heart of Christian society. The Council of Paris of 1213 condemned usurers as being even worse than heretics. All usurers were assimilated in ecclesiastical vocabulary with Jewish moneylenders. In this atmosphere Jews were finding it more difficult to conduct their business. However rapacious and unreliable the king was, they needed the co-operation of his officials to collect their debts and the interest owed on them. The new ordinance renewed its official support to Jewish moneylending, but at a cost. Again, following Jordan's interpretation, the ordinance ruled that loans were to be granted on a fixed-term basis, which presumably included the usual interest of two pennies a week per pound. If the loan was not repaid on time then, as a penalty, interest at two pennies a week per pound would accrue for a year. What was new was that this would happen for only one year; once the year was up, the debt would not accrue any more interest. This would prevent debts taking on vast proportions. Royal officials would henceforth make copies of any loan contracts they sealed. It is clear that the king wished to keep his own record of Jewish lending. It is also clear that at this stage of his reign Philip was not prepared to lose the income he derived from taxing 'his' Jews on account of ecclesiastical ideas about the kind of service they provided within Christian society. One only need think of the challenges Philip was facing around 1212 when he and his son, Prince Louis, were garnering support against King John and his allies. Victory at the Battle of Bouvines in 1214 by Philip and Frederick II of Germany against John and Frederick's rival Otto of Brunswick was as decisive as it was expensive. Consolidation of his extended domain had come at last and Philip could turn his full attention to finding a way to respond to ecclesiastical concerns about usury without undue damage to his royal prerogative. And this brings us neatly to Philip's comprehensive constitution concerning the Jews of February 1219.[9]

To begin with, as Jordan has argued, the fact that Philip dubbed this ordinance a Constitution for Jews must be significant. The term constitution brings to mind the name that Innocent III attached to *Sicut Iudeis*, when he reissued the bull in 1199. When his successor, Honorius, reissued

it in 1217 he addressed [all] faithful Christians. In a technical legal sense a
constitution is a ruling which accords its promulgator supreme authority;
obedience to it is absolutely prerequisite; disobedience would amount to
treason. When Philip used the words 'this is the constitution which the lord
king has made concerning the Jews under his power' he must have meant
to emphasise his and his authority alone as 'most Christian king' to deal
with these matters. Neither the Pope nor any of the French magnates could
to his mind, prevent him from doing so. Yet again, Philip's constitution has
no preamble offering 'his' Jews protection in a general sense. Instead, as
usual, he launches straight into regulations about their moneylending activities. Loans were to be for one year only at a maximum rate of two pennies
per pound per week. New were the careful rules about the types of people
who were allowed to borrow money from Jews such as manual labourers,
who could not fall back on land or chattels to sustain them. A three-year
moratorium was granted to manual labourers with outstanding debts. Jews
were also not permitted to lend money to monks without written consent
from their abbots; nor were they allowed to accept ecclesiastical ornaments
or clothes which were wet or blood-stained. Complicated rules regulated
the repayment of loans made to burghers, merchants and knights; Jews
were to be awarded an agreed portion of the income of the debtor from his
lands or rents. Prior consent of the creditor's lord was needed. If the debtor
played foul, the Jewish creditor could turn to royal officials for help and
repayment would be rescheduled at two pennies a week per pound with a
fine payable to the king. Large loans were at play here, and 43 per cent
interest would be an unwelcome burden. Details were given for the specific
ways in which Jewish debts were administered in Normandy. Although
Philip continued to permit Jewish moneylending in his constitution, he
clearly went out of his way to respond to ecclesiastical worries concerning
vulnerable members of Christian society.[10]

Louis VIII

Philip might have thought that he had successfully regulated Jewish service
to suit his Christian royal persona and his Christian subjects, but his son
clearly did not. When Louis VIII succeeded Philip in 1223, he scrapped the
constitution. The deeply religious Louis seems to have regarded royal protection of Jewish moneylending (and indeed Christian – Louis regulated

but did not provide official back-up to Italian moneylenders in Paris either) as incompatible with the duties of a Christian king. Less than four months after his accession to the throne Louis drew up a new ordinance on Jewish moneylending on 1 November. He did not follow his father's lead in calling it a constitution. One week later, on 8 November, he had 26 magnates of his kingdom, who held Jews under their lordship, add their names to the ordinance, which had to undergo some revision in order to obtain their acquiescence. Louis's ordinance ruled that from now on neither he nor the lords who were co-signatories to the document would allow Jews to use seals for their debts. This amounted to nothing less than the removal of official enforcement of Jewish loans. As far as Jewish debts were concerned, those which were active, that is to say, were still attracting interest according to the regulations of Philip's constitution, would no longer accrue usury. The principal of the debt, and not any of the accumulated interest, would be repaid over the next three years in nine instalments to the lord in whose dominion the Jewish creditor tarried. Bad debts, that is to say, debts which had been incurred since 1219 and which had ceased to attract interest in accordance with Philip's rules, which Jews were actively pursuing, would be repaid to the Jewish creditor. This clause only applied to royal Jews and, as Jordan has shown, was only included in the original version of the ordinance. As far as Jewish mobility was concerned, the ordinance stipulated that neither Louis nor his lords would retain each other's Jews. As Jordan has noted, the language of this clause reads as if it was the king's prerogative to demand this of his lords, whether or not they had signed up to the ordinance. This might well be one of the reasons why the Count of Champagne was not one of the signatories. He signed a separate treaty confirming the older agreement between king and count about non-retention of Jews and a second one agreeing the same with regard to the Jews of the lords who had signed the ordinance. Louis's ordinance did not outlaw Jewish moneylending. What it did do in the short term was, yet again, to seize a good chunk of their financial resources; in the long term it made their moneylending activities considerably more precarious. In so doing it raised serious questions about royal amenability to this particular form of Jewish service. What it also did was, in the tradition of Philip, use dominion over Jews as a marker of the king's authority over his barons.[11] But it was Louis's activities in the field of battle which had much graver consequences for the future of the Jews of France.

Louis's acquisition of the rest of Poitou from the English in 1224 affected some Jews. His gains in Languedoc affected many more. Languedoc was a hotchpotch of rivalling lordships and urban centres. The Jews of Languedoc were part of the political, socio-economic and cultural world of the Latin Mediterranean. Far more Jews lived south of the Loire than in Zarfat. Languedoc is where from the second half of the twelfth century the Cathar heresy had taken hold. Cathars were dualists who maintained that all material things had been created evil by an evil force other than the good God. This was in variance with Catholic thinking which taught that all things were created good by the good God; sin is what made things bad. Cathars developed their own churches and rituals in opposition to Catholicism and were perceived as a serious threat to universal Christendom by the institutional Church. The sense of threat was exacerbated by the fact that magnates in Languedoc, such as Count Raymond VI of Toulouse, offered a safe haven to Cathar heretics. Things came to a head when Innocent III's legate was murdered in Toulouse in January 1208. In March the Pope preached a crusade against the Cathars; by 1209 many northern French knights had arrived in the south. One of them, Simon de Montfort, titular Earl of Leicester, took the lead. Crusaders came and went in a bloody series of sieges and battles. By spring 1216 Simon had been accepted by the Pope and Philip Augustus as Count of Toulouse and lord of other southern lands. This did not, however, prevent a comeback from Count Raymond of Toulouse and his son, Raymond VII. Indeed, when in 1218 Simon de Montfort fell in battle, he had already lost much of his authority. By 1224 Simon's son had to make way for Raymond VII, passing on to King Louis his claims to southern lands. In 1226 Louis decided to go to war to make those claims good. Once Avignon had fallen, other cities followed suit. The king's triumphal path was only stopped by his sudden death in November 1226. It was left to his widow, the redoubtable Blanche of Castile, who was acting as regent to Louis IX, to broker a peace with Raymond VII. In 1229 Languedoc passed into royal hands. Raymond remained count and kept most of his county but the line of succession shifted to his daughter and her husband-to-be, Alphonse, a younger brother of Louis IX. Thousands upon thousands of Jews who had hitherto enjoyed the protective southern approach to Christian–Jewish relations would now experience the hardline policies of the Capetians. But before we go on to explore how Louis IX continued the policies of his short-lived father, we need to turn back to the

Jews of Champagne where significant Jewish settlements had flourished since the early eleventh century.[12]

Champagne

By the end of the eleventh century Jews had settled in Troyes and in the sees of Reims, Sens, Châlons, Auxerre and Soissons, where prelates exercised ecclesiastical and temporal authority under differing degrees of royal influence. Reims or Sens was where the Capetians were crowned. Other important places of Jewish settlement were in smaller towns such as Vitry on an offshoot of the river Marne, and Ramerupt on the Aube. The twelfth and especially the first half of the thirteenth century saw many more settlements in towns of all sizes throughout the different lordships which made up the county. Towns with a particularly strong comital presence, such as Provins, were especially attractive. The community in Troyes, the capital of the county, continued to grow, while the communities in the other bishoprics did not. Troyes was the main seat of the counts of Champagne and the bishop was confined to an ecclesiastical role. Provins was second seat of residence of the counts. In the annual cycle of the Champagne fairs both Troyes and Provins housed a fair twice a year. The fairs attracted merchants and moneychangers from across Europe. In Champagne, as elsewhere in France, Jewish livelihood depended on the goodwill and authority of the prince in whose lands the Jews lived. Thus we see that in Champagne Jews tended to live in the middle of towns in the neighbourhood of the count's castle or palace. In Troyes, for example, the Jewish quarter lay in the oldest part of the fortified town; from 1172 Jews were living in the upper city inside the counts' fortifications near the old market. Civic structures in these important centres and others did not challenge comital authority in the way that cities vied for power in Germany. The Jews had primarily to look to the count for protection, and not to civic authorities. This does not mean Jews failed to interact with their Christian neighbours on an everyday basis. They lived near to each other and did business with each other in markets and fairs. As in royal lands, moneylending was the main Jewish economic activity. Soloveitchik has demonstrated that in Champagne too Jews were not players of any significance in viticulture. Although the region produced wine, it was not a major trading commodity and most of it was used locally. Twelfth-century merchants travelled the length and breadth of Europe to buy cloth at the Champagne fairs, not wine.

The counts of Champagne exploited 'their' Jews through tallages and compulsory loans over and above the taxes they demanded, but on the whole they were less punitive in their regulation of Jewish moneylending than the king. As we have seen, Blanche of Champagne and the lord of Dampierre joined Philip Augustus in issuing the 1206 ordinance regulating Jewish moneylending. And Blanche renewed the non-retention treaty between Champagne and the royal lands in 1210. She drew up similar treaties with neighbouring regions such as Burgundy and Nevers. But the counts did not subscribe to Philip's later Jewish ordinances and, as we have seen, Count Theobald IV of Champagne was not one of the co-signatories of Louis VIII's ordinance of 1223. William of Dampierre was, and unsurprisingly the male Jews of Dampierre fled to Theobald's domain to seek his aid. William was on bad terms with Theobald at the time. They did not expect Theobald to confirm a non-retention treaty with all of the 26 lords who had signed Louis VIII's ordinance, which, of course, included their own lord of Dampierre. Apart from that Theobald and William also reached an agreement in which they used each other's Jews to their own advantage. According to the agreement the count alleviated the debts which the lord of Dampierre and others in his domain owed to the Jews of Dampierre. In return, the count seems to have been given the Jews of Dampierre as a surety. These were not just the men who had hoped to obtain the count's help but also their wives and children whom they had left behind. In other words, as Jordan has explained, the Jews of Dampierre, who had thought to avoid seizure of their goods by their own lord by fleeing to the count, ended up having themselves and their families seized on behalf of the count. What made matters particularly perilous for the Jews was that the count had large outstanding debts to royal Jews, and according to Louis's ordinance these had to be paid to the Jews. The count needed money and word got out that he was prepared to torture the Jews of Dampierre in his hands to get it. The male Jews of Dampierre did what they could to prevail on their lord not to send their families to the count. The end of the sorry story was that many Jews of Dampierre lost what they had in money and lands with the spoils divided between the count and their lord. The point of rehearsing this incident is to show that although comital regulation of moneylending in many ways helped Jews earn their living, the counts made use of 'their' Jews for their own purposes. In other words, however mutually beneficial the relationship between the count and 'his' Jews could be for much of the time, the trump card always remained in comital possession. When, for example, in 1217 Blanche took issue with the pressure exerted by Peter of Corbeil, Archbishop of Sens (1199–1221) on Jewish usury, she did so as much in her own interest as in the interest of the Jews affected. She was not prepared to carry the brunt of ecclesiastical disapproval of Jewish usury and lose Jews to neighbouring lands in the process, just because Philip Augustus had been able to curb Robert of Courson and his followers in royal lands. In Sens itself, Archbishop Peter fanned hostility against the Jews. Pope Innocent III's harsh letter of 16 January 1205 to Philip Augustus concerning Jewish usury seems to have been inspired by him. Innocent had been Peter of Corbeil's student in Paris. The Pope complained about the new synagogue which had been constructed next to an old church in Sens and was higher than the church. Apart from that the Jews conducted their services in loud voices to the detriment of the order of services in the church. According to Innocent, Jews blasphemed against God and mocked Christians for their faith in Christ. Of particular concern was the report that they did this during Holy Week. In short, Innocent felt that the Jews were abusing the king's patience and were posing a real threat to the Christians amongst whom they lived. A murdered Christian scholar had been found dead in their latrine. The Pope admonished the king to make sure that Jewish servitude was not better than Christian liberty. In July 1205 Innocent sent the Archbishop of Sens and the Bishop of Paris the *Etsi Iudeos* bull we have already touched on. This bull coined the idea that the Jews had brought everlasting servitude upon themselves through their actions against Christ. Innocent urged the recipients of the bull to prevail upon the king, the Countess of Champagne (and the Duke of Burgundy) to see to it that Jews served Christians rather than the other way around. If Jews did not dismiss their Christian servants, Christians should refrain, under pain of excommunication, from doing any business with them. As we have seen, both Philip and Blanche seemed to have taken this kind of rhetoric in their stride. But on one crucial point they were at one with Innocent. Jews were meant to serve their lords. Exactly how that service should be defined was another matter.[13]

Rashi and the *Tosafists*

The most remarkable feature of Jewish life in Champagne was its scholarship at the end of the eleventh century. It was in Troyes that Rabbi Solomon
ben Isaac (d. 1105), who is known as Rashi, set up his school after having
studied in Mainz and Worms. Rashi was a brilliant commentator on the
Hebrew Bible and the Talmud. His special gift was the way he analysed the
language and syntax of the Bible in all its permutations in relationship to
existing rabbinical interpretations. In so doing, he often used Judaeo-French
words to help his readers understand the meaning of biblical Hebrew
terms. Rashi's work is, in fact, an important source for scholars of medieval
French. This proves that Jews in Champagne used Judaeo-French as their
daily language. Rashi's grandson, Samuel ben Meir (*c.* 1080/5–*c.* 1158/74)
developed Rashi's exegetical approach and promoted the plain reading of
the words of the Bible within their own context (*peshat* in Hebrew) as
opposed to figurative and allegorical rabbinical explanations (*derash*). The
readiness of northern French practitioners of the *peshat* method in the
twelfth century to move away from rabbinical interpretations and forge
their own understanding of the text is of particular interest.

As far as the Talmud was concerned, the method Rashi and his students
used went far beyond previous scholarship which was more exegetical or
explanatory in nature. The *Tosafists* (writers of the *tosafot* ['additions'], as
Rashi's pupils were called), challenged the complex material of this vast
corpus of rabbinical writings through analytical comparisons between disparate passages. They sought for contradictions in the text and tried to
solve them. They made it their business to tease conclusions from obscure
passages and in the process they added many novel interpretations of their
own. The tractates over which the *Tosafists* pored concerned all aspects of
Jewish life and ritual, including Sabbath observance, laws concerning food
and drink, marriage and divorce. From its first printing in the fifteenth century, the Talmud has appeared with *Tosafist* commentaries in the margin of
the text. In the 1080s Rashi's pupil and son-in-law, Meir ben Samuel set up
a school in Ramerupt. His sons Samuel and Jacob ben Meir (*c.* 1100–1171,
known as Rabbenu Tam) built up the Ramerupt *yeshiva* to be the most
important centre of learning until the time of the Second Crusade.
Ramerupt was one of the few places where Jews lost their lives in 1146.
Another pupil of Rashi was Simha of Vitry. Simha's grandson was Isaac ben

Samuel of Dampierre (*c.* 1120–1195/8) who had studied under Rabbenu Tam and was Tam's nephew. He set up an important academy in Dampierre around the middle of the twelfth century. The school was developed by his pupil, Isaac ben Abraham of Dampierre. These *Tosafists* were an elite within the Jewish community, bound together by their scholarly activities as well as by their family connections.

Tosafist activity was put into practice through the compilation of guides for living and prayer. Simha of Vitry with others, for example, brought liturgical and halachic (legal) matters together into the so-called *Machzor* (prayer-book) *Vitry*. In the middle of the thirteenth century Moses of Coucy composed the *Sefer Mitzvot Gadol* ('the large book of the command-ments'), in which he tried to connect Maimonides's (see Chapter 6) overview of Jewish law with the *Tosafists'* interpretations. Isaac of Corbeil (d. 1280) produced a simplified version of this and called it *Sefer Mitzvot Katan* ('small book of the commandments'). This was a runaway success and became the standard halachic guide for French Jewry. From the names of these scholars it is plain that the study of the Bible and Talmud was not confined to Champagne. In the Île-de-France there were schools in Orléans, Étampes, Melun, Pontoise and, of course, Paris, the greatest of them all. Schools in the outskirts of Paris, such as Corbeil, and schools in Évreux, Touques and Falaise in Normandy gained in importance after the burning of the Talmud in Paris in 1242.

What we have, then, are vibrant Jewish communities with a keen sense of their own importance. Rashi's biblical commentaries and those of the *peshat* school, frequently claimed that their reading of the Hebrew Bible proved that Christian interpretations were wrong. Augustine might have decided that Jews should serve Christians as witnesses to Christian truth, but that is not a role Jews actually accepted. Rashi's commentaries on the Hebrew Bible were so well received that they became the standard accom-paniment to the text. Much is to be said for comparing his commentaries with the work of late-eleventh- and twelfth-century Christian scholars in northern France in providing glosses for the books of the Old and New Testaments. The interest of Rashi and his school in the language of the Bible also brings to mind the work of Christian scholars on the historical meaning of the biblical text in, for example, the school of St Victor. We shall return to this in Chapter 9. *Tosafist* study of the Talmud was not the work of people who accepted the Christian view of a fossilised Judaism.

Their endeavours were not dissimilar to those of Christian scholars exploring Roman and canon law in the twelfth and thirteenth centuries. The *Tosafists* were determined to work out what rabbinical material had to say about their own individual lives and the lives of their communities. Judah ben Isaac of Paris, who was known by his French nickname, Sirléon, and who died in 1228, for example, advised Jews who were required by their lords to swear that they would not leave their domain, silently to add to their oath 'today' or, if they had to swear not to leave as long as they lived 'unless it is necessary'. Jews did not accept the legality of lords restricting their freedom of movement or seizing their property. Referring to an earlier ruling by Rabbi Isaac of Dampierre, Meir of Rothenburg wrote:

> ... *the ruler had no right to confiscate real property that belonged to the Jews for generations. Such an act on the part of the ruler is not considered 'law of the land' [to which Jews by Jewish law had to adhere] but is rather outright robbery, and, therefore, illegal.*

Isaac claimed that 'every Jew had the right, according to the law of the land, to leave his home town at will, and freely to move from place to place' and compared Jewish freedom of movement with that of lords.[14] A great deal was to change after Isaac's death in 1195/8.

Louis VIII's inheritance

It would be a grave mistake to think that the military and diplomatic successes of Philip Augustus, Louis VIII and Blanche of Castile meant that Capetian territorial expansion had been secured once and for all for the young Louis IX. Although Capetian authority radiated far beyond the Île-de-France to the east and west and would from now penetrate deep into the south, southern lords continued to resist royal domination and Aragon's influence was as strong as ever. Gascony continued to be hotly contested with the English. The will of Louis VIII had stipulated that some of Louis IX's younger brothers would hold several of the newly acquired territories. In the event Charles gained Anjou and Maine; Alphonse, who stood to inherit Toulouse through his wife, Poitou and the Auvergne. The idea was to prevent discord among the brothers and to promote Capetian family power in newly acquired lands. In reality it also meant that younger brothers engaged in their own alliances and politics. Constant negotiation was needed to sustain a royal grip on these lands; Louis's successors, Philip III and IV, would insist that that such gifts to cadet members of the royal family should revert to the crown upon the death of the prince in question. When Alphonse died in 1271 without an heir Philip III reclaimed his lands. But Charles of Anjou did have an heir and, as we shall see, both father and son would become important players in late thirteenth-century politics. Further complexities arose from the fact that both Henry III of England and Louis IX had set their sights on Brittany, and relations with Champagne were anything but straightforward. How did Louis IX's policies towards the Jews intermesh with all of these intricate alliances and rivalries?[15]

Louis IX

Louis took the duty of a Christian prince to defend Christendom and safeguard the fabric of Christian society very seriously. He was a devotee of the Virgin Mary and went on two ill-fated crusades in 1248 and 1270. He legislated against prostitution and supported the work of the new papal inquisition against heresy which was especially active in the newly conquered regions in the south. His royal policies were, in other words, infused by his Christian outlook. It is not for nothing that he was remembered as Saint Louis; he was canonised in 1297. As far as Jews were concerned, his biographer, Joinville, quoted Louis as having said that only learned clerks should ever attempt to dispute religious matters with Jews. Laymen should thrust a sword deep into the belly of a Jew if they heard him malign the Christian faith. Louis had no patience for Jewish moneylending activities and was anxious for Jewish conversion. As the new lord of so many Jews he used them to strengthen his position vis-à-vis his magnates. It is striking, for example, how the Ordinance of Melun of 1230 made Jewish policy binding for the whole kingdom. This was made plain by the long list of lords who co-signed the document. The lords included Theobald of Champagne: his own circumstances in 1230 necessitated his co-operation with the crown. As Jordan points out, this was also emphasised by the clause which declared that anyone who disobeyed the ordinance would be considered a rebel to the crown.

It is striking, too, how unwilling Louis was to avail himself of the Jewish service of moneylending. In his eyes usury was immoral and he was determined to cleanse his Christian kingdom of its evils. The exact details of the ordinances that he and his mother – Louis was 12 when his father died – enacted to achieve this need not detain us. Suffice it to say that when Jewish debts were seized in 1227 and 1228, considerable care was taken to distinguish between the principal of the debts and any interest that had accrued. The crown did not want to be tainted by accepting usurious gains. In the Ordinance of Melun Christians were instructed not to pay interest on their loans. In 1235 Jews were admonished to 'live from their own labours or from commerce without usury'. And they were, yet again, forbidden to employ Christian wet-nurses and other servants. Unsurprisingly, Jewish (and Christian) moneylending did continue; not only were alternative economic opportunities for Jews limited, people continued to require capital for their business ventures. Royal advisers seem to have argued that it was preferable for Jews to perform the necessary service of moneylending than Christians because Jews were already damned. But Louis argued that he was responsible for the Jews who were subjected to the yoke of his servitude. As such it was his Christian duty to protect his Christian subjects from being oppressed by Jewish usury. If Jews wished to remain in his kingdom they had to stop lending money at interest. In other words, Louis had a very clear idea about the principles underlying Jewish service in Christian society. From 1244 to 1248 Louis made preparations to go on crusade. From 1245 his Jewish policy began to be applied in Languedoc, while at the same time renewed efforts were made in the north to settle complaints about Jewish debts and any accrued interest. Jewish debts were seized, with any usury returning to the debtors and the principal going to the crown. In 1254 the rulings of Melun were repeated, and Jews were commanded to earn an 'honest' living from the work of their own hands or from trade without engaging in usury. Those who continued the practice of usury were told to leave the kingdom. The obvious hope was that Jews would convert sooner rather than later. Investigations to root out all kinds of usury, Christian as well as Jewish, were carried out until the king again took the cross in 1270. Christian usurers were just as unwelcome as Jewish ones. The complaint by R. Meir ben Simeon of Narbonne gives a Jewish perspective from the south where these hardline ideas about usury seemed particularly incongruous:

Since your wealthy [Christians] refrain from lending free of interest, how will the common people and the needy make a living? Or isn't it true that many [of these less privileged] bring livelihood to their households through [the help of] a loan of money [to purchase] one single [cow] for plowing or a bit of cereal or wheat for sowing and [also] for the protection of their families?

The resistance of the viscount and the Archbishop of Narbonne to Capetian domination actually safeguarded the Jews of Narbonne from the excesses of Louis's Jewish policy. Many Jews looked longingly to Narbonne as the place to escape the king's demands.[16]

The concept of Jewish service is clearly expressed in the clause of the Ordinance of Melun, which concerns non-retention of Jews:

Nor shall anyone in all our kingdom be permitted to retain the Jew of another lord. Wherever anyone shall find his Jew, he may legally seize him like his own serf (tanquam proprium servum), *whatever length of time the Jew was under another's lordship or in another kingdom.*

Much has been written on the meaning of *tanquam proprium servum*. Langmuir and Jordan rightly concluded that the words did not mean that Jews were serfs in any legal sense. What Louis is doing is comparing one aspect of Jewish existence to that of serfs: the fact that they did not have freedom of movement. The comparison was multilayered. On one level it emphasised to his barons that only the king had the authority to make pronouncements such as this one over Jews *and* serfs. As Jordan has pointed out, all serfs could be emancipated by their lords, but the king by now claimed the prerogative to ratify this. On another level the analogy surely echoed Innocent III's *Etsi Iudeos* bull of 1205 where Jews were described as *tamquam servi* to emphasise the implications of perpetual Jewish servitude for their day-to-day existence. We have already suggested that Philip Augustus's biographer might have been influenced by this concept when he described the possessions of Jews as the possessions of the king's servants. On this level the words embodied the concept of Jewish service to the king. Jewish service was not the same as any other kind of service. It was governed by its own rules and ultimately it was the king who called the shots.[17]

But there was another aspect of Jewish life which troubled Louis greatly. In 1240 Gregory IX sent out letters via the Bishop of Paris to princes throughout Latin Christendom to investigate the Talmud. He had heard to his horror that Jews adhered to the Talmud rather than to the Bible. Louis

IX was the only Christian prince to respond, but perhaps it was unsurprising that it was in France, where Talmud studies had reached such heights, that the Talmud was first attacked in this way. Moses of Coucy and Yehiel of Paris were summoned to explain the role of the Talmud in Jewish life. They also had to defend the Talmud against charges of blasphemy. Nicholas Donin, a Jewish convert to Christianity, had warned the Pope that the Talmud contained passages denigrating the Virgin and Jesus. It is not hard to imagine how these *Tosafist* scholars must have felt discussing the work they had dedicated their life to in front of a hostile court who had already made up their mind to condemn the Talmud. In 1242 cartloads of volumes of the Talmud and other books were publicly burnt. Yet again the French king (rather than his mother – there are indications that Blanche had her doubts) had committed violence against 'his' Jews, this time by burning their authoritative texts. In the wake of the burning, Yehiel and many other Jewish scholars escaped from France and travelled to the Holy Land.[18]

Philip III and Charles II of Anjou

Louis IX died on crusade in 1270; his son and heir Philip III returned to France with his remains. Philip himself died in a papally sanctioned war against Aragon in 1285. At stake was the future of Sicily which had been held by Charles of Anjou, Louis IX's brother, from 1266. In 1282 there was an uprising in Sicily, the so-called Sicilian Vespers. Against the Pope's wishes, the King of Aragon laid claim to Sicily, and Charles and the French were driven from the island. Philip was battling for French interests in the Mediterranean. As far as Jews were concerned, Philip followed his father's policies. He continued to demand that Jews wear a sign on their clothes to distinguish them from Christians, according to the ruling of the Fourth Lateran Council. His ordinance of 1282 further regulated Jewish pawnbroking by stipulating how long unredeemed pledges had to be kept before being sold. As Jordan emphasises, there was no return to permitting any form of usury.[19] Indeed, throughout France lords were faced with a paradoxical situation. Usury was deemed unacceptable, and so Jews had been told to choose between giving up moneylending or packing their bags. This brought severe economic hardship to Jews; as Jews they could not freely undertake any kind of manufacturing or other trade among Christians. The point of the policy was to urge them towards the baptismal font. But many

Jews did not convert and moneylending in one form or another continued to exist surreptitiously. Lords had, in other words, to decide what to do with Jews whose moneylending services were no longer welcome. Increasingly, lords saw expulsion as the solution. Brittany had already expelled its Jews in 1240. In 1289 Charles II of Anjou expelled the Jews from Anjou and Maine. The words of his ordinance are revealing. Using the well-known proverb Innocent had also employed in his *Etsi Iudeos* bull about the perils of harbouring a mouse in one's pocket or a snake in one's lap or fire in one's bosom, Charles claimed that Jews had been a subversive force in Anjou and Maine. Through their usury they reduced Christians to beggars; through their licentiousness they corrupted Christian womenfolk. Charles saw it as his Christian duty to purge his lands of this evil. Rather than benefit from Jewish moneylending he preferred to act for the good of his Christian subjects. And to show how deep his loathing for usury was, he also expelled Christian usurers. In exchange for doing his pious duty for his Christian people and in compensation for the financial losses he would incur in so doing, he was granted a special tax from his subjects. But however adamant Charles was about ridding Maine and Anjou of its Jews, he did not expel the Jews from the imperial county of Provence, which he had inherited through his mother Beatrice of Provence. For his part, the English king expelled the Jews from Gascony in 1287 before ordering their expulsion from England in 1290. The Count of Nevers expelled 'his' Jews in 1294.[20] What would Philip IV the Fair do?

Philip IV

Philip, who became Count of Champagne and King of Navarre in 1284 through his marriage to Joan I of Navarre, also insisted that Jews wear the Jewish badge and he too legislated against usury. The host-desecration accusation in Paris of 1290, which we shall discuss in Chapter 8, increased the king's concerns about 'his' Jews. Nevertheless he wanted to benefit from them financially. Philip still drew considerable levels of revenue from the south where most Jews lived. He defended royal jurisdiction to tax Jews against local magnates and he insisted that inquisitors should not overstep their mark and act unlawfully against the king's Jews to the king's disadvantage. Inquisitors had received extra powers through Pope Clement IV's bull *Turbato corde* ('with troubled heart') of 1267 which enabled them to seek out relapsed Jewish converts to Christianity and any Jews who might have supported them in their return to Judaism. The bull was frequently repeated by subsequent popes. War with England over Gascony between 1294 and 1297 increased Philip's need for money. Taxes were exacted from the Church without seeking papal approval; large sums were borrowed from the burghers of French cities and from the Lombards; the Jews throughout the kingdom were milked for what they had. In addition the king increased his available cash by revaluing his coinage at three times its original value. In response to the ensuing inflation the procedure was reversed in 1305, with the coinage brought down to its original value. This in turn brought disarray to the economy and anger over the way the crown tried to manipulate coinage to its own advantage. As Jordan has explained, by 1306 Philip had to do something to prove his mettle and what he did was to order the expulsion of all the Jews of his kingdom after seizing all their properties and chattels.

Expulsions

The expulsion order was followed in most territories of what is now France, including Narbonne. Jews were not expelled from Provence and Avignon, which were both ruled by Charles II of Anjou, the Comtat-Venaissin, which was under papal control and where Carpentras was an important centre of Jewish settlement, and Cerdagne and Roussillon, which were held by the King of Majorca from the King of Aragon (the King of Majorca did follow Philip's wishes with regard to Montpellier, which he held as a vassal of the French crown). Indeed a number of French Jews immigrated to these regions at that time. Others went to Navarre which was held by Philip's son, Louis. Although Louis expelled the Jews from Champagne, his other fiefdom, he did not follow his father's suit in Navarre. Still others went to Catalonia and Aragon; some to areas in the East which fell under German hegemony. The power of Philip to have his expulsion order followed by so many lords in his kingdom proves how successfully the Capetians had used their Jewish policy to enhance the position of the crown. Expelling the Jews was meant to increase the reputation of the hard-pressed king as a most Christian king acting for the good of Christian society. Sharing the confiscated goods of the expelled Jews with his nobles enhanced the point. This was particularly important to Philip following his violent encounter with Pope Boniface VIII in 1301 over his right to arrest a troublesome bishop. Vicious arguments ensued about royal sovereignty as opposed to papal claims of plenitude of power. Under Boniface's successor the seat of the papacy moved to Avignon where it stayed under French influence till 1378.

Another way Philip tried to shore up his royal prestige and, it must be said, fill his ever-empty coffers, was to arrest and despoil the Knights Templar, one of the great crusading orders of military monks. After the fall of Acre in 1291 and the end of the crusader states in the Middle East, the focus of the activities of Knights Templars shifted to France and the rest of Europe, where they had a large number of monastic houses. They were highly successful bankers and advised Philip as his treasurers. In 1307 Philip accused them of all kinds of sexual abuses. His attack on the order was supposed to prove how careful he was in protecting the proper fabric of the Church. As far as coinage was concerned, Philip revalued it in 1311, hoping that this time the procedure would be successful. It was not. When he died in 1314, the crown faced rebellion. The partial re-admission of Jews under Philip the Fair's son, Louis X (r. 1314–16), in 1315 was directly connected to his need for money to deal with the rebellions he had inherited from his father. The few Jews who were re-admitted had to pay heavily for the privilege. They were severely restricted in what they could and could not do; but, contrary to years of Capetian policy, they were allowed to engage in interest-earning pawnbroking by charging two pennies a pound per week. Louis had promised the Jews that they could come back for 12 years, but after the anti-Jewish violence of the Shepherds' Crusade of 1320 and the violence unleashed by the so-called Lepers' Plot of 1321 in which Jews and lepers were accused of colluding with the Muslims of Granada to poison wells, Louis's idea of re-admission lay in tatters. They were again expelled in 1322 by Charles IV (r. 1322–8). In 1359 the crown did re-admit some Jews with the express purpose of making money for the king. They were supposed to function as self-contained communities solely to serve the crown. Finance was again a huge problem, this time due to the high cost of the continuing war with England, the so-called Hundred Years' War. The final expulsion came in 1394 at the hand of Charles VI (r. 1380–1422). Jews continued to live in Provence, Navarre, Roussillon and Cerdagne for another one hundred years or so; the so-called *Juifs du Pape* ('the Pope's Jews') remained in Avignon and Comtat-Venaissin. Avignon

became a papal possession in 1348. By the end of the fifteenth century the
'Pope's Jews' were confined to separate areas in the towns they inhabited.
They became French citizens after the French Revolution.[21] It is time we
crossed the channel to examine the history of the Jews of medieval England.

Notes and references

1 William Chester Jordan, 'Jews, Regalian Rights, and the Constitution in
  Medieval France', in Jordan, *Ideology and Royal Power in Medieval France.
  Kingship, Crusades and the Jews* (Aldershot, 2001), XV, 1–16.

2 Michael Toch, 'The Jews in Europe, 500–1050', in Paul Fouracre (ed.), *The
  New Cambridge Medieval History*, vol. 1 (Cambridge, 2005), 553–5; Gérard
  Nahon, 'Zarfat: Medieval Jewry in Northern France', in Cluse, 205–20;
  JLSEMA, 402–3; Gérard Nahon, 'From the *Rue aux Juifs* to the *Chemin du
  Roy*: The Classical Age of French Jewry', in Michael A. Signer and John Van
  Engen (eds), *Jews and Christians in Twelfth-century Europe* (Notre Dame, IN,
  2001), 311–39; Rigord, *Histoire de Philippe Auguste*, ed. and trans. Élisabeth
  Carpentier, Georges Pon and Yves Chauvin. Sources d'Histoire Médiévale, 33
  (Paris, 2006), 144–7; Simonsohn, no. 59, p. 62.

3 William Chester Jordan, *The French Monarchy and the Jews from Philip
  Augustus to the Last Capetians* (Philadelphia, PA, 1989), 4–10, 52.

4 William Chester Jordan, 'Princely Identity and the Jews in Medieval France',
  in J. Cohen (ed.), *From Witness to Witchcraft. Jews and Judaism in Medieval
  Christian Thought* (Wiesbaden, 1996), 257–73; idem, 'Jews, Regalian Rights',
  1–16.

5 Jordan, *French Monarchy*, 30–2; Rigord, 130–3, 144–55, 311; *Oeuvres de
  Rigord et de Guillaume le Breton, Historiens de Philippe Auguste*, vol. 2, 194,
  22; Gavin I. Langmuir, ' "Tanquam Servi": The change in Jewish Status in
  French Law about 1200', in idem, *Toward a Definition of Antisemitism*
  (Berkeley, CA, 1990), 185 reads William the Breton's statement slightly
  differently. John A Watt, 'Jews and Christians in the Gregorian Decretals',
  in Diana Wood (ed.), *Christianity and Judaism*. Studies in Church History,
  29 (Oxford, 1992), 103–5; Grayzel I, no. 18, pp. 114–17. On usury see
  Chapter 9.

6 Jordan, *French Monarchy*, 38–60; Robert Chazan, *Medieval Jewry in Northern
  France. A Political and Social History* (Baltimore, MD, 1973), 70–4, 207–20;
  Nahon, 'Documents sur les juifs de Normandie médiévale au public Record
  Offices de Londres', *Archives Juives* 11(1975), 3–10; Norman Golb, *The Jews
  of Normandy. A Social and Intellectual History* (Cambridge, 1978), 154–69;

among the many items Bernhard Blumenkranz wrote on the subject see his 'Synagogues en France du haut moyen-âge', *Archives Juives* 14 (1978), 37–42; see Chapter 5 note 5.

7 Jordan, *French Monarchy*, 61–3, 69; for Chazan's reading see *CSJMA*, 205–7; John W. Baldwin, *The Government of Philip Augustus. Foundations of French Royal Power in the Middle Ages* (Berkeley, CA, 1986), 230–3.

8 Jordan, *French Monarchy*, 64–7.

9 Jordan, *French Monarchy*, 73–82; *Recueil des Actes de Philippe Auguste*, vol. 2 (Paris, 1943), no. 955, pp. 549–51, vol. 4 (1979), nos 1554–5, pp. 188–91; Chazan's reading in *CSJMA*, 207–8; Kenneth R. Stow, 'Papal and Royal Attitudes toward Jewish Lending in the Thirteenth Century', *AJS Review* 6 (1981), 178–9; John W. Baldwin, *Masters, Princes and Merchants. The Social Views of Peter the Chanter and His Circle*, 1 (Princeton, NJ, 1970), 296–9.

10 Jordan, 'Princely Identity', 265–8; Jordan, *French Monarchy*, 82–90; Chazan's reading in *CSJMA*, 209–10.

11 Jordan, *French Monarchy*, 93–104; Chazan's reading in *CSJMA*, 211–12.

12 Jordan, *French Monarchy*, 105–27.

13 Sonja Benner and Alexander Reverchon, 'Juden und Herrschaft: Die Champagne vom 11. bis frühen 14. Jahrhundert', in C. Cluse *et al.* (eds), *Jüdische Gemeinden und ihr christlicher Kontext in kulturräumlich vergleichender Betrachtung von der Spätantike bis zum 18. Jahrhundert* (Hanover, 2003), 151–213; Haym Soloveitchik, *Principles and Pressures: Jewish Trade in Gentile Wine in the Middle Ages* (Tel Aviv, 2003), 91–8 [Hebrew]; Jordan, *French Monarchy*, 80–1, 98–102; Grayzel I, nos 14, 18, pp. 104–9, 114–17; Simonsohn, nos 79, 82, pp. 82–4, 86–8; Watt, 'Jews and Christians', 103–5. See Chapter 8 for accusations against Jews of using their latrines to store bodies or desecrate Christian religious objects.

14 Benner and Reverchon, 'Juden', 157–60; Kenneth R. Stow, *Alienated Minority. The Jews of Medieval Latin Europe* (Cambridge, MA, 1992), 135–56; Nahon, 'Zarfat', 210–13; Haym Soloveitchik, 'Catastrophe and Halakhic Creativity: Ashkenaz – 1096, 1242, 1306 and 1298', *Jewish History* 12 (1998), 71–6; Barry D. Walfish, 'An Introduction to Medieval Jewish Biblical Interpretation', in Jane Dammen McAuliffe a.o., *With Reverence for the Word. Medieval Scriptural Exegesis in Judaism, Christianity, and Islam* (Oxford, 2003), 4–5; Simon Schwarzfuchs, 'La Vie interne des communautés juives du nord de la France au temps de Rabbi Yéhiel et de ses collègues', in Gilbert Dahan with Élie Nicolas (eds), *Le Brûlement du Talmud à Paris 1242–1244* (Paris, 1999), 29; Irving A. Agus, *Rabbi Meir of Rothenburg. His Life and His Works as Sources for the Religious, Legal, and Social History of the Jews of Germany in the Thirteenth Century* (Philadelphia, PA, 1947), vol. 1, 141 and

vol. 2, 552–3; see also Emily Taitz, *The Jews of Medieval France.*
The Community of Champagne (Westport, CT), 1994.

15 Elizabeth M. Hallam and Judith Everard, *Capetian France 987–1328*, 2nd edn
(Harlow, 2000), 177–8, 267–75, 318–22.

16 Jordan, *French Monarchy*, 128–76; Chazan, *Medieval Jewry*, 102–4; *CSJMA*,
216–17; Jordan, 'Jews, Regalian Rights', 7; A. Teulet a.o., *Layettes du Trésor
des Chartres*, vol. 2 (Paris, 1866), no. 2083, pp. 192–3; Chazan's reading in
CSJMA, 213–15; Meir's quotation from: Joseph Shatzmiller, *Shylock
Reconsidered. Jews, Moneylending, and Medieval Society* (Berkeley, CA, 1990),
80–1. On Narbonne see Chapter 6.

17 Jordan, *French Monarchy*, 133; Jordan, 'Jews, Regalian Rights', 8; Langmuir,
'Tanquam Servi', 178–94; John A. Watt, 'The Jews, the Law, and the Church:
The Concept of Jewish Serfdom in Thirteenth-century England' in Diana
Wood (ed.), *The Church and Sovereignty c. 590–1918. Essays in Honour of
Michael Wilks.* Studies in Church History, subsidia, 9 (Oxford, 1991), 155–6,
172 which stresses the importance of the concept of Jewish service. See also
Gilbert Dahan, 'Le Pouvoir royal, l'église et les Juifs, ou de la condition
politique du Juif en occident médiéval', in D. Tollet (ed.), *Politique et
religion dans le judaïsme ancien et médiéval* (Paris, 1989), 96–100.

18 Jordan, *French Monarchy*, 137–41; Jordan, 'Marian Devotion and the Talmud
Trial of 1240', in Friedrich Niewöhner (ed.), *Religionsgespräche im Mittelalter.*
Wolfenbütteler Mittelalter-Studien, 4 (Wiesbaden, 1992), 61–76; Nahon,
'Zarfat', 216; Colette Sirat, 'Les Manuscrits du Talmud en France du Nord au
XIIIᵉ siècle', in Dahan, *Le Brûlement du Talmud*, 127. The literature on the
Talmud trial is vast, see for example Jeremy Cohen, *The Friars and the Jews.
The Evolution of Medieval Anti-Judaism* (Ithaca NY, 1982), 62–76; texts in
Hyam Maccoby (ed. and trans.), *Judaism on Trial. Jewish–Christian
Disputations in the Middle Ages* (London, 1982), 19–38, 153–67.

19 Jordan, *French Monarchy*, 150–1.

20 Jordan, *French Monarchy*, 72; Chazan, *Medieval Jewry*, 184–6; *CSJMA*,
314–17.

21 Jordan, 'Jews, Regalian Rights', 9–16; Jordan, *French Monarchy*, 179–251;
Grayzel II, no. 26, pp. 102–4; Simonsohn, no. 230, pp. 236–7; Chazan,
CSJMA, 181–2; Jordan, 'Home Again: The Jews in the Kingdom of France,
1315–1322', in *Ideology and Royal Power in Medieval France*, XIV, 27–45.
Nahon, 'Zarfat', 216–18; Esther Benbassa, *The Jews of France. A History from
Antiquity to the Present*, trans. M.B. DeBevoise (Princeton, NJ, 1999), 25,
41–7. Much has been written about the trial of the Templars, see for example,
Malcolm Barber, *The Trial of the Templars*, 2nd edn (Cambridge, 2006).

chapter 5

The Jews of England

When it comes to the Jews of England we are geographically on much firmer ground than we could ever be in France and Germany. Politically we are dealing with more effective concepts of royal authority. Chronologically we have greater clarity because we are considering a Jewry with beginnings in 1066 and an end in the expulsion of 1290. We also have a wealth of documentary evidence concerning Jewish moneylending. All of these factors set the Jews of England apart from the Jews of Ashkenaz and Zarfat and indeed, as we shall see in the next chapter, the Jews of the Latin Mediterranean. But having so much clear-cut evidence for English Jewry does not mean we can extrapolate evidence from England to other parts of Latin Christendom, for example, about the role of Jewish moneylending.[1] The rich evidence for England gives us the opportunity to see with particular clarity the ambiguities which underlay medieval Christian–Jewish relations and the importance of Jewish service in Latin Christendom. For, prosperous as the English Jewish community was, its fortunes proved to be precarious. And the key to both Jewish prosperity and uncertainty was the nature of Jewish service to the crown.

Changing money and trading in plate

It is likely that William the Conqueror brought Jews from Rouen to London on account of their expertise in the trade in luxury items and their experience in moneychanging. As Stacey has argued, William may have hoped to use 'his' Jews as some kind of counterweight against the Anglo-Saxon merchant community in London. But new Jewish immigrants did not make their mark as traders. By the first half of the twelfth century they seem to have created successful businesses through dealing with plate and coin together with moneylending. People needing cash had to pawn or sell all kinds of items including silver or gold objects, jewels and items of clothing. Dealing with plate was particularly lucrative in England because of its ready availability and because English coins, which were minted under strict royal control, contained a very high percentage of silver as a result of the massive sale of wool to the continent. This meant that moneyers, who continued to be Anglo-Saxons, were in constant need of good-quality plate. Jews and non-Jews, including the moneyers themselves, were heavily involved in providing plate for coins. But Jews gained an edge in the moneychanging business because they were allowed to travel from county to county to visit fairs, in order to ply their trade. Christian moneyers were only allowed to act as moneychangers in their own county. This meant that Jews could seek out the best deals to foreign merchants at different fairs who had either to exchange their coins for expensive English ones or to sell their plate so that it could be converted into the requisite English coins. For in England the crown did not allow the use of foreign coins, but made a profit from reminting foreign coins into English ones. And because Jews could, therefore, attract foreign business, they became profitable to the lords of fairs. As Stacey has pointed out, this provides a good explanation for Jewish migration from London to other market and minting towns from around the middle of the twelfth century. Even the unsettled reign of King Stephen seems to have been beneficial for the Jews, though it is possible that Jews started moving into the provinces by the end of Henry I's reign. We know from the *donum* of 1159, through which Henry II collected monies from the Jews, that Jewries existed outside London in Norwich, Lincoln, Cambridge, Winchester, Thetford, Northampton, Bungay, Oxford, Gloucester and Worcester. Jews were probably in Bury too by this time. Many of these towns were ports, but not major ones. Most of them had mints and either hosted fairs of their own or were located close to important fairs. All of these towns had Norman castles, offering protection to incoming Jews.[2]

Moneylending in the king's service

Further opportunities beckoned when Henry II divested himself of his Anglo-Saxon moneyers and their moneylending in 1158 and when he began to disadvantage other Christian moneylenders as well. The Constitutions of Clarendon of 1164, in which Henry tried to reclaim prerogatives which the Church had been granted under Stephen, denied ecclesiastical courts the right to deal with debt pleas. Henry also started to claim the estates of open usurers. In 1166 he proceeded to confiscate the estate of the great Flemish moneylender William Cade. Together with growing ecclesiastical strictures against usury, this meant it became ever less lucrative for Christians to specialise in moneylending. As for Jews, they had full royal backing to collect their debts, especially when from around 1180 Henry taxed them rather than use them as a source for borrowing money, and after 1186 when he confiscated the huge estate of Aaron of Lincoln and proceeded to use his royal muscle to collect the outstanding debts for himself. By the end of Henry's reign a Jewish financial network, comprising some two dozen Jewish communities, spread from London to Norwich and Lincoln and reached into the developing areas around York, where Aaron of Lincoln lent substantial sums to the elite of the land, which included prominent landowners, knights and religious houses. Additional provincial Jewries now included Lynn, Stamford, York, Canterbury, Warwick, Colchester, Chichester, Bristol and Hereford.[3]

As Jews set up Jewries outside London, some local lords seem to have gained rights over them. But the notion that all Jews in fact 'belonged' to the king was never lost. The so-called *Leges Edwardi Confessoris*, a twelfth-century legal collection, made it plain that all Jews fell under royal jurisdiction and protection because Jews and all their possessions belonged to the King. As Roger of Howden (d. 1201–2) phrased it in his Chronicle:

> *Let it also be known that all Jews, wherever they may be in the kingdom, must be under the guardianship and protection of the lord king, nor can anyone of them subject himself to any prominent person without the king's licence. Jews and all they have belong to the king. But if anyone will have detained [money] from them, the king may demand their money as his own.*

By the end of the 1170s the crown was determined to make sure practice accorded with theory. The case of Bury St Edmunds illustrates this well.

We learn from Jocelin of Brakelond's Chronicle of Bury St Edmunds about the financial difficulties of the abbey. A great deal of money had been borrowed and the treasures of the monastery had been used as pledges. Jocelin mentions a very large debt owed to William FitzIsabel, one of the leading Christian moneylenders after the death of William Cade. Large loans were also taken from Jews. It is interesting that a prominent Christian lender was used by the monastery as well as Jewish moneylenders. Jocelin claimed that whenever the abbot was travelling, Jewish *and Christian* lenders would clamour for their money. Abbot Samson (r. 1182–1211), the hero of Jocelin's work, was determined to settle the monastery's affairs. In 1190 Samson sought permission from Richard to expel the Jews from Bury; apart from anything else, Samson did not want anyone in town who did not fall under his jurisdiction: 'the Jews should be St Edmund's men or they should be banished from the town'. Permission was granted on condition that the Jews would be allowed to take their movable possessions with them and retain the value of their immovable property. Samson ruled that anyone giving accommodation to Jews in Bury would henceforth be excommunicated. Richard, however, insisted that if Jews needed to plead their cases against their debtors at the abbey's 'great court of pleas' (which functioned in Bury as the royal county court) they would be allowed to stay for two nights and two days. The jurisdictional aspect of the Jews' presence rather than the savage attacks on the Jewry earlier that year or the report of ritual murder ten years before, to which we shall return, seems to have weighed heaviest on Samson's mind.[4]

In England then, unlike Germany and France, the king was able to claim exclusive jurisdiction over 'his' Jews. The Jews were in England on royal sufferance. He looked after them so that they could serve him. We can get an overview of the privileges given to the Jews by looking at the provisions of Richard's charter of 22 March 1190 and John's of 1201. The charters are virtually identical. Richard's refers to privileges granted to the Jews by Henry II; John's to those granted by Henry I. This is important because no charters concerning Jews survive from Henry I and Henry II. Richard and John's charters allowed the Jews to reside freely and honourably in England and Normandy, and they were given free passage throughout these lands. Jews were permitted to receive or to buy any pledges brought to them except ecclesiastical items and blood-stained cloth. Their goods were to be protected in the same way royal possessions were. Jewish witnesses as well as Christian ones were to be used in court cases between Christians and Jews. Jews were expected to swear oaths on the Torah.[5]

So far we have an image of a Jewry which had successfully expanded from its earliest beginnings as an imported group of Jews from Rouen. Jews from other areas of Normandy augmented the community over the years, as did Jews from northern France and the Rhineland. By the end of Henry II's reign English Jewry possessed considerable wealth which was concentrated in the hands of a small number of prominent Jews, such as Aaron of Lincoln. English Jews lent out large capital sums to the elite within Anglo-Norman/Angevin society: aristocratic landholders, knights and, crucially, religious houses, such as Bury St Edmunds. Many Cistercian monasteries in Lincolnshire and York borrowed considerable sums from Aaron of Lincoln. Less well-off Jews dealt in very much smaller loans to townspeople and peasants. Wealthy and poorer Jews were also occupied with other affairs such as medicine and the trade in wine – we shall return to that. But behind the façade of this success lay a host of ambiguous attitudes within Anglo-Norman and Angevin society towards a group of newcomers under the special protection of the king, who not only continued to speak French but also used Hebrew and who, crucially, were adherents of a different religion.[6]

Inklings of this emerged in 1144 when rumours started circulating that Jews ritually murdered little boys to mock Jesus. Details of this are the subject of another chapter. These rumours first arose in Norwich after the body of a twelve-year-old boy was found. This warrants a closer look at the situation in Norwich in this period. As was true for many towns of Anglo-Saxon England, the Norman influx into Norwich fundamentally changed the town's appearance. The Norman castle and cathedral displaced scores of Anglo-Saxon houses. It is worth recalling that in the mid-twelfth century all towns containing Jewries had a Norman castle. In Norwich a new Norman borough was created. This borough was in direct competition with the existing Anglo-Saxon market. The Norman cathedral was also in competition with older Anglo-Saxon parishes. Competition existed not only between Normans and Anglo-Saxons; there was tension too between the Norman cathedral and castle. Into this medley came French-speaking Jews some time before 1144, settling in the new Norman borough. Lipman thought they arrived around 1135, at the start of Stephen's turbulent reign. In these circumstances it is possible to see such shocking accusations against Jews as deliberate mechanisms to bind together different sections of the Christian community through their hostility against Jews.[7] It is, however, important to stress that in twelfth-century England Jews were not murdered on account of these libels.

Violence in 1189–90

But they were murdered in the violence connected with Richard's coronation in September 1189 and the departure of crusaders on the Third Crusade in 1189–90. The Jewries affected included London, Norwich, Lynn, Stamford, Lincoln, York and Bury. The particulars of what happened will be discussed in Chapter 7. At this stage it is interesting to analyse how William of Newburgh discussed the Jews in his description of the riots, in order to get a better sense of the ambiguities underlying the Jewish presence in England. William was an Austin canon at Newburgh in York. He was the author of an important commentary on the *Song of Songs* in which he made numerous references to Jews. His *History of the English*, which he probably wrote in the year or so before his death in late 1198, gives an extensive account of what happened to the Jews at the start of Richard's reign. William wrote about these events at greater length and with more concern than all the others who mentioned them. William was faced with the problem that he had to rhyme acts perpetrated against the Jews of which he clearly did not approve with his belief that Jews were a 'perfidious and blasphemous race' carrying collective responsibility for the Crucifixion. Although he was convinced that those who attacked the Jews acted out of greed, he did feel that the Jews of England had been getting above themselves by the end of Henry II's reign. So he introduced the subject by stating that Henry II had cherished the Jews more than he should have on account of the profits he made from their usury. This had allowed the Jews to act insolently towards Christians and impose hardship on them. William felt that it was important to record what had befallen the Jews as a memorial of divine judgement against that 'perfidious and blasphemous race'.

William felt that even if the attackers of the Jews were driven by zeal to serve God, they ignored the basic Christian maxim that Jews should not be killed: 'slay them not' (Psalm 58[9]: 12). According to William, Jews were the crucifiers of Christ and, as such, they were allowed to live among Christians for the express purpose of reminding them of Christ's Passion. He compared their presence to the presence of crosses in churches which reminded the faithful of the Passion. But on account of their guilt for the Crucifixion Jews must *serve* Christians. What mattered in Christian–Jewish relations was that they were useful to Christians; Jewish service was the key concept underpinning this. William had hard words to say about those who attacked the Jews in 1189–90, but he did feel that an inversion had occurred in the correct hierarchy within Christian–Jewish relations. Jews existed in order to serve Christians until they converted. This meant that Jews should not have a hold over Christians by lending them money; Jews should not be wealthier than Christians; the king should not strengthen the position of the Jews by making them the king's usurers; he should not profit from their moneylending. William implied that the topsy-turvy state of affairs had caused widespread resentment among Christians, especially among the gentry of Yorkshire who were heavily indebted to Jews and those who were going on crusade. Reading William's views on the position of Jews within Christian society in this way is confirmed by his references to Jews in his commentary on the *Song of Songs*. William called Synagogue the mother of the Church. By taking his flesh from Mary, Christ had been born of the Jews. By rejecting Christ, Synagogue betrayed her Lord. William said in so many words that Jews were guilty of deicide, and that all contemporary Jews shared in this guilt because the Jews at the time of the Crucifixion called Christ's blood upon their children. But those Jews unwittingly served Christ. For Christ used their wickedness to redeem the Gentiles. The true Israelites were now the Christians. William was careful to point out that no amount of enmity towards Jews should cause people to forget that salvation came from the Jews because it was from them that Christ took his flesh. As a punishment for killing Christ Jews were burdened with the yoke of service in this world. Once they converted, the burden would be lifted.[8]

We have before us the built-in complexity of translating the theological concept of Jewish service into temporal realities. Heavy taxation was the price the English crown exacted from 'its' Jews in return for royal support for moneylending. Jews needed to be successful to pay these taxes. Yet any success they enjoyed could be seen as upsetting the right order governing the relationship between Christians and Jews. Having said that, we know that the Jews did build up successful businesses. This means that for all the existing ambiguities Jews and Christians must have lived side by side quite comfortably for much of the time. Jocelin of Brakelond complained that Jews were free to wander around the monastery, even during services.

Although many Jews in Bury lost their lives in 1190, they had found safety in the monastery in previous turbulent times.[9] It is striking how during the crusading riots the perpetrators are primarily the indebted gentry of York and crusaders passing through. Locals did join in, for example in London once the riots started. The so-called *Chronicle of Benedict*, which was probably an earlier version of Roger of Howden's *Chronicle*, not only states that the *plebs* of London took their cue from the *curiales* (courtiers) but also that some Jews managed to save themselves by hiding in the castle or *in the houses of their friends*.[10] In York the elite of the city held off, as did the inhabitants of King's Lynn and Stamford.

Recovery

The Jews recovered rapidly from the crusade riots and were able to expand their business with considerable success. But royal control over English Jewry was greatly enhanced by ordinances Richard put in place in 1194. The clear objective of these rulings was to prevent the possibility of debtors ever again destroying the evidence of their debts to the Jews. This is what happened in York after the Jews had been killed in Clifford's Tower; the indebted knights had burnt the bonds the Jews had put into safekeeping in York Minster. The ordinances required Jews to register everything they owned, including their debts, rents and houses. All loans would be recorded in double charters (chirographs); one half would be kept by the Jewish lender, the charter would be sealed with the seal of the Christian debtor; the other half would be kept in chests (*archae*) which would be kept in royally licensed places such as London, Lincoln and Norwich. The chest would have three locks and keys: one key would be kept by two Christians, the second by two Jews, the third by clerks of the crown. Transcripts of all these charters would be kept on rolls. These regulations led to the formalisation of the Exchequer of the Jews, a special royal department to deal with Jewish affairs, which had started its activities in the pursuit of the debts of Aaron of Lincoln. The Exchequer had its own personnel of justices and clerks. It dealt with the taxes and tallages Jews had to pay to the crown; it was also the place where court cases were heard on behalf of Jews or against them.[11] The records of the Jewish Exchequer provide us with extremely rich documentation about Jewish life in the thirteenth century, predominantly with regard to its economic aspects.

Jewish life

What about the Jews themselves? Jewish communities had synagogues with schools of different levels in which males studied Hebrew, the Bible and Jewish law. From 1177 provincial Jewries were allowed to set up their own cemeteries so that they did not have to rely on the Jewish cemetery in London. These cemeteries were to be built outside the city walls.[12] This means that Jewries would have had local burial societies. Jewish courts made up of scholars of Jewish law would legislate on all internal Jewish matters, including rulings on food and drink. The courts would also hear matrimonial cases, handle all kinds of contracts and deal with any internal disputes. Numerous *shetaroth* ('deeds') have survived from these court proceedings.[13] Female Jewish participation in moneylending is extensively documented and it appears that Jewish women played an active role in their families' economic endeavours. Many did business together with their husbands, others acted independently, often after they had been widowed.[14] Jewish scholars based their rulings on their interpretation of the Talmud and were in close contact with their counterparts in France. Throughout the time that Jews lived in medieval England there were close familial, religious and intellectual relations between English and French Jewries. The Jewries managed somehow to maintain these contacts even after the loss of Angevin lands to the French crown.

Although moneylending together with pawnbroking became the chief occupation within the Jewish community, one must not forget that many Jews were also doctors, teachers and scribes. Jewish bakers, butchers, wine traders etc. must also have serviced their communities.[15] In many cases Jews would have engaged in moneylending or pawnbroking alongside another occupation. As for literary activities, we have very little English Jewish material for the twelfth century. It was left to Ephraim of Bonn (d. after 1196), the author of *Sefer Zekhirah* ('Book of Remembrance') to praise King Stephen for protecting the Jews at the time of the Second Crusade and to commemorate the martyrs of London and York; Menachem ben Jacob and Joseph of Chartres wrote elegies for the martyrs of York.[16] We do know that the Spanish poet, philosopher, exegete and grammarian Abraham ibn Ezra (d. 1164) visited London in the course of his many travels and it is possible that the French author of the renowned twelfth-century Hebrew *Fox Fables*, Berechiah haNaqdan, spent time in England.

For the thirteenth century we have some Hebrew poetry by Meir ben Elijah of Norwich and the remarkable halachic compendium, the *Etz Hayyim*, which R. Jacob ben Judah Hazan of London composed just before the expulsion in 1290. It is very likely that the extant MS of the text is, in fact, his autograph. Although this work is hardly a masterpiece of its kind, it does provide us with a snapshot of Jewish daily life and liturgical practices in England just before the expulsion. From the *Etz Hayyim* we learn, for example, that at Passover Jews tried to acquire all the fruits mentioned in the *Song of Songs* to make their *charoset*, the paste representing the mortar the Israelites used when enslaved in Egypt. We have in the *Etz Hayyim* a copy of a *get* (Jewish bill of divorce) from which we learn some technical legal details. We have the record of a number of English rabbinical rulings. We gain a deeper insight into the close religious ties between English Jews and those living in northern France through the use of French words throughout the text; English Jews seem to have shared their order of service of the *Seder* (the service in the home on the eve of Passover) with the Jews of Normandy. We also have three poems by Jacob and a fourth anonymous one which laments the depletion of scholars and synagogues.[17]

John and the first half of Henry III's reign

The volatile nature of Jewish business fortunes was exacerbated in the thirteenth century, with a period of expansion in the first half of Henry III's reign following a precarious time under John and preceding increasing problems in the second half of Henry III's reign. These came to a head under Edward. John's need for money was a burden for both his Christian and Jewish subjects, but whereas Christians were taxed for 1/13th of their chattels in 1207, yielding about £60,000; Jews had to pay 4,000 marks (1 mark = $\frac{2}{3}$rds pound) as well as transferring to the king 1/10th of the bonds they held. In order to fulfil this requirement, Jews were put under the obligation to produce a list of all the bonds and their values. But the king also claimed the prerogative to buy any bond he wanted to at the value given. The result of this was that John started chasing repayment of bonds Christians had originally arranged with Jewish moneylenders, much as Henry II and Richard had done with Aaron of Lincoln's confiscated bonds. Following the heavy tallage of 1207, John ordered a *captio* (seizure) of all Jews and their bonds in 1210. A ransom of 60,000 marks was demanded over the next few years. Jews who fell behind in their share of payment of this tallage were imprisoned. Once again, this led to even more bonds coming into royal hands and Christian debtors coming under increasing pressure to settle their debts. More and more lands were ceded to the crown in the process. It is not for nothing that Jewish property, including synagogues in London, came under fire during the turbulent years of the Magna Carta rebellion. The circle was complete: hardship imposed on the Jewries by the king led to hardship among his prominent subjects, this in turn led to their violence against Jews and their property.

Matters quickly improved during Henry III's regency and in the early years of his reign. Jews once again experienced the more benevolent side of royal protection and were able to recoup their losses. It is interesting that the king did not insist that Jews wear the *tabula*, the English version of the Jewish badge featuring two white tablets representing the tablets of the law. This had been required in 1218 during his regency, following Lateran IV. Over the next decades English Jewry was able to produce a number of male and female Jewish magnates who made fortunes by lending money to the upper echelons of Christian society. The names that come to mind are David of Oxford (d. 1244) and his widow Licoricia of Winchester (d. 1277), Leo of York (d. 1245), Aaron of York (d. after 1255), Hamo of Hereford (d. 1231) and David Lumbard of Nottingham (active in the 1220s). Hereford, Oxford and York had become important centres for Jewish finance. Most other Jewish moneylenders would have done business on a smaller scale with the members of the local gentry, their fellow city dwellers and people living in the surrounding villages.[18] But even in these years of plenty there were significant signs of trouble ahead. In 1232–4 Bishop Peter des Roches of Winchester used his position at court to lead a campaign against the Jews. A straightforward explanation for this campaign was Henry III's desperate need for money to fund his attempts to win back his French lands. Thus an onerous tallage was placed on the Jews in 1233 after they had already been heavily taxed in the previous year for operations in France and after they had been paying regular tallages since 1221.[19]

Nicholas Vincent rightly links Peter des Roches's campaign to theological issues. In Paris the circle of Peter the Chanter had expressed itself forcefully against moneylending by Christians and Jews. An active proponent of this school was Thomas Chobham, who fulminated against princes benefiting from Jewish usury in his handbook for confessors of around

1215. He found it hard to credit that the Church put up with such affairs. Jews, according to him, were supposed to serve Christians by performing lowly jobs in society; they were not supposed to lord it over Christians. The sentiments of William of Newburgh echo in our ears. Another member of this circle was Stephen Langton, who as Archbishop of Canterbury did his best to introduce the anti-Jewish canons into England. At the Council of Oxford in 1222 rulings were passed reiterating the earlier canonical prohibitions against Jews employing maidservants and the building of new synagogues. Jews were forbidden to enter churches or to ask for their property to be stored in churches for safekeeping. Jews had to wear the *tabula* badge. But however much ecclesiastics such as Langton supported these canons, their enforcement relied on temporal power. Christians could be put under pressure through threats of excommunication, but the king made sure that the Church did not wield power over 'his' Jews. Thus efforts to boycott Jews who did not follow the canons were blocked by royal officials. As we have seen, the wearing of the *tabula* was not enforced at this stage. But that does not mean that the ecclesiastical concerns about Jewish moneylending and service went away. When in 1231–2 Simon de Montfort expelled the Jews from Leicester for much the same reason as the Abbot of Bury had done so in 1190, the Jews moved into the lands under the jurisdiction of the Countess of Winchester. Robert Grosseteste, who at that stage was Archdeacon of Leicester, proceeded not only to instruct the Countess of Winchester about the evils of profiting from Jewish usury but also to insist that Jews should serve by living from the toil of their hands from the land rather than waxing rich from charging usury. King Henry himself took the lead in encouraging Jewish conversion by establishing the *Domus Conversorum* (House for Converts) in Chancery Lane in London in 1232. The pious idea was that Henry would use a proportion of the property which came his way when a Jew converted to provide for the convert's future upkeep. The chapel of the House was dedicated to the Trinity; its patron saint was the Virgin Mary. The *Domus* bore many similarities to a monastery. It provided communal life for its male and female inmates and was designed to ease converted Jews into Christian society. In the event, it was chronically under-funded and overcrowded and in many ways became a kind of no-man's land between Christian and Jewish society, from which converts and their children found it hard to emancipate themselves fully. Converts who could not be accommodated in the *Domus* were parcelled out to reluctant monasteries by the king for care. One year after founding the *Domus* Henry passed a Statute of the Jewry in April 1233 which limited the interest Jews were allowed to charge on their loans to two pennies per pound per week (i.e. 43 per cent per annum). Compound interest was forbidden. Jews who were unable to provide service to their king were to leave by the following Michaelmas. At the end of 1234 Jews were expelled from Warwick, High Wycombe and Newcastle upon Tyne.[20]

Stacey has described the 1233–4 years as a brief hiccup in the good years under Henry, which lasted until 1239; Vincent has charted the decline of English Jewry in the thirteenth century from these years.[21] It would seem more helpful to argue that the sentiments expressed by Thomas Chobham, Langton and Grosseteste, the actions precipitated by des Roches and also Henry's own measures reveal the time bomb threatening the presence of Jews in thirteenth-century England. The unsolved conundrum of how temporal Jewish service could or should follow theological guidelines while being at the same time profitable to the king made Jews vulnerable to any political exigency. That Jews could still be prosperous in the years leading up to the *captio* of 1239 does not mean they were in no danger.

The second half of Henry III's reign

The second part of Henry III's reign showed all the familiar traits. After the crippling seizure of their goods in 1239, the Jews faced massive and crippling tallages in the 1240s. In 1239, the rule limiting interest charges to two pennies per pound per week was reiterated; in addition, a six-month moratorium was placed on accumulating interest on Jewish debts. Increasing pressure on Jewish lenders once again resulted in heavy pressure on Christian debtors to pay up. Many had to forfeit their lands and see them pass into the hands of the king's favourites.[22] In 1253 the king passed a Statute of the Jewry, taking on board many of the ecclesiastical canons which had been so keenly promoted by Langton at the start of his reign. As before, Jews were defined by the service they provided to the king: no Jewish man or woman was to remain in England unless he or she served the king in some way. Wearing of the *tabula* became a requirement; Jews were not allowed to employ Christian servants; Christians were not permitted to live in Jewish houses; Jews were not allowed to move to other towns without the king's permission; there were to be no synagogues in towns that did not have them under John; Jews had to keep their voices down during their synagogue services; Jews had to join Christians in abstaining from meat in Lent.[23] Aaron of York went bankrupt in 1255; by 1258 Licoricia had fallen into penury.[24] In 1255 a ritual-murder libel gained royal support for the first time. Henry commanded a royal investigation into the accusation that Jews had ritually murdered 'little Hugh of Lincoln'. Nineteen Jews were executed for the alleged crime; others were eventually released by the king.[25] Stacey reckons that between about 1240 and about 1260 as many as 10 per cent of the English Jewish population might have converted. His calculations are based on the assumption that there were probably about 3,000 Jews in England in 1240. In the 1280s the population had shrunk to less than 2,000. Others have suggested higher figures for the mid-thirteenth century of 4,000 or 5,000; still others much higher figures of 16,000. As for individual towns, Stacey suggests 500 to 700 Jews lived in London. Other English Jewish communities would have numbered between 50 and 300 people.[26]

Many barons joined forces with Simon de Montfort in 1263–4 when Henry's reign fell apart. They lashed out against the Jews: the Jewries of London, Canterbury, Worcester, Lincoln, Bedford, Bristol, Northampton, Winchester and Nottingham were attacked. Jews were forced to choose between death and the font. *Archae* were seized and bonds were destroyed to prevent the king from appropriating more lands through confiscating Jewish loans. When Henry had regained power he responded to these fears by stipulating in 1269 among other things that Christians taking over Jewish debts could only lay claim to the original sum lent. In 1271 he not only confirmed this but also determined that Jews should not be allowed to own land in freehold.[27]

Edward I

When Edward I came to the throne in 1272 he quickly discovered that his Christian subjects were unwilling to bear the brunt of indirect burdens caused by renewed heavy royal tallages on the Jews. This reinforced his own reservations concerning usury and prompted him to change gear and issue his Statute of the Jewry in 1275. The statute acknowledged that English kings had profited from Jewish usury at the expense of their Christian debtors. It attempted to rectify some of these abuses at the expense of

Jewish lenders. Thus Christian debtors were guaranteed that they could keep enough back from their debt for maintenance without concern for the maintenance of the Jewish creditor. It spelt out repeatedly that Jews owed exclusive service to the king and it tried to make sure Jews did not 'lord over Christians'. It tried to do this by directing Jewish economic endeavours away from moneylending towards trade or working on the land. We are reminded of Grosseteste's views on the latter. Although it envisaged Jews going about this business under the king's protection, it hampered Jews' freedom of movement by limiting them to living in the *archae* towns. They were to be distinguished from Christians by the *tabula* badge and to pay a poll tax. In short, one could say that apart from all the reasons of expediency Edward had for drawing up this statute, he was also trying to work out a way in which to find an acceptable format for temporal Jewish service.

English Jews were not slow to point out their concerns about the statute to the king, but to no avail. Their problems were aggravated when in 1283 Edward set up a new system for recording and enforcing Christian loans, which copied many features of the Exchequer of the Jews. By this time Christian moneylenders, including the French Cahorsins and the Italians, had been filling the gaps left by ruined Jewish moneylenders. The system was not open to Jews. This made it harder than ever for Jews to compete successfully. Nonetheless, Mundill has argued that a number of Jewish moneylenders were able to shift their business interest to trade in grain and wool. Stacey suggests that some Jews went back to trading in plate and coins. We must remember that many moneylenders would have maintained some trading activities in addition to moneylending. Both point out that whatever the statute said, certainly (small-scale) moneylending did continue, as bishops pointed out in their complaints to the king in 1285. In any case, any speculative trading in commodities would have been considered usurious as well. The bishops also complained that converted Jews lapsed back to Judaism. John Peckham (Archbishop of Canterbury, 1279–92) was particularly concerned about this kind of apostasy. It is worth noting that after 1280 the crown made Jews submit to hearing weekly conversion sermons delivered to them by Dominican friars.[28]

Stacey has argued that a revival in Jewish involvement with bullion, plate and coins might be one of the reasons that so many Jews were arrested and tried in 1278–9 for coin-clipping offences. It is indeed likely that some

Jews, as indeed some Christians, were involved in the crime. At the same time it is patently obvious that Jews were punished disproportionally for the offence. Zefira Rokeah has demonstrated that for every Christian who was executed almost ten Jews were condemned.[29] Whatever the case may be, there can be no doubt that the coin-clipping trials depleted an already shrinking English Jewry.

How did English Jews respond to the different expressions of royal control and protection they were exposed to? We have seen that it was possible for some English Jews to amass remarkable wealth at the end of the twelfth century and towards the middle of the thirteenth century. It was their wealth that made it possible for the king to extract so much money from 'his' Jews. But just as their success often led their Christian contemporaries to assume that all Jews were wealthy at the expense of Christians, so should modern historians look beyond the success of a few to try to gauge how the communities coped as a whole. William of Newburgh records how concerned English Jews were to ensure that Richard would continue his father's favourable treatment of them. It is not for nothing that the leaders of the York Jewry, Benedict and Josce, had come down to London for Richard's coronation. In the event, the king did not allow Jews to share in the festivities. The riots had started when courtiers pushed back a Jew who himself had been pushed forward by the crowds. With their French connections English Jews would have been all too well aware of the fact that the new king of France had inaugurated his reign by expelling the Jews of his kingdom. They would have known of the violence perpetrated against the Jews of Blois in 1171 when the Count of Blois burnt about 30 Jews on a trumped-up ritual murder accusation. In other words, they would have been well aware that royal protection could be capricious and unreliable. Nor were these sentiments confined to Jews. A number of twelfth-century sources mention the possibility of Jews being expelled from England. These include an allusion in Thomas of Monmouth's *Life of William of Norwich* and a passage in Gerald of Wales's *Concerning the Instruction of Princes*. Stacey has argued that the crusading riots should be interpreted as widespread disappointment that the new king did *not* expel 'his' Jews.[30]

As far as the thirteenth century is concerned, we should recognise that for all the wealth that was accumulated by the most successful Jewish financiers, the fact that royal hostility recurred under John and before all too long under Henry meant that English Jews realised that they could not rely on royal protection for any length of time. This caused considerable insecurity and resentment. One of the poems by Meir ben Elijah of Norwich, for example, which, according to Susan Einbinder, was probably written after 1275 lamented the crippling taxation inflicted on English Jews and the hatred Jews had incurred. It also showed that Jews understood the negative knock-on effects which royal pressure on them had had on their Christian debtors: 'The land exhausts us by demanding payments, and the people's disgust is heard.' Concern is expressed over the decline of the Jewish community through conversion. Hopes of redemption are loudly voiced by invoking God to save his people: 'You are mighty and full of light, you turn the darkness into light.'[31]

In 1290 Edward was making strenuous efforts to negotiate a grant of tax from his subjects. Concessions had to be made. One of these was the expulsion of the Jews. But as we have seen, the concept was hardly a novel one. Apart from the French expulsion of 1182 and local expulsions under Henry III, Edward's own mother had insisted in 1275 that Jews should be expelled from the towns which provided her with income. This resulted in Cambridge Jews moving to Norwich, Marlborough Jews to Devizes, Gloucester Jews to Bristol and Worcester Jews to Hereford. In 1287 the Jews had been expelled from English Gascony. The fact that Edward no longer profited from 'his' Jews was one of the reasons he was prepared to countenance the concession. But English Jewry was also depleted on account of royal rapacity. And royal rapacity had as its premise the concept of Jewish service, which owed so much to ecclesiastical ideas about the correct relationship between Christianity and Judaism. Thus we see once again the intimate interface between Christian–Jewish relations and general political, economic and religious concerns.[32] Let us now move southwards to examine the pragmatic attitudes of the Christian kings of Iberia towards their Jews.

Notes and references

1 Robert C. Stacey, 'Jews and Christians in Twelfth-century England: Some Dynamics of a Changing Relationship', in Michael A. Signer and John Van Engen (eds), *Jews and Christians in Twelfth-century Europe* (Notre Dame, IN, 2001), 351.

2 Robert C. Stacey, 'Jewish Lending and the Medieval Economy', in
   R.H. Britnell and B.M.S. Campbell (eds), *A Commercialising Economy.*
   England 1086 to c. 1300 (Manchester, 1995), 82–7; Joe Hillaby,
   'Jewish Colonisation in the Twelfth Century', in Patricia Skinner (ed.),
   Jews in Medieval Britain (Woodbridge, 2003), 20–2.

3 Stacey, 'Jews', 345–54; idem, 'Jewish Lending', 87–97; Hillaby, 'Jewish
   Colonisation', 27–9; H.G. Richardson, *The English Jewry under Angevin*
   Kings (London, 1960), 121, 161–3.

4 Stacey, 'Jews', 348–50; Roger of Howden, *Chronica*, ed. William Stubbs,
   RS 51.2, 231; Stacey, 'Jewish Lending', 89; Jocelin of Brakelond, *Chronicle*
   of the Abbey of Bury St Edmunds, trans. Diana Greenway and Jane Sayers
   (Oxford, 1989) x, xvi, xx, 3–4, 28–9, 41–2; H.E. Butler (ed. and trans.),
   The Chronicle of Jocelin of Brakelond Concerning the acts of Samson, Abbot of the
   Monastery of St. Edmund. Nelson Medieval Texts (Oxford, 1949), 1–2, 32,
   45–6.

5 *CSJMA*, 67–9, 77–9.

6 Stacey, 'Jewish Lending', 92–7; Hillaby, 'Jewish Colonisation', 27–8; Stacey,
   'Jews', 343–5.

7 V.D. Lipman, *The Jews of Medieval Norwich* (London, 1967), 4; J.J. Cohen,
   'The Flow of Blood in Medieval Norwich', *Speculum* 79 (2004), 26–65.

8 *The History of William of Newburgh*, in *Chronicles of the Reigns of Stephen,*
   Henry II and Richard I, ed. R. Howlett, RS, 82.1 (London, 1884), 280,
   293–322; online translation by Joseph Stevenson (*The Church Historians*
   of England, vol. 4.2, London, 1856), edited by Scott McLetchie (1999):
   http://www.fordham.edu/halsall/basis/williamofnewburgh-intro.html;
   William of Newburgh's Explanatio sacri epithalamii in matrem sponsi, ed.
   J.C. Gorman (Freibourg, 1960), 151–3, 228, 238, 299–302, 341–2;
   Michael J. Kennedy, ' "Faith in the one God flowed over you from the Jews,
   the sons of the Patriarchs and the Prophets": William of Newburgh's writings
   on Anti-Jewish violence', *Anglo-Norman Studies* 25 (2003), 139–52.

9 Jocelin of Brakelond, *Chronicle*, trans. Greenway and Sayers, 10;
   ed. Butler, 10.

10 R.B. Dobson, *The Jews of Medieval York and the Massacre of March 1190*,
   Borthwick Papers, 45 (York, 1974), 23; *The Chronicle of the Reigns of Henry II*
   and Richard I of Benedict of Peterborough, ed. William Stubbs, RS 49.2, 84.

11 R.R. Mundill, 'The Medieval Anglo-Jewish Community: Organization
   and Royal Control', in C. Cluse *et al.* (eds), *Jüdische Gemeinden und ihr*
   christlicher Kontext in kulturräumlich vergleichender Betrachtung von der
   Spätantike bis zum 18. Jahrhundert (Hanover, 2003), 273–81; Roger of
   Howden, *Chronica*, ed. Stubbs, RS 51.3, 266–7; J. Jacobs (ed.), *The Jews*

of Angevin England (New York, 1893; repr. 1977), 156–9; see also
Paul Brand, 'The Jewish Community of England in the Records of English
Royal Government', in Skinner, 73–83.

12 Roger of Howden, *Chronica*, ed. Stubbs, RS 51.2, 137.

13 Mundill, 'Medieval Anglo-Jewish Community', 267–75; Hans-Georg von
Mutius (trans.), *Rechtsentscheide Mittelalterlicher Englischer Rabbinen,
Judentum und Umwelt*, 60 (Frankfurt am Main, 1995); M.D. Davis, *Hebrew
Deeds of English Jews before 1290* (London, 1888).

14 R.B. Dobson, 'A Minority within a Minority: The Jewesses of Thirteenth-
century England', in S.J. Ridyard and R.G. Benson (eds), *Minorities and
Barbarians in Medieval Life and Thought* (Sewanee, 1996), 27–48; idem,
'The Role of Jewish Women in Medieval England', in D. Wood (ed.),
Christianity and Judaism (Oxford, 1992), 145–68. My PhD student,
Hannah Meyer has written a fascinating thesis on the role of female Jewish
moneylenders in thirteenth-century England.

15 Mundill, 'England: The Island's Jews and Their Economic Pursuits', in Cluse,
219–32.

16 Jacobs, 107–8, 130–1, 258–9; A.M. Habermann, *Gezerot Ashkenaz ve-Zarfat*
(Jerusalem, 1945), 121, 127, 147–54; Cecil Roth, 'A Hebrew Elegy on the
York Martyrs of 1190', *Transactions of the Jewish Historical Society of England*,
vol. 16 (1945–1951), 213–20; Susan L. Einbinder, 'Meir b. Elijah of
Norwich: Persecution and Poetry among Medieval Jews', *Journal of Medieval
History* 26 (2000), 146.

17 Einbinder, 'Meir b. Elijah', 145–9; Cecil Roth, *The Intellectual Activities
of Medieval English Jewry*. The British Academy, Supplemental Papers, 8,
London, [1950]; Moses Hadas (trans.), *Fables of a Jewish Aesop, Translated
from the Fox Fables of Berechiah ha-Nakdan* (New York, 1967); Rabbi Jacob
ben Jehuda Hazan of London, *The Etz Hayyim*, ed. I. Brodie, 3 vols,
Jerusalem, 1962–7, for *charoset* see vol. 1, p. 321; M. Beit-Arié, *The Only
Dated Medieval Hebrew Manuscript Written in England (1189 CE) and the
Problem of Pre-expulsion Anglo-Hebrew Manuscripts* (London, 1985); David
Kaufmann, 'Etz Chayim of Jacob B. Jehudah of London, and the History of
His Manuscript', *JQR* 5.3 (1893), 353–74, 'The Prayer-Book According to
the Ritual of England before 1290', *JQR* 4.1 (1891), 20–63, 'The Ritual of
the Seder and the Agada of English Jews before the Expulsion', *JQR* 4.4
(1892), 550–61.

18 Stacey, 'Jewish Lending', 92–7; Stacey, 'The English Jews under Henry III',
in Skinner, 41–6; Dobson, 'A Minority', 43–4; John A. Watt, 'The English
Episcipate, the State and the Jews: The Evidence of the Thirteenth-century
Conciliar Decrees', in P.R. Coss and S.D. Lloyd (eds), *Thirteenth-century*

England. Proceedings of the Newcastle upon Tyne Conference 1987 (Woodbridge, *c.* 1988), 140.

19 N.C. Vincent, 'Jews, Poitevins, and the Bishop of Winchester, 1231–1234', in Diana Wood (ed.), *Christianity and Judaism* (Oxford, 1992), 119–32; Stacey, 'English Jews', 48–9.

20 Vincent, 'Jews', 128–32; Richardson, *English Jewry*, 180–9, 293–4; Watt, 'English Episcopate', 140–3; Watt, 'Grosseteste and the Jews: A Commentary on Letter V', in M. O'Carroll (ed.), *Robert Grosseteste and the Beginnings of a British Theological Tradition. Papers Delivered at the* Grosseteste Colloquium *held at Greyfriars, Oxford on 3rd July 2002* (Rome, 2003), 201–16; Thomas of Chobham, *Summa Confessorum*, 7. 6. 11. 4 and 7. 4. 6. 11, ed. Frederick Broomfield. Analecta Mediaevalia Namurcensia, 25 (Louvain, 1968), 434, 510; Watt, 'Parisian Theologians and the Jews: Peter Lombard and Peter Cantor', in P. Biller and B. Dobson (eds), *The Medieval Church: Universities, Heresy, and the Religious Life. Essays in Honour of Gordon Leff* (Woodbridge, 1999), 72–4; R.C. Stacey, 'The Conversion of Jews to Christianity in Thirteenth-century England', *Speculum* 67 (1992), 263–83; Stacey, 'Jews', 350–1.

21 Stacey, 'English Jews', 48–9; Vincent, 'Jews', 119, 132.

22 Stacey, 'English Jews', 48–50.

23 Watt, 'English Episcopate', 143–5; *CSJMA*, 188–9; Stacey, 'English Jews', 52.

24 Stacey, 'English Jews', 50, Dobson, 'Minority', 44.

25 G.I. Langmuir, 'The Knight's Tale of Young Hugh of Lincoln', *Toward a Definition of Antisemitism* (Berkeley, CA, 1990), 258–9.

26 Stacey, 'Conversion', 269, 279.

27 Stacey, 'English Jews', 52–4.

28 Stacey, 'English Jews', 53–4; R.R. Mundill, *England's Jewish Solution. Experiment and Expulsion, 1262–1290* (Cambridge, 1998), 119–45, 291–3; Mundill, 'Edward I and the Final Phase of Anglo-Jewry', in Skinner, 62–70; Stacey, 'Jewish Lending', 98–100; Watt, 'English Episcopate', 144; Stacey, 'Conversion', 268–9; 282–3.

29 Stacey, 'Jewish Lending', 99; Zefira E. Rokeah, 'Money and the Hangman in Late-13th-century England: Jews, Christians and Coinage Offenses Alleged and Real', *Jewish Historical Studies* 31 (1988–90), 83–109; 32 (1990–2), 159–218; Willis Johnson, 'Textual Sources for the Study of Jewish Currency Crimes in Thirteenth-century England', *British Numismatic Journal* 66 (1996), 25–6, 30–1; Sophia Menache, 'Matthew Paris's Attitudes toward Anglo-Jewry', *JMH* 23 (1997), 153–6.

30 William of Newburgh, *Chronicles*, ed. Howlett, RS, 82. 1 , 294; Stacey, 'Crusades, Martyrdoms, and the Jews of Norman England, 1096–1190', in

A. Haverkamp (ed.), *Juden und Christen zur Zeit der Kreuzzüge* (Sigmaringen, 1999), 243–51; Cohen, 'Flow of Blood', 55; August Jessopp and Montague Rhodes James (ed. and trans.), *The Life and Miracles of St. William of Norwich* (Cambridge, 1896), 25; Gerald of Wales, *Concerning the Instruction of Princes*, trans. J. Stevenson (Felinfach, 1991 [repaginated facsimile reprint of 1858]), 31.

31 Einbinder, 'Meir b. Elijah', 145–62; analysis: 153–6; translation of text with notes: 156–9; Hebrew 160–2.

32 Mundill, *England's Jewish Solution*, 23, 249–85.

chapter 6

The Jews of the Latin Mediterranean

The history of Jewish–Christian relations in the lands of the Latin Mediterranean is intimately linked to the history of the Muslim conquest of Spain from 711, Sicily in 827, the Balearic Islands in 902 and Muslim incursions to southern France. The sway of the Umayyad caliphate of Cordoba, which was established in 929, reached deep into the north of Spain where the fledgeling Christian kingdoms of Leon, Navarre, Castile and Aragon were emerging. Christian rule had already been restored to Barcelona by 802. As the caliphate disintegrated into numerous competing states or *taifas* from the start of the eleventh century, the Christian kingdoms and *taifas* vied with each other for territorial gains and tribute. The capture of Toledo in 1085 by Alfonso VI of Leon and Castile gave Christians an important edge in the frontier area between the Tagus and Guadiana rivers. The Muslims of al-Andalus responded to this by calling in the help of the Berber Almoravids from north-west Africa. Although the Almoravids resisted further Christian advances, they were not able to retake Toledo. The annexation of al-Andalus to their African empire stretched their resources. This situation was exacerbated when the fundamentalist Almohads from Morocco replaced them. The Almohads did win an important victory at Alarcos in 1195 which gave them the upper hand along the Guadiana. But in the long run they could not consolidate their gains. Both the Almoravids and the Almohads espoused strict forms of Islam which had little sympathy for the tolerant Muslim courts of the *taifa* states of al-Andalus. Their hardline policies not only caused Jews and Christians to move northwards to Christian Spain and southern France or Jews to migrate eastwards to more tolerant Muslim lands, it seems to have stimulated Christians within Spain to be more receptive to ideas which had already stimulated French knights to fight Muslims in Spain from the 1060s. With hindsight one can see the battle at Las Navas de Tolosa in 1212 as the turning point in the gradual but steady Christianisation of Spain. Gathered at Las Navas de Tolosa were the kings of Castile, Navarre and Aragon together with French crusaders. The mastermind behind the operations was the Archbishop of Toledo, Rodrigo Jiménez de Rada (r. 1209–47), who had garnered backing for the battle with papal support from within and outside Spain and who in his later writings presented the battle as a mighty confrontation between Christianity and Islam. Over the following years it became clear that the Almohads were not able to retaliate; their hold over Spain dissipated when in 1224 the caliphate became embroiled in a power struggle after the death of Yusuf II. As different *taifa* kings competed with each other and with different scions of the Almohad dynasty to take the lead in Iberia, Fernando III was able to combine Leon and Castile under his rule. All these factors made it possible for Fernando to take Cordoba in 1236 and Seville in 1248. Majorca had been seized by King James I of Aragon-Catalonia in 1229; the city of Valencia was conquered in 1238; the kingdom of Murcia was taken over by Castile in 1265–6. By the end of the thirteenth century Muslim power in Spain had been effectively restricted to the kingdom of Granada.[1]

A tradition of *convivencia*

The circumstances under which these Christian kings formed their attitudes towards the Jews of their territories, known by the Hebrew term *Sefarad*, were entirely different from those in which their Visigothic predecessors had developed their punitive policy of enforced conversion. For one thing, they were taking over Muslim lands where there had been a tradition of tolerance for the Peoples of the Book. The *laissez-faire* atmosphere of the Cordoban caliphate and the courts of the *taifa* kingdoms had given Jews and Christians considerable opportunities to partake in all aspects of their host cultures. Many Jews had risen to high administrative positions in Muslim courts, as for example, Samuel ibn Naghrila (d. 1056) who served the king of Granada as vizier, and possibly as a general too. The literary output of

Samuel and other poets and scholars such as Bahya ibn Paquda (writing
c. 1080), Solomon ibn Gabirol (d. 1054–8), Moses ibn Ezra (d. after 1138),
Judah Halevi (1075–1141), who was born in Toledo, but who spent much
of his life in Muslim Spain before leaving for the Holy Land, Moses ben
Maimon (Maimonides [1138–1204]) exudes the mixing of cultures for
which the Muslim courts of al-Andalus remain so renowned. These people
also wrote in Arabic, even if they used Hebrew script; their Hebrew poetry
followed the metre and literary conventions of Arabic verse; their thinking
was moulded by Arabic translations of Greek philosophical and scientific
texts. That even under mainstream Muslim rule Jewish preferment did not
always find approval with all sections of society is attested by the fact that
Samuel's son Joseph, who inherited his father's positions, was assassinated
by disaffected Muslims who put the Jewish community of Granada to
the sword in 1066. Maimonides had to flee Almohad rule in his native
Cordoba; it was in Cairo that he composed his major philosophical work,
The Guide for the Perplexed, in which he attempted to synthesise the ideas of
Aristotle to the teaching of the Torah. But temporary setbacks in eleventh-
century Granada and the fundamentalist approach of the Almohads do
not take away from the fact that generally medieval Muslim society had
room for monotheists such as Jews and Christians who accepted the divine
revelation of scriptural authority, as long as they accepted their subjection to
Muslim rule. Jews and Christians were so-called *dhimmis*, protected people
who paid an annual poll tax, or *jizya*, as a symbol of their subjection and
in exchange for their protection. Although these measures meant that Jews
and Christians were second-class citizens – to use the phrase so aptly coined
by Bernard Lewis – the vital point is that they *were* citizens. Medieval Islam
could find a concrete, practical place for Jews in its societies. Unlike
medieval Christianity, it did not have to struggle with defining the practical
position of contemporary Jews in the light of the theoretical role they were
supposed to play as theological reminders of the past and portents of
the future. This outlook enabled what modern historians have dubbed
convivencia, the 'living together' of Muslims, Jews and Christians.[2]

Opportunities in newly conquered territories

As important as the broad framework of *convivencia*, which the Christian
kings inherited from Islam, was the immediate practical need for them to

consolidate their authority over extensive new territories and to make those lands economically productive. Lands from which Muslims fled had to be resettled. Newly conquered lands needed a strong presence of royal authority. These lands were on the frontiers of what had so recently been Muslim territory; at the same time, they created new frontiers between the competing Iberian kingdoms. The challenge of absorbing them into their existing kingdoms gave the Christian kings the opportunity to develop strategies to expand their authority throughout their realms. And, as Jonathan Ray has recently argued, the royal conquerors were more than happy to make use of Jews to act as royal vanguards in the resettlement of Muslim areas brought under Christian rule. Jews who had retained their knowledge of Arabic were of especial use to them in the complicated negotiations which accompanied Muslim surrender and the intricate administrative realignment of landholding and taxation which followed. Jewish translators were often rewarded with considerable estates. Jewish courtiers of the interior, like their Christian counterparts, were granted large tracts of land which were often managed from afar. An obvious example of this is the gift of Alfonso X (r. 1252–84) of a prosperous village of Paterna Harah just outside Seville to some of his Jewish tax collectors and officials. The efforts of the Castilian kings to repopulate the city itself after it had been abandoned by so many Muslims is reflected by the strong presence of Toledan Jews in Seville. Jewish settlement was actively encouraged not just by grants of land; their lives and property were safeguarded by the crown and they were given rights of free passage to facilitate their trading activities, as for example in the 1239 privilege granted to the Jews of Valencia by James I of Aragon (r. 1208–76):

> *We receive you all . . . and your property under Our protection, custody and command, and under Our special safe-conduct wherever you may go, remain, or return in all places of Our kingdoms and dominions on land and on the sea. . . .*

Tax exemptions were another welcome inducement to settle the frontier, as is attested by James I's privilege to Jews settling in Morella in Valencia. These Jews were exempted from paying tax in the first year after their arrival and liable to a tax reduction for another four years.

The economic activities of Jewish and Christian settlers were very similar. Jews like Christians owned houses in cities and plots of land outside the city walls. Others had more rural landholdings. They made their living from the vegetables, fruit and wine which they produced like everyone else. Some Jews were landlords; some owned shops, others ran bath houses, others owned mills; there were Jewish long-distance and short-distance merchants, artisans, bakers, butchers, teachers and doctors. Wealthier Jews would have been involved in property transactions and some would have also been moneylenders, but economic diversification was the rule of the game. Moneylending was certainly not the predominant activity of Iberian Jews in this period. The composite image which emerges from the available source material is that large numbers of Jews set out for the frontier to take advantage of the economic opportunities on offer. As Ray has demonstrated, it seems that many were not even that concerned about seeking out existing Jewish communities. Jewish presence in some areas was sparse, lacking communal amenities such as synagogues, cemeteries and butcher shops. In Elche in Aragon in 1312, for example, Jews still had to call on the help of Christian butchers to have access to animals and slaughtering facilities. All of this shows how integrated Jews were in these areas and how their presence there was an integral component of royal policy for settlement of the frontier. The singular advantage to the crown, however, of using Jews was that Jewish property was much more likely to remain under royal control. Jews were, at least in theory, not supposed to alienate the property they had been granted, as we see, for example, in a document of 1301 in which a Jewish couple in Lisbon and their successors are told 'not to sell nor . . . alienate the aforementioned houses . . . to any bishop, nor clergyman, nor order, nor to any religious person, nor to any knight, nor lady, nor squire'. This is only one example of how Jews were caught up in the power manoeuvres between the Iberian monarchs and their magnates, the institutional Church and emerging civic communities.[3]

As far as the Church was concerned, there were numerous aspects of Jewish life in Iberia which caused concern. The use of Jews as royal officials was unsurprisingly considered problematic. Already in 1081, Gregory VII had admonished Alfonso VI of Leon and Castile (r. 1065 [Leon], 1072 [Castile]–1109) against this practice:

. . . you should no longer in any way allow Jews in your land to rule over Christians or to hold power over them. For what is it to place Christians below Jews and to subject them to their judgement but to oppress the

*church of God and to exalt the synagogue of Satan, and, while you wish to
please the enemies of Christ, to set at naught Christ himself?*

Notwithstanding Roman and Visigothic precedent and even their own
laws, Iberian monarchs, as indeed many bishops, continued to make use
of Jewish officials to the chagrin of successive popes. Jewish tax collectors
continued to be used in Castile by Alfonso X and in Aragon by James I
and Peter III (r. 1276–85) for this purpose. It is only at the end of the
thirteenth century that the monarchs slowly began to pay some heed to
ecclesiastical complaints, and indeed those of civic councils. Nonetheless,
Jews continued to hold office in Iberia until their expulsion in 1492.[4]

The presence of Muslim labour in the Peninsula made it easier for
Jews to circumvent prohibitions against Jews employing Christians and to
cultivate the lands they were granted than elsewhere in Europe. Problems,
however, arose when preachers encouraged Muslim slaves who were in the
temporary or permanent possession of Jews to convert to Christianity.
As we have discussed in previous chapters, these slaves had technically to be
given their freedom. Even churchmen sometimes suspected that slaves had
ulterior motives for seeking the font. This, of course, presented financial
hardship to the Jews who owned them. In 1231 James I promised the Jews
of Majorca compensation; in 1273 he tried to stem the conversion of slaves
by ruling that they would exchange Jewish ownership for royal ownership.[5]

The payment of tithes by Jews was a major bone of contention. Jews
were unwilling to be lumbered with yet another form of taxation. As far as
the kings were concerned, they did not relish any Jewish money being
diverted from royal coffers and they were loath to force Jews to accede to
ecclesiastical demands for payment. In 1205 Innocent III wrote to Alfonso
VIII of Castile (r. 1158–1214) complaining how he not only did not make
Jews pay the tithes owed to the Church, he continued to grant them more
land on which tithes were due. Innocent also accused him of making the
Church pay exorbitant compensation to Jews for their converted slaves:
'Thus while the Synagogue grows in power the Church becomes weaker,
and the handmaid is openly preferred.' Jewish liability for tithes on proper-
ties that had passed to them from Christian hands was incorporated by
Innocent III in the Fourth Lateran Council in 1215 and he and his successors expected lay authorities to help the Church get its due. Thus we have
Honorius III complaining to Archbishop Rodrigo in 1218 and again in

1219 that Jews were not paying their tithes. He demanded that Rodrigo sever relationships between these Jews and Christians until they paid up. Rodrigo took it upon himself to settle the matter by brokering an agreement with the Jews of Toledo whereby the Jews became liable to a poll tax instead of tithes on the Christian property already in their possession. The agreement was sanctioned by Fernando III of Castile (r. 1217–30). The poll tax was to be paid by the Jews of Toledo in return for Rodrigo's protection. This made it very similar to the *jizya* payment Muslim rulers had exacted from *dhimmis*. In 1254 Alfonso X finally decreed that the Jews (and Muslims) of Cordoba should pay tithes on the Christian dwellings and land they acquired inside and outside the city. In 1255 he granted the church of Seville the same privilege for the Christian houses which Jews owned outside the Jewish quarter. As far as property within the Jewish quarter was concerned, that was considered by the king ultimately to belong to himself. But he gave the church the right to collect a poll tax from the Jews of Seville, a tax which the Jews did everything they could to resist.[6]

As elsewhere in Europe, the demand made by Lateran IV that Jews (and Muslims) wear clothes that distinguished them from Christians was another area of contention between popes and kings. Although he had been insistent on Jews paying tithes, Pope Honorius conceded that the Jews of Castile would not be required to wear a sign to mark them out as Jews. His concession of 1219 reveals that both Ferdinand and Rodrigo had asked him to waive the new requirement. The reason they produced was that the ruling was, in effect, unworkable. They claimed that some Jews would pack their bags and move to Muslim lands, causing financial hardship to the king; others might plot against the crown. In 1220 Honorius showed the same leniency to James I of Aragon for similar reasons after James had assured him (probably mendaciously) that the Jews of his kingdom were already distinguishable through what they wore. James had complained that the new rule was being misused to extort money from the Jews. When in 1221 Honorius received a report that in Toledo Jews could not be distinguished from Christians, he insisted that Rodrigo make sure that they wore clothes that did distinguish them. It is unlikely that Rodrigo complied. As Lucy Pick has shown, Rodrigo is an excellent conduit into understanding some of the dynamics of the interchange between Christians, Jews and Muslims in thirteenth-century Spain. As we recall, Rodrigo Jiménez de Rada was the mastermind of the battle of Las Navas de Tolosa of 1212. He began the construction of the magnificent cathedral of Toledo to take the place of the mosque that had served as a cathedral since 1085 and he composed histories of Spain. It is clear from his oeuvre how committed he was to the programme of Christianising Spain and how convinced he was of the continuing threat from Muslims. In his work Rodrigo consistently portrayed Jews in alliance with Muslims. His feeling that Jews might be conspiring against the crown over the new dress regulations would fit into this mindset. Rodrigo also penned a Christian–Jewish disputation, in which he underlined the differences between the two faiths and the superiority of Christianity. But all of this did not mean that in practical terms he oppressed the Jews of his archbishopric. On the contrary, his amicable relations with the Jews of Toledo and his use of Jewish administrators are consistent with the practical workings of *convivencia*. But as Pick suggests, it is clear that for Rodrigo *convivencia* was a far cry from the ideal modern historians have made of it. For him it seems rather to have been a pragmatic interim solution until Christianity could fully triumph. As for the dress code for Jews, it seems that Alfonso X of Castile began to insist on it within the framework of regulations on Christians and Jews showing off too much wealth in their attire. This had to do with economic problems in his reign. But in Castile as elsewhere both Jews and Christians could buy exemptions to the rules.[7]

The *Fueros* of Cuenca and Teruel

Fueros were the codes which the Iberian monarchs used to make new towns attractive to new settlers. In the course of the twelfth century *fueros* developed into substantial municipal law codes. The *fueros* of Cuenca and Teruel are of particular importance because they (especially the Cuencan one) served as models for many other settlements. Both cities, which lay either side of the north-central border between Castile and Aragon, played an important part in the southward expansion of each kingdom. Cuenca was finally taken from the Muslims in 1177 by Alfonso VIII of Castile; Teruel was taken by Alfonso II of Aragon (r. 1162–96) in 1171. Both cities were given very similar *fueros* by their kings, Cuenca probably between 1189 and 1193, Teruel in 1177. Whether the Cuenca code was based on the *fuero* of Teruel or whether both codes derived from similar sources does not concern us here. What does concern us is that these *fueros* reflect much of what we have already discussed: the attempts of the conquering monarchs to establish their authority throughout their expanding lands and the evolution of new Christian communities. The codes offer excellent insights into the daily interaction within these towns between Christians, Jews and Muslims. Although there was a clear royal presence in these towns the cities were granted a remarkable level of independence. The kings evidently needed the military support of these towns and others to consolidate their gains and allow them to pursue further conquests in Muslim territory.

The *fuero* of Cuenca comprises 43 chapters detailing royal representation, civic offices, criminal and civil legal procedures, security measures, agricultural regulations, rules concerning the buying and selling of goods and moneylending, military service and so on. Apart from Chapter 29 which deals with cases between Christians and Jews, the code mentions Jews a number of times in conjunction with Christians and/or Muslims. Thus members of all three faiths are urged to settle in the town (1.10); neither Christians, Jews nor Muslims should charge too much for harvested cereals (41.5); Jews and Christians are prohibited from selling unripe grapes (4.11); if a Christian woman is found with a male Jew or Muslim both are to be burned alive (11.48). Bathing is regulated in 2.32: Christian males were free to use the bath house on Tuesdays, Thursdays and Saturdays; Christian females could do so on Mondays and Wednesdays. Jews were allotted Fridays and Sundays. (Christian) men who dishonoured (Christian) women in the bath house faced the death penalty. The one instance when Jews are mentioned on their own outside Chapter 29 is in 1.17 where the stipulation is made that neither citizens nor Jews should function as *merinos* (royal rent collectors) or *telonearii* (collectors of market tolls payable to the king and city). It is clear from the *fuero* of Cuenca that some Jews like some Christians were citizens of the town while others were not (29.8). In light of the use the Iberian monarch made of Jews as tax collectors, it is interesting to see that in Cuenca they were not welcome to perform this function. It is equally interesting to note that the analogous clause in the *fuero* of Teruel which bars citizens from these functions does not go on explicitly to bar Jews.

Chapter 29 regulates cases between Christians and Jews in a remarkably even-handed way. The cases needed to come before Christian and Jewish judges, with equal numbers of both (1). The same rule applied for witnesses (2). Christians swore their oath on the cross; Jews on the Torah

POLITICAL AND SOCIO-ECONOMIC REALITIES

(17). Cases were heard at the gate of the *alcacería*, the area where Jews rented houses and shops from the king, and not the synagogue. As David Abulafia has pointed out, this might have served as a reminder of the king's interest in Jewish affairs. Jewish cases were not heard on the Sabbath or Jewish festivals (26). Jews like Christians owned real estate (8); Jews and Christians borrowed money from each other (18). Accruing interest on loans was not allowed to exceed the amount which had originally been borrowed (20). The final two clauses (32–3) concern the fines payable by Christians who killed Jews and vice versa. And it is in clause 33 that the key to the Jews' position in Cuenca is revealed when an explanation is given why neither Jews, nor the town's *iudex* (municipal officer), were owed any part of the penalty money paid by a Christian in such cases. The reason given is that 'Jews *servi regis sunt et fisco deputati* (are *servi* of the king and they are entrusted to his treasury)'. The Teruel code gives virtually the same text. As David Abulafia has emphasised in a number of recent articles, the term *servi* in the *fueros* of Cuenca and Teruel was not pejorative. The conditions Jews enjoyed in both towns were extremely favourable. But those conditions hinged on the service they performed for their king. Indeed the remarkable extent to which Jews were allowed to integrate themselves into the socio-economic and political life of these towns was underpinned by Jewish service to the crown. As we have seen in the charters of the German emperors, *servi* does not mean slaves here. To be sure, there were slaves in Cuenca but they were Muslim slaves (e.g. 1.23, 16.51); other Muslims were free.[8]

The *fuero* of Cuenca was granted to many towns by Ferdinand III of Castile. Alfonso X made unsuccessful attempts to substitute these *fueros* and others which granted such wide-reaching municipal benefits with his *Fuero Real* which combined Roman and Visigothic legal tradition with municipal material. Alfonso XI was more successful in the endeavour to impose royal standardisation on the laws of Castile. Among the many jurisdictional issues between monarchs and municipalities was the continuing royal insistence on the monarchs' prerogative over Jews (and Muslims) and their belongings and their duty to protect them throughout their extensive kingdoms. Thus we see, for example, how in 1288 Alfonso III of Aragon (r. 1285–91) admonished the civic authorities of Majorca against exacting municipal taxes from the Jewish community there. Needless to say municipal dissatisfaction continued unabated. In a similar vein James II of Aragon

(r. 1291–1327) was not interested in the Bishop of Tortosa's concerns about the activities of Jewish moneylenders in that town. The kings of Castile also ignored ecclesiastical condemnation of usury. In 1258 annual interest rates of up to 33.3 per cent were established in Castile; 20 per cent seemed to be the acceptable rate in Aragon and Valencia.[9] But that is not to say that ecclesiastical concerns counted for nothing. This is clear when we turn to the so-called *Siete Partidas* ('Seven Divisions or Parts') of Alfonso X of Castile, known as Alfonso the Wise.

The *Siete Partidas*

The *Siete Partidas* developed from Alfonso X's *Fuero Real* and his *Espéculo de las Leyes* ('Mirror of Laws') and attempted to extend the remit of royal authority by creating an all-encompassing and uniformly applicable set of laws. Alfonso's imperial pretensions in the interregnum which followed on the death of Emperor Frederick II may have prompted its production. The year 1257 witnessed the double election of Alfonso and Richard of Cornwall, the brother of England's Henry III, as German king. The *Siete Partidas* was encyclopaedic in its extensive coverage of every aspect of Christian society from matters of belief and ecclesiastical organisation to the laws concerning government matters, as well as private, commercial and criminal law. The nature of Alfonso's contribution to the *Siete Partidas* is not entirely clear. It would seem likely that at the very least he would have had a redactor's hand in what must have been a collective effort of many civil and canon lawyers working at his court. Alfonso seems not to have officially enacted the *Partidas* upon its completion between 1256 and 1265. O'Callaghan has argued that he may not have thought this was necessary because he had reserved the right to revise the contents of the *Espéculo* when he promulgated it in 1254. Be that as it may, the opposition by Castilian magnates and municipalities in 1272 to his new laws scuppered many of his legal aspirations. It was left to Alfonso XI formally to promulgate the *Partidas* in 1348. The code offers us particularly valuable insights into the tensions which existed between Christian theory and the practicalities of *convivencia* in Alfonso X's reign. In practice Jews continued to be held in high esteem by the king who not only benefited from their administrative, financial and medical skills, but also collaborated with them on so many of his intellectual and scientific projects. In theory the legislation incorporated traditional material which was unfavourable to Jews. Much of this material was collected in the 11 laws of title 24 of the seventh part of the laws.[10]

The first law sets out clearly why Jews were allowed to live in Christian society by 'the Church, emperors, kings and princes'. It is so

that they might live forever as in captivity and serve as a reminder to mankind that they are descended from those who crucified Our Lord Jesus Christ (. . . como en catiuerio pora siempre e fuesse remembrança a los omnes que ellos uienen del linaje daquellos que crucificaron a Nuestro Sennor Jhesu Christo).

This statement simply reflects the standard Christian position on the role of Jews in Christian society which we have highlighted throughout this book. A Jewish view on the matter can be gleaned from the words of R. Asher ben Yehiel, a refugee from Germany who arrived in Toledo by the early fourteenth century:

It seems to me that all types of taxes must be considered defence expenditures. For it is they that preserve us among the Gentiles. For what purpose do some of the Gentile nations find in preserving us and allowing us to live among them if not the benefit that they derive from Israel in their collection of taxes and extortions from them.

The *raison d'être* of Jews throughout Christendom was to serve their king through their taxes. And in the peculiar circumstances of Reconquest Spain the Christian monarchs freely availed themselves of Jewish expertise in their efforts to consolidate and expand their separate kingdoms. As we have seen, the nature of this service was on the whole positive. But any benefits accrued by the Jews underlined just how much they depended on the goodwill of the crown they served. Having established why Jews were permitted to reside among Christians, the law code proceeded to outline how Jews were supposed to conduct themselves.[11]

Law 2 instructed them to behave meekly and to forbear from any insulting behaviour against the Christian faith on pain of death. In compliance with the rulings of Lateran IV and earlier canonical material Jews were prohibited from leaving the Jewish quarter on Good Friday. Startling is the inclusion in this law of the report that in some places Jews steal Christian children on Good Friday and crucify them or use waxen images if there is no child to hand. This, of course, refers to allegations of ritual murder which by the middle of the thirteenth century were common in northern Europe, as we shall see in a following chapter. The crucifixion of a waxen image is intriguingly similar to the twelfth *cantiga* in the *Cantigas de Santa Maria* ('Hymns of Saint Mary'), written, set to music and illustrated at Alfonso's court. The *Cantigas* constituted one of the most important vernacular renderings of the miracles of the Virgin. *Cantiga* 6 tells of a Jew murdering a child singing praises to the Virgin Mary. Other songs presented Jews as greedy, guilty of deicide, maligning Jesus, his mother and Christianity in general and as allying with the devil. For our purposes it is enough to emphasise with Dwayne Carpenter that the law in the *Siete Partidas* makes it crystal clear that it is the king and no one else who would deal with any accusations of ritual murder. However, as Carpenter also points out, Alfonso's accommodating approach in his day-to-day practical dealings with the Jews at his court and in his kingdom did not mean he distanced himself from pejorative conceptions of Jews and their religion. Indeed it would be anachronistic to expect Alfonso's practical toleration of Jews to encompass the kind of tolerance we would expect in the twenty-first century.[12]

But that does not mean that Alfonso's law code slavishly followed negative precedents of canon, Roman and Visigothic law. As Carpenter points out, the *Siete Partidas* allowed Jews to employ Christian labourers to help them cultivate their fields and to engage Christians to protect them on their travels, even though Jews were not allowed to hold any office over Christians lest they 'oppress Christians'. Christians were not allowed to obtain medicines from Jewish doctors *unless* they were very learned and the potion was prepared by a Christian. Nor were Jews allowed to have Christian domestics in their homes or to have Christian slaves (laws 3, 8, 10). As far as synagogues were concerned, no new ones were to be built *unless* the king had given his permission. Christians were prohibited from damaging synagogues because they were places where 'the name of God is praised' (4). Jewish court cases were not to be heard on the Jewish Sabbath (5). Forced conversion of Jews was forbidden; Jewish converts would keep their property and should be honoured; no one was to 'disparage them or their descendants concerning their Jewish past' (6). Jews who lay with

Christian women faced the death penalty (9). Finally, in the spirit of Lateran IV, Jews were obliged to wear distinguishing headgear to mark them from Christians (11). As we have already said, it is unclear to what extent any of these laws were enacted during Alfonso's reign and, in any case, we know that he himself did not adhere to them. It is, however, important to recognise that even in theory the laws made sure that Jews could continue to function as doctors and landowners. Their religious observance was protected. Even Alfonso's theoretical approach seems to have been aimed at finding a workable pragmatic balance between theological ideas and concrete day-to-day exigencies, in which the crown required Jewish service.[13]

Jewish quarters

The balance which the Iberian kings brokered between a concrete pragmatic approach to the benefits of Jewish service and the ambiguities of theological concepts about the place of Jews in Christian society can also be glimpsed through the evolution of the physical space they set aside for their Jews in towns throughout the peninsula. These quarters were called *juderías* in Castile, *calls* in Catalonia and *judiarias* in Portugal. To be sure, Jewish areas had existed under Muslim rule, and in that sense the *judería* can be seen as an extension of previous custom. A separate physical space does not in itself have to signify anything hostile, especially in a society where there is concrete, practical space for Jews in the here and now. Even under Christian rule separation does not in itself have to have negative connotations. For one thing, many Mediterranean cities had separate areas for merchants from different regions. Anyone visiting present-day Acre in Israel, for example, can move between what were once the Pisan, Genoese and Venetian quarters. And, as we have seen, in northern Europe too Jews of their own accord tended to gravitate towards particular areas in the towns they inhabited, usually those in easy reach of the lord who protected them. For another, Christians were forever buying houses and running shops in the Jewish quarters, whether or not they were supposed to. And Jews owned property outside their section of the city. These breaches underlined the ambiguities of the system as well as the ever-present gulf between theory and practice. In theory, the *judería* was supposed to demarcate the separation between Jews and Christians, if only to allow the crown to pay lip service to theological ideas concerning the role of Jews in Christian society. In practice, it assisted the crown to strengthen its hold over its Jews in opposition to magnates and civic authorities. It is important to remember that walls enclosing the *juderías, judiarias* and *calls* of Iberia were much more a feature of the fourteenth and fifteenth centuries than the thirteenth. But the evolution of designated open Jewish quarters into closed ones points to the adder in the grass. The nature of physical separation could be just as changeable as the nature of service. Let us illustrate this by turning to the chequered history of the *call* of Majorca.

Majorca

In his examination of Jewish settlement in Ciutat de Mallorca, which is now known as Palma, David Abulafia has traced how gradually Jews were separated from Christians. Immediately after his conquest James I of Aragon welcomed Jewish merchants to Majorca and gave them generous privileges. The Jewish community or *aljama* was a self-regulating entity where Jewish law held sway. Only the gravest judicial matters concerning Jews had to be referred to the crown. They seem to have congregated around the palace. In 1273 James allowed Jews to buy Christian houses but Jews and Christians were not permitted to share them. As we have seen, the crown was jealous of its jurisdiction over Jews and forbade the municipality from levying their own taxes from the *aljama* in 1288. It was Alfonso III of Aragon who started moves to create a specific Jewish quarter. By 1290 a spacious area was set aside in the south-eastern part of the old city. Jews were permitted to construct a new synagogue and they were granted their own butcher's shop. Previously they had made use of Christian premises. Having their own shop would have been a mixed blessing, because it probably meant that they could no longer sell meat on to Christians which was not ritually permitted to Jews. They also got their own bake-house, again making Jewish existence a little less reliant on Christian facilities. A wall with doors and gates was put around the *call*, a word which probably derives from the Hebrew *kahal*, meaning community. The *call* was presented to the Jews as a special privilege and they had to pay a fortune to receive it. Henceforth no Jews were supposed to live outside the *call*. To be sure, as long as it could comfortably accommodate growing numbers, the *call* had its advantages for the *aljama*. Community leaders could more easily regulate its affairs if Jews lived in one designated area. And the king's protection gave it added security as, for example, in the ruling in 1296 of James II of Aragon that preachers were only to enter the *call* with the permission of the king's representative. No more than 10 Christians were allowed to come along. But the key to the conditions in the *call* was the king's goodwill. In the wake of the scandal of the conversion of two German Christians to Judaism in Majorca, King Sancho of Majorca (r. 1311–24) imposed a heavy fine on the Jews in 1315, removing all their privileges and confiscating their property, including the synagogue, which was turned into a church dedicated to the holy faith. Things began to improve in 1323 and still further under Sancho's successors. The fact that the Jews were again allowed a synagogue under King James III of Majorca (r. 1324–43) was a testimony to their continuing contribution to the island's economy.[14] In Majorca too pragmatism at this stage counted more than theology. Let us now move on to explore some of the cultural benefits of pragmatic *convivencia* in twelfth- and thirteenth-century Castile and Aragon.

Jewish cultural life

Jewish cultural life in Toledo was greatly enriched by the Jewish refugees from al-Andalus who brought the learning of al-Andalus to their new home in Toledo. By the early thirteenth century the poet Judah Alharizi was already implying that Toledo was the new Jerusalem of Spain. Its Jewry appears to have been the largest and most prosperous of Latin Christendom. It was there that Abraham ibn Daud was writing in the middle of the twelfth century, armed with his expertise in Arabic philosophy, astronomy, medicine and literature. His *Book of Tradition*, which offers much valuable information on the history of the Jews in Spain, included bitter comments on the destruction of the Jewish world of learning by the Almohads: 'the world became desolate of academies of learning'. His philosophical tome, *Exalted Faith*, tried to show how Aristotelian philosophy was compatible with the teachings of the Jewish faith. There was no need for scholars to feel that they had to choose between the two. His work, was, however, soon overtaken by Maimonides's much more comprehensive treatment of the relationship between Aristotle and revealed religion in *The Guide for the Perplexed*. Maimonides may have known ibn Daud's work. At the turn of the century the towering intellectual figure in Toledo was Rabbi

Meir ha-Levi Abulafia (*c.* 1165–1244). Meir hailed from Burgos, about 300 kilometres to the north of Toledo. He was the son-in-law of Alfonso VIII's Jewish treasurer, Joseph ibn Shushan. The Abulafia family was part of a Jewish elite, which included the Alfakars, ibn Ezras and ibn Shushans, who combined their service to the crown as administrators and colonisers, doctors, scholars and translators with their own studies, as well as their roles in the Jewish community. Conversant with Arabic philosophy and literature as he was, Rabbi Meir chose to expend his talents on halachic matters. He was the first important Talmudic scholar of Christian Spain; his acquaint-ance with the work of the *Tosafists* was novel; his work on the correct orthography of the Torah was instrumental in finalising its text. It was probably with him that Archbishop Rodrigo negotiated the Jewish poll tax to be paid in lieu of tithes and it is not impossible that Rodrigo had Meir in mind when he composed his Christian–Jewish disputation. Meir's own poetry reflects his disdain for Christian beliefs presented to Jews: 'You preach vanity and lies. . . . To my face, always.' Whatever the exact relation-ship was between Meir and Rodrigo, a pupil of Meir's, Judah ha-Cohen ibn Malkah (b. 1215) exchanged letters with a Christian at Frederick II's court about mathematical problems. This might have been Michael Scot, one of the many scholars and translators working in Toledo under Rodrigo's patronage.[15]

Christian Spain was an important hunting ground for northern scholars in search of Arabic texts on medicine and philosophy. It was from here that Peter Alfonsi, a Jewish convert to Christianity, brought knowledge of Greek and Arabic astronomy when he journeyed to England and France in 1106. And it was he who introduced Latin Christendom to the tales of the Orient through his collection of didactic stories, the *Disciplina clericalis.* It was in Spain that Abbot Peter the Venerable of Cluny (d. 1156) com-missioned the first translation of the Koran into Latin by Robert of Ketton (or Chester) and other works concerning Islam in 1142–3. Peter's aim was not to study Islam for its own sake. He wanted to collect the material he needed in order to launch a polemic against Islam. Peter's collection is known as the Toledan collection, but Robert and his fellow translator Hermann of Carinthia worked in northern Spain. By the second half of the twelfth century Toledo started to feature as a centre of translation activity. At this stage translations seem often to have been a collaborative effort, with a Jew translating the Arabic into the vernacular Romance, which was then translated by a Christian into Latin. The texts imported by Jews from al-Andalus could only have enriched the available corpus. Ibn Gabirol's work of pure philosophy in Arabic, *Fountain of Life*, for example, was used by Michael Scot by way of the translation of Dominicus Gundisalvi, who was working in Toledo in the second half of the twelfth century. This work was widely disseminated in Latin Christendom under the title *Fons Vitae* and ascribed to 'Avicebron'. Christians scholars such as Thomas Aquinas (d. 1274) who used it had no idea they were quoting a Jew. Dominicus also translated a treatise on the soul by the Muslim philosopher Avicenna (d. 1037) with the help of a certain 'Avendauth' who called himself an '*israelita philosophus*' and who wrote the prologue to the text. It is possible that this Jew was in fact Abraham ibn Daud. Michael Scot himself produced a second Latin translation of the Koran in 1210 at the behest of Rodrigo. Rodrigo clearly felt that arms in itself were not sufficient to conquer Islam; verbal arguments based on knowledge of the Koran were needed as well. Scot collaborated with a Jew on an astronomical translation; while working for Frederick II he collaborated with Jacob Anatoli, a scion of the ibn Tibbon family of translators in Provence. We recall that Provence was another area to which Jews had fled from the Almohads. Among the myriad of Arabic and scientific texts which Samuel ibn Tibbon (d. *c.* 1232) translated into Hebrew was Maimonides's *The Guide for the Perplexed*. Alharizi produced an inferior translation. This Hebrew version of *The Guide* reached Frederick's court and it was there that it was put into Latin, possibly by Michael Scot and presumably with Jewish assistance. Aquinas was one of the many Christian scholars throughout the West who quoted from the *The Guide*. Aquinas's attempt to synthesise Aristotle with religion bore many similarities to the work of Maimonides, as indeed to that of Averroës (ibn Rushd [d. 1198]), the Muslim scholar, whose works were also translated into Hebrew and Latin in this period. Collaboration between Christians and Jews on translations and other scholarly endeavours continued in the Toledan court of Alfonso X.[16]

Controversy over the writings of Maimonides prompted bitter disputes about the role of rational thought within Judaism. An important figure in the discussion about the relationship between faith and reason was Moses ben Nachman, known as Nachmanides, (1194–1270), who came from Gerona but was active in Barcelona, two centres of Jewish scholarship in this period. The Catalan county of Barcelona had been ruled jointly with

Aragon since the reign of Alfonso II in 1162. As part of the Aragonese-Catalan world, which included Valencia and Majorca, these centres possessed close ties with regions of what is now southern France such as Cerdagne, Roussillon, Montpellier, Languedoc and Provence. Although Nachmanides had worked hard to vindicate Maimonides's orthodoxy, he was a mystic with no love for rationalism. Mysticism, or Kabbalah, had by this time become an important stream of thinking in Catalonia, in what is now southern France and in Castile. There were many levels to Kabbalah. At a basic practical level it engaged ordinary Jews in greater dedication to following the dictates of their religion. It also gave new meaning to their experience of living in the diaspora. An important aspect of the Maimonidean controversy had been the clash between a learned philosophical elite and others who felt at a loss when faced with the challenge which philosophy seemed to pose to religion. At a much higher level Kabbalah comprised an esoteric system of contemplation of the divine nature through which the learned few sought visionary experiences of God. The major Kabbalist of this period was Abraham Abulafia (1239–after 1291), whose visionary experiences led him to believe that he was the Messiah who would be acclaimed as such by Jews and Christians in 1290–1. His prophetic mission included his attempt to communicate his ideas to the Pope in 1280. Nicholas III's unexpected death after refusing to see him seemed to confirm his teachings. Abulafia disappeared off the map when 1291 came and went without the messianic manifestations he had predicted.[17]

To return to Nachmanides, as the leader of Barcelonan Jewry it was he who was called upon to defend the Talmud in 1263 in the public disputation at the court of James I with the Dominicans, who by this time were actively proselytising among Jews and Muslims in southern Europe. Their spokesman was a convert from Judaism called Paul. At this stage in our investigation it is fascinating to gauge King James's ambivalent behaviour throughout the proceedings. On the one hand, he presided over the event; on the other, he seems to have allowed Nachmanides considerable latitude in presenting his case. In the aftermath of the debate, James did at first stipulate that Jews had to listen to conversion sermons by the Dominicans and expose their religious texts to Dominican scrutiny for blasphemy. But before long Jews were allowed to absent themselves from these sermons and regained control over their books. Nor was the king willing to accede to repeated demands from the Dominicans to deal harshly with

Nachmanides on account of the report he had produced of the disputation which contained anti-Christian sentiments. The Dominicans had not been placated by the two-year sentence of exile James had meted out. In the end Nachmanides left for the Holy Land in 1267.[18] We shall return to this disputation in Chapter 9.

Southern France

The littoral regions of southern France accommodated a variety of persons who were not in tune with ecclesiastical orthodoxy. This was in a large part due to a combination of fragmented political power and the lack of a strongly co-ordinated ecclesiastical presence within the region. It is not for nothing that the Cathar heresy was able to spread throughout this area. Very large numbers of Jews lived here and they were fully integrated in the urban economies where they partook in a variety of economic pursuits besides moneylending. Jews ran their own businesses; they were doctors, tailors, masons and rag dealers; they worked in the leather industry; they bound books and illuminated them. As in Iberia, some ran their own estates; others acted as agents in the trade in grain and cattle. In Languedoc, Narbonne was one of the most vibrant Jewish centres. Jews had lived there since the fifth century. The Jews of Narbonne were led by the Kalonymides, who claimed that they were descendants of King David. Elaborate legends imagined that Charlemagne had taken Narbonne from the Muslims and narrated how Charlemagne had granted a third of Narbonne to the ancestor of the Kalonymides, whom he had deliberately recruited from Babylonia as a Jew of Davidic descent. The Kalonymides possessed a large amount of property on which no tax had to be paid and they were able to wield a considerable amount of authority. As in Spain their status was recognised by the title *nasi* ('prince'). In Latin texts this exceptionally powerful head of the community was referred to as the *rex Judeus* ('Jewish king'). In the thirteenth century R. Meir ben Simeon of Narbonne broadened the legendary material to claim that the Jews of Narbonne owed their special position to the fact that they had aided Charlemagne against the Muslims in his battle for Narbonne. Meir was clearly doing his best to claim enduring protection for the Jews of his city. As we have seen, circumstances for Jews gradually began to deteriorate as Capetian hegemony increasingly took hold in the south in the generations after Languedoc nominally passed into royal hands in 1229. The Jews of Narbonne were expelled in 1306 along with the Jews in the rest of France. But the ancient Jewries of Marseilles and Arles in Provence would flourish until well into the fourteenth century. Jews were granted citizenship in Marseilles in 1257, in Arles in 1385.[19]

Southern Italy and Rome

The twelfth-century Norman crown of Sicily combined areas of southern Italy which had been wrested from Byzantine rule and Sicily which had been taken from the Muslims in the second half of the eleventh century. Together with the Greeks and Muslims who now fell under Norman rule came many Jews who had lived in these territories for centuries. Except for Rome, this is where most Jews lived in Italy in this period. As in al-Andalus, the Jews of Sicily had been an integral part of Islamic society. Little changed in this respect under Norman rule. Jews continued to own land and many Jews were artisans. Dyeing cloth was a particular speciality. Moneylending did not dominate Jewish economic concerns. Sicily fell under Hohenstaufen rule when Frederick II's father, Henry VI, gained the Sicilian crown in 1194. We have already touched on collaborative cultural activities between Jews and Christians under Frederick II. As in Germany, Frederick was ever anxious to make plain that he had the ultimate control over the Jews of Sicily, and indeed, Muslims. The difference with Germany was that his power in Sicily was much greater. As far as the Sicilian Jews were concerned, for all the royal protection they enjoyed, they were supposed to wear distinguishing clothing in compliance with Lateran IV. Rejection of papal or ecclesiastical claims over 'his' Jews did not mean he rejected their ideas about the correct relationship between Christians and Jews. As far as Muslims were concerned, Frederick decided to respond to the Muslim resistance he had encountered by deporting all Muslims from the island to Lucera on the mainland from 1223 onwards. Under the rule of Charles I of Anjou preaching campaigns started to convert Jews. Under Charles II, whose father lost Sicily to the Crown of Aragon-Catalonia, forced conversions took place in Apulia in the 1290s. The Muslims of Lucera were sold into slavery in 1300. In Sicily itself Christian–Jewish relations continued along the same lines as elsewhere in the Christian Iberian kingdoms with its special mix of political and economic pragmatism and theological constraints.

It is fitting to end this chapter with Rome, the oldest Jewish community of Italy. Rome was the seat of the papacy which, as we shall shortly see, made valiant strides to expand its ecclesiastical say throughout the institutional Church as well as affect the rule of princes throughout Latin Christendom. But in Rome too there was a gulf between theory and practice when it came to legislation concerning Jews. For example, notwithstanding papal posturing towards Latin princes about the importance of Jews wearing clothing to mark them out from Christians, the Jewish badge was not introduced in Rome until 1257. And when it was imposed, exceptions could be bought. Jewish life in Rome was, in fact, remarkably similar to the circumstances of Jews elsewhere in southern Italy. On the whole, they were well integrated in the life of the city. Immanuel of Rome (1261–1328), for example, knew Dante's work and composed poems in Italian and Hebrew. In other words, in Rome, as elsewhere in Latin Christendom, there were manifold ambiguities concerning the role of Jews in Christian society.[20] It is high time we deepened our understanding of those ambiguities by examining how Christian religious and cultural manifestations of the period affected the concept of Jewish service in Latin Christendom.

Notes and references

1 Lucy K. Pick, *Conflict and Coexistence. Archbishop Rodrigo and the Muslims and Jews of Medieval Spain* (Ann Arbor, MI, 2004) 21–70; David Abulafia, 'The Rise of Aragon-Catalonia' and Peter Linehan, 'Castile, Portugal and Navarre', in David Abulafia (ed.), *The New Cambridge Medieval History* (Cambridge, 1999), 644–67 and 668–99.

2 Daniel H. Frank and Oliver Leamon (eds), *The Cambridge Companion to Medieval Jewish Philosophy* (Cambridge, 2003). The literature on the Jews of al-Andalus is vast, see for example Eliyahu Ashtor, *The Jews of Moslem Spain*, 3 vols, trans. Aaron Klein and Jenny Machlowitz Klein (Philadelphia, PA, c. 1973–84) and Jane S. Gerber, *The Jews of Spain* (New York, 1992); on a comparison between Muslim attitudes towards Jews and Christian ones see Mark R. Cohen, *Under Crescent and Cross. The Jews in the Middle Ages* (Princeton, NJ, 1994) and his 'Anti-Jewish Violence and the Place of the Jews in Christendom and in Islam: A Paradigm', in Anna Sapir Abulafia (ed.), *Religious Violence between Christians and Jews: Medieval Roots, Modern Perspectives* (Houndmills, 2002), 107–37; Bernard Lewis, *The Jews of Islam* (Princeton, NJ, 1984), 62.

3 Jonathan Ray, *The Sephardic Frontier. The* Reconquista *and the Jewish Community in Medieval Iberia* (Ithaca, NY and London, 2006), 1–71; 98–104; quotations: 28–9, 42.

4 Quotation from: H.E.J. Cowdrey, *The Register of Pope Gregory VII, 1073–1085. An English Translation* (Oxford, 2002), 400 (cf. Revelations 2:9, 3:9); Ray, *Sephardic Frontier*, 93–4.

5 Ray, *Sephardic Frontier*, 65–6.

6 Ray, *Sephardic Frontier*, 46–52; Pick, *Conflict*, 172–3, 177–9; Grayzel I, nos 17, 36, 37, pp. 112–13, 145–7; Simonsohn, nos 81, 99, 102, pp. 85–6, 103, 105–6.

7 Ray, *Sephardic Frontier*, 156–64; Pick, *Conflict*, vii, 172–7; Grayzel I, nos 38, 44, 51, pp. 150–1, 156–7, 168–9; Simonsohn, nos 102, 108, 115, pp. 105–6, 111, 118–19.

8 Ray, *Sephardic Frontier*, 77; James F. Powers (trans.), *The Code of Cuenca. Municipal Law on the Twelfth-century Castilian Frontier* (Philadelphia, PA, 2000); Maz Gorosch (ed.), *El Fuero de Teruel* (Stockholm, 1950), 105, 320; [Yitschak] Fritz Baer, *Die Juden im Christlichen Spanien. Erster Teil: Urkunden und Regesten*, vol. 1: *Aragonien und Navarra* (Farnborough, 1970 [reprint of 1929 edn]), 1037–43; see for example, David Abulafia, ' "Nam Iudei servi regis sunt, et semper fisco regio deputati": The Jews in the Municipal Fuero of Teruel (1176–7)', in H.J. Hames (ed.), *Jews, Muslims and Christians in and around the Crown of Aragon. Essays in Honour of Professor Elena Lourie*, (Leiden, 2004), 97–123.

9 Powers, *The Code of Cuenca*, 22–3; Ray, *Sephardic Frontier*, 85–8, 57.

10 Robert I. Burns, 'The *Partidas:* Introduction' and Joseph F. O'Callaghan, 'Alphonso X and the *Partidas*' in Samuel Parsons Scott (trans.) and Robert I. Burns (ed.), *Las Siete Partidas*, vol. 1 (Philadelphia, PA, 2001), xi–xii, xxx–xl; Dwayne E. Carpenter, *Alfonso X and the Jews: An Edition of and Commentary on* Siete Partidas *7.24 'De los judíos'*, (Berkeley, CA, 1986).

11 Carpenter, *Alfonso X*, 28, 59–61; R. Asher ben Yehiel, commentary on *Baba Bathra* 1.29 in the Babylonian Talmud, translation from Bernard Septimus, *Hispano–Jewish Culture in Transition. The Career and Controversies of the Ramah* (Cambridge, MA, 1982), 13.

12 Carpenter, *Alfonso X*, 29, 63–6, 105; idem, 'The Portrayal of the Jews in Alfonso the Learned's *Cantigas de Santa Maria*', in Bernard Dov Cooperman (ed.), *In Iberia and Beyond. Hispanic Jews between Cultures. Proceedings of a Symposium to Mark the 500th Anniversary of the Expulsion of Spanish Jewry* (Newark, NJ, 1998), 15–42.

13 Carpenter, *Alfonso X*, 30–7, 67–105.

14 Ray, *Sephardic Frontier*, 145–56. David Abulafia, 'From Protection to Persecution: Crown, Church and Synagogue in the City of Majorca, 1229–1343', in David Abulafia, Michael Franklin and Miri Rubin (eds), *Church and City, 1000–1500. Essays in Honour of Christopher Brooke* (Cambridge, 1992), 111–26.

15 Colette Sirat, *A History of Jewish Philosophy in the Middle Ages* (Cambridge, 1985), 141–55; Septimus, *Hispano-Jewish Culture*, 1–38; Pick, *Conflict*, 164–71, 178, 79–80.

16 Marie-Thérèse d'Alverny, 'Translations and Translators', in Robert L. Benson and Giles Constable with Carol D. Latham (eds), *Renaissance and Renewal in the Twelfth Century* (Oxford, 1982), 421–59; Dominique Iogna-Prat, *Order and Exclusion. Cluny and Christendom Heresy, Judaism, and Islam (1000–1150)*, trans. Graham R. Edwards (Ithaca, NY, 2002), 338–9; Pick, *Conflict*, 79–80, 94–5, 102–26; Sirat, *Jewish Philosophy*, 158–9, 212–18; David Abulafia, *Frederick II. A Medieval Emperor* (London, 1988), 255–7.

17 Harvey J. Hames, *Like Angels on Jacob's Ladder. Abraham Abulafia, the Franciscans and Joachimism* (Albany, NY, 2007), 8, 29–53; Septimus, *Hispano-Jewish Culture*, 27–8.

18 Yitzhak Baer, *A History of the Jews in Christian Spain*. Volume 1: *From the Age of Reconquest to the Fourteenth Century*, trans. Louis Schoffman with introduction by Benjamin R. Gampel (Philadelphia, PA, 1992), 155–6; see note 24 of Chapter 9.

19 William Chester Jordan, *The French Monarchy and the Jews from Philip Augustus to the Last Capetians* (Philadelphia, PA, 1989), 110–16, 162–8; Joseph Shatzmiller, 'Politics and the Myth of Origins: The Case of the Medieval Jews', in Gilbert Dahan (ed.), *Les Juifs au regard de l'Histoire. Mélanges en l'honneur de Bernhard Blumenkranz* (Paris, 1885), 54–8; Gilbert Dahan, 'Le Pouvoir royal, l'église et les Juifs, ou de la condition politique du Juif en occident médiéval', in D. Tollet (ed.), *Politique et religion dans le judaïsme ancien et médiéval* (Paris, 1989), 101; Danièle Iancu-Agou, 'Provence: Jewish Settlement, Mobility, and Culture', in Cluse, 175–89.

20 David Abulafia, 'The Italian Other: Greeks, Muslims, and Jews', in David Abulafia (ed.), *Italy in the Central Middle Ages, 1000–1300* (Oxford, 2004), 222–36; Abulafia, *Frederick II*, 146–8; Shlomo Simonsohn, 'Sicily: a Millennium of *Convivenza* (or Almost)', in Cluse, 105–21.

part 3

The religious and cultural ambiguities of Jewish service

'Although Jews are enemies of our faith, they serve us and are tolerated and defended by us.'

(Hostiensis, *Apparatus, ad* 5.6.9, adapted from John A. Watt,
'Jews and Christians in the Gregorian Decretals', in Diana Wood [ed.],
Christianity and Judaism Studies in Church History, 29 [Oxford, 1992], 105.)

chapter 7

Jewish experience of
the crusades

Crusades were wars preached by the papacy in defence of Christendom. Knights were called upon to serve Christ as his own knights, defending him against his enemies. This service would make up for the sins they had committed; if they died in battle they would be rewarded in heaven as holy martyrs. The First Crusade and its successors were deemed to be just and holy because they were fought with the right intention, that is love for God, and preached by the right authority, namely the Pope, against those who were seen to have attacked Christian interests. The combination of service for Christ with sanctioned warfare proved to be a heady and a popular cocktail with wide-ranging ramifications for the development of Christian life and thought and for Christian relations with Muslims and Jews.

Reform

An important aspect of crusading was the manner in which it transcended the lay and ecclesiastical frontiers within medieval Europe. It was a concrete manifestation of late eleventh-century papal rhetoric concerning a universal institutional Church which was headed by the Pope and which was led by him from its centre in Rome. This kind of rhetoric developed in Rome from 1046 when the first of four German reforming popes was installed at the behest of Emperor Henry III of Germany. Their election followed years of monastic reform which had radiated out to Germany from Cluny in

Burgundy and its daughter-houses throughout France. Henry III (r. 1039–56) keenly supported reformers who attempted to reinvigorate monastic life through closer attention to the Benedictine rule, unencumbered by lay interference. In time new monastic orders such as the Cistercians (1098) would intensify this kind of reform by finding new ways for monks to express personal inner conversion to Christ and to live out their personal devotion to Christ. An important aspect of monastic reform and, indeed, of the Reform Movement in general, was a closer engagement with the figure of Christ. Men and women closely identified with the life of Christ and his suffering on the cross as a method of enhancing their own spirituality. As we shall see in the next chapter, the figure of the Virgin Mary also played a vital role in this kind of religious activity.

One main concern of papal reformers was the desire to safeguard the institutional Church as a whole from lay control. Another principal concern was the relationship between the Pope and the rest of the ecclesiastical hierarchy. Where should the seat of ecclesiastical power be? Should it lie in the centre with the Pontiff or in the dioceses with the bishops? It was during the reign of Pope Gregory VII (r. 1073–85) that these issues were articulated with uncompromising enthusiasm. One of Gregory's key concepts was that of righteousness (*justitia*). For him it was paramount that righteousness be established throughout Christendom so that it would be worthy of being headed by Jesus Christ himself. What did he mean by righteousness? For Gregory righteousness encompassed everyone doing God's will at all times in every walk of life. Princes played a crucial role by acting righteously themselves and ruling righteously over others. But princes themselves needed the sustained guidance of the Pope and his priesthood in these endeavours. Gregory insisted that, for this to happen, the institutional Church needed to be led from the centre by the Pope instructing the rest of the ecclesiastical hierarchy through his chosen legates. Essential to the programme was a clergy that itself was righteous. This meant to Gregory that bishops should, therefore, be elected for their piety through the correct ecclesiastical processes and that they should be obedient to him as the representative of St Peter. They should not be appointed by emperors, kings or princes for lay political purposes or any other lay interests. They should not be able to buy their ecclesiastical office from anyone. And all clerics who had the rank of deacon or higher had to be celibate so that they could devote their lives to Christ and to Christ's ministry to the laity. The institutional Church had to be free from lay concerns if it was to establish righteousness throughout society.

Pious papal rhetoric is one thing, the reality of contemporary temporal and ecclesiastical politics is another. This is not the place to rehearse the battles between Gregory and Henry IV of Germany concerning the choice of bishops and their investiture; nor is there space to enumerate the widespread inefficacies of papal attempts at ecclesiastical centralisation. For us it is sufficient to note that when Urban II (r. 1088–99) preached the crusade on 27 November 1095 at the Council of Clermont, the Church was anything but a unified front; on the contrary, it was in schism. In retaliation for Gregory's support of a rival king in opposition to him, Henry had called a council of German and Italian bishops in 1080 to censure Gregory and to designate Clement III (r. 1080–1100) as Pope instead. It was Clement who finally crowned him emperor in March 1084 after Clement himself had been crowned as rival Pope. Urban was Gregory's successor but one, all the while that Clement continued to reign as antiPope. Things were not satisfactorily resolved until 1122 when a compromise was agreed between the German emperor and the papacy on the election and installation of bishops. In England both Williams had wavered between rival popes until William Rufus made up his mind in 1095 not to recognise Clement. His political goals in Normandy made Urban, who had French support, the better candidate. As for Philip I of France, he was actually excommunicated at Clermont in 1095 by Urban for putting aside his long-standing wife in order to marry another. It is, therefore, hardly surprising that when Urban II preached what we now call the First Crusade, he was not addressing the French king or German emperor.[1]

Preaching the First Crusade

As is well known, we lack a transcript of the sermon Urban preached at the closing session of the Council of Clermont. We do know that he preached it in the open air, so that a large lay audience could hear him as well as the large numbers of bishops and abbots attending the council, together with the lay magnates ecclesiastical lords had been asked to bring with them. We can work out from Urban's preparatory work for the council and his subsequent preaching programme what his message was. Urban called upon Christian knights to use their special expertise to serve Christ in this world.

He called for their assistance to regain the Holy Sepulchre in Jerusalem from the Saracens and in so doing to battle for the liberation of Christendom and alleviate the hardship of Christians living in the East. He described the knightly assistance he was seeking as a penitential exercise which would cancel penance owed in this world and the next for past sins. The exercise had all of the trappings of a pilgrimage and, whatever Urban himself might have had in mind, it was interpreted as an armed pilgrimage. It was Urban's meticulously planned, theatrical preaching tour following the Council of Clermont that made sure that the new message of penitential warfare in service of Christ caught on as well as it did. Through taking the crusader's vow to liberate Jerusalem as a personal penitential exercise, knights were transforming themselves into 'knights of Christ' by internalising the message of the Reform Movement. By cleverly tapping into currents of lay spirituality, Urban had, in other words, managed to make concrete the programme Gregory VII had promoted of implanting righteousness into society at large. Lay spirituality was married to ecclesiastical reform, and the papacy was playing a leading role in Christianising society in novel ways.[2]

Urban's message of crusade was widely disseminated by like-minded reformers and by rumours of the new venture. Important princes such as Robert of Normandy and Bohemund of Taranto in southern Italy took the cross. Adherents of Henry IV were also attracted to the cause. Godfrey of Bouillon (d. 1100), who would later briefly rule Jerusalem, was a vassal of the emperor. The role of abbots in the ensuing recruitment drive was vital not only on account of the intimate ties between monastic foundations and local aristocratic families. Many crusaders had to turn to the monasteries in the hope of raising the necessary funds to go to Jerusalem. The wealth of the monasteries, as it were, bankrolled the First Crusade. Lay aristocratic crusaders in turn stimulated enthusiasm for the crusade among the wide range of their dependants, which included people living in the cities in which they had influence and authority. The scale of response was startling. Within a year of Urban's sermon at Clermont, many thousands of crusaders had started their march to the East. They included recruits of populist preachers such as Peter the Hermit who spread the word in the Orléanais, Champagne, Lorraine and the Rhineland. Although Peter and fellow populist preachers did attract some important local lords to the cause such as Walter Sans-Avoir, who was lord of Boissy, Count Emicho of Flonheim and Count Hartmann of Dillingen-Kybourg, the armies which came into being through this kind of preaching seem to have been less well regulated through the influence and social control of magnates than the other assembling armies. That is why in the secondary literature they are often given the misnomer of the 'People's Crusade' or the 'Popular Crusade'. These armies left Europe in spring and early summer 1096 before the harvest and marched overland to the East before the main armies left some months later. Their encounter with the thriving Jewish communities in Rouen and the Rhineland brings us back to the subject of this book, Christian–Jewish relations.[3]

By discussing the crusades in relationship to the ideals of Christian reform, we have naturally emphasised the religious and spiritual aspects of crusading. This does not mean that other motives played no role in taking the cross. It would be foolish to discount the love of adventure or the hope of material gain as motives for becoming a soldier of Christ. Yet, going on crusade was hardly a prudent financial investment. Although the possibility of booty and the traffic in Holy Land relics might have been lucrative, families received a poor material return on the money they invested in crusading. What matters to us, however, is what effect all this emotive religious rhetoric had on Christian–Jewish relations. How did the idea of knights serving Christ by fighting his enemies mesh with the idea that Jews had a place in Christian society as long as they served Christians and Christianity? How robust would the uneasy equilibrium of Christian–Jewish relations prove to be in the face of heady calls to Christianise self and society? With so much ecclesiastical rhetoric assuming that *ecclesia* (church) and society were one and the same, what kind of real space could there be left in lay society for Jews? And crucially, how did Jews themselves respond to all these new forces and ideas?

The dangers of crusading rhetoric

The dangers posed to Jews by Christian knights taking up arms against Muslims were already apparent in Spain in the 1060s. Spanish bishops had been called upon to safeguard Jewish communities from attack from northern knights who had come to help expand Christian territories at the expense of Islam. Pope Alexander II deftly expressed the official ecclesiastical position on this by emphasising that Jews should not be attacked because unlike the Saracens they were 'prepared to serve (*parati sunt servire*)'. His words of protection were included in Gratian's Decretum (1140s–1150s) as *'Dispar nimirum est'* (23.8.1). He wrote to the bishops of Spain:

> *We have been pleased with the rumour that we have lately heard about you, how you have protected the Jews who live among you, that they should not be destroyed by those who went out against the Saracens in Spain. Inspired by stupid ignorance or perhaps out of blind cupidity, they wanted to kill them in their rage, though divine piety might have predestined them to salvation. In this way did the blessed Gregory prohibit some who were inflamed in their wish to destroy them, denouncing as impious those who wished to destroy people who were [preserved (servati sunt)] by God's mercy; for since the loss of their freedom and fatherland they live dispersed in all parts of the world, condemned to lasting penance for the crime of their fathers in the effusion of the saviour's blood. There is, assuredly, a difference between the case of the Jews and that of the Saracens. It is just to fight those who persecute Christians and who expel them from their cities and houses, while these people are everywhere ready to serve. He even prohibited a certain bishop from destroying their synagogue.*[4]

The highly emotive language the Pope used to safeguard Jews helps us to appreciate how susceptible Christian–Jewish relations, which were premised on this kind of Jewish service, were bound to be to the types of religiosity we have just been describing. How realistic was it to imagine that Christian fighters, who had been fired up to wage holy war on the enemies of Christ, would abide by theological subtleties which demanded the preservation of the lives of those who were considered guilty of the greatest crime of all, the Crucifixion?

It must be emphasised at the start that the fact that attacks against Jews did *not* occur in southern France where there were large Jewish communities or in important Jewish centres such as Troyes or Reims in northern France is as important as the fact that attacks *did* occur in the German cities along the Rhine and Danube in spring and early summer 1096 but not again in August 1096 when Godfrey of Bouillon took his army through on his way to Jerusalem.[5] As with so many other aspects of Christian–Jewish relations, the key to upholding the ambiguous Pauline/Augustinian policy of toleration towards Jews at any one moment and in any one place lay in the hands of those in command. It is not for nothing that attacks against Jews occurred where crusading armies were least effectively controlled by their commanders. That these selfsame armies were desperate for provisions because they had started their journey before the main harvest no doubt exacerbated the situation. Seen from this perspective the anti-Jewish pogroms of the First Crusade did not signal a sea-change in Christian–Jewish relations. Instead, in an odd sort of way, the outbursts of violence allow us greater insight into the underlying tensions and incongruities governing those relations. For when violence takes place, all kinds of unresolved paradoxes and ambiguities come into sharp relief and those experiencing the violence as protagonists, spectators or *post factum* commentators are called upon to make sense of what happened. Their accounts then in turn become part of the complex web of ideas and measures governing relations between Christians and Jews. So although the pogroms did not substantially change Christian–Jewish relations, they did in an oblique way affect them. After all, it is a lot easier to open Pandora's Box than to close it.

Rouen

As far as France is concerned, we effectively have only one account of one instance of violence against the Jews in Rouen by Guibert of Nogent (d. *c.* 1125). The affair is described in Guibert's *Autobiography* which he penned almost twenty years after the event. Guibert tells us that when men started taking the cross to undertake the journey to Jerusalem, they began to question the logic of marching countless miles to the East to attack the enemies of God when right in front of them there were Jews who were 'more inimical to God than any other people'. They proceeded to put Jews to the sword; the only escape was acceptance of baptism. One little boy, who allowed himself to be baptised, was rescued.[6]

We cannot be sure exactly when the killing took place in Rouen and which of the 'unofficial' bands of crusaders were responsible. There is only the briefest mention of the episode in the continuation of the Annals of Rouen.[7] In his *Historia novorum* Eadmer records reports that Jewish converts to Christianity in Rouen paid William Rufus money to gain his permission to return to Judaism.[8] This must refer to people who were converted against their will in 1096. The Hebrew chronicles on the crusades, which predominantly concern Germany, record the serious threat French Jews felt they were under, but no specific mention is made of Rouen. One of the chronicles clearly traces the genesis of the crusading movement to France.

In words which bear a remarkable resemblance to Guibert's, the Jewish chronicler states that the princes, knights and ordinary people who took the cross thought it made more sense to avenge the Crucifixion on the Jews at home before attacking the Muslims in faraway lands. The French Jews sent letters to the Rhineland communities to warn them of the impending danger and to ask for their prayers. Ironically, the communities who would suffer most at the hands of crusaders thought that the Jews of France stood to lose more than the Jews of Germany. After all, the Jews of Speyer and Worms had just been granted handsome privileges by Henry IV.[9]

The Hebrew chronicles of the First Crusade

The Hebrew chronicles of the First Crusade offer unique insights into the mindset of German Jewish communities about their own sense of identity and their relations with Christians living in their locality. They cast light on relations between the Jews of Ashkenaz and the Christian lords to whom they owed service and from whom they expected protection and, more generally, on the future of their position in Christian society. The chronicles are three in number; the most extensive of the three narratives was compiled by the otherwise unknown Solomon bar Simson. A much shorter text was written by a halachist (Jewish legal expert) from Mainz called Eliezer bar Nathan (c. 1090–1170). Woven into his narrative are four liturgical poems. The third narrative is also short. Because it mainly concerns Mainz, it is known as the Mainz Anonymous. The narratives give detailed accounts of what happened when the armies that had been recruited by the populist preachers encountered German Jewish communities on their way to Jerusalem. The many similarities as well as the subtle differences between the narrative accounts have prompted many different complex theories about the interrelationship between the three texts. Are they indirectly related to one another through usage of common material such as inter-communal letters or, indeed, a no-longer-extant report? Or are they directly related to one another with the longer text drawing from the shorter ones? Alternatively, is it possible that the opposite occurred with the shorter texts drawing material from the longer ones? The finer details of this discussion need not concern us here. Suffice it to say that the recent editor of an entirely new and definitive edition of the texts, Eva Haverkamp, has argued convincingly that the relationship between the chronicles is both direct and indirect, with Solomon bar Simson drawing material from the Mainz Anonymous and, in addition to other no longer extant material, a contemporary source which was also used by Eliezer bar Nathan. As far as dating is concerned, she concludes that Solomon bar Simson compiled his work around 1140; that Eliezer bar Nathan completed his work by 1146 and that the Mainz Anonymous was written soon after the events of 1096. All three chronicles were written in Mainz.[10]

The most striking aspect of the chronicles is their passionate account of the defiant response of hundreds of Jews facing attack by the crusaders. Confronted by crusaders who had made up their minds to wipe Jews off the map either by murdering them or by forcing them to convert, the Jews, according to the chronicles, did not just decide to kill themselves. In an impromptu manner, they decided that group martyrdom would be the most appropriate response to this Christian onslaught on their Jewish identity. The chronicles take the reader from family to family, as parents slaughter their children and then each other. The manifold deaths of babies, children, women and men are depicted as *Kiddush ha-Shem*, sanctification of God's name, the holiest duty of every Jew to God. The chronicles stress how remarkable this kind of response was to a novel scale of attack. Indeed, notwithstanding the fact that sporadic local persecutions might well have taken place before 1096 and the fact that there are records of varying reliability which record occurrences of Jewish martyrdom, this was the first time medieval Jews outside Spain had been exposed to such a level of persecution.[11] What do we make of all of this?

Many scholars have pointed to the obvious fact that however many Jews died in 1096, a sufficient number survived to tell the tale. Most of the survivors must have been forcibly baptised in one way or another. We know that in 1097 Henry IV allowed the Jews who had been forced to convert to live again as Jews. It is highly likely that the survivors of the pogroms would have had every reason to transmit a particularly heroic account of the deaths of those who had perished. For one thing, it would give them an opportunity to work through their own conflicting emotions about what had happened during the pogroms and help them come to terms with their feelings of guilt and ambivalence towards those who had died, for another it gave them an opportunity to rally the spirits of other survivors within their communities, who were reeling from the shock of the unexpected onslaughts. The historical narratives of the chronicles are infused with liturgical nuances and it would seem that they were in part written to make theological sense of the carnage. In their anguished search for an answer as to why the God of Israel could have allowed such outrages to happen, they devised ideas about an elite generation, who God knew would be strong enough to resist Christianity and in so doing earn a heavenly reward for themselves and build up credit in God's eyes for generations to come. In other words, the detailed scenes of self-martyrdom probably tell us more about the way the survivors memorialised those who died than how their actual deaths occurred. But that does not mean no self-martyrdoms occurred, nor does it have to imply that those who killed themselves did not share in any of the feelings ascribed to them by the chroniclers. The Latin sources say very much less about the attacks on the Jews, but what they do say corroborates the evidence that many Jews took their own lives in order to avoid facing death or baptism at the hands of the crusaders. Contemporary Jewish litur-gical poetry (*piyyutim*) also confirms the occurrence of self-martyrdom, as do entries in the *Memorbücher* (Books of Remembrance) compiled by com-munities to commemorate the dead. Whether as many Jews died at their own hands as the chronicles would have us believe or not, Jews did martyr themselves and their children. The question which then follows is how this extreme response to persecution can be explained within the framework of *halachah* (Jewish law), which is so stringently opposed to suicide and so fiercely protective of the lives of children.[12]

The terminology used in the chronicles to denote Christianity and the imagery with which the chroniclers depicted the enactment of ritual slaughter offer us clues as to why the Jews of Germany might have acted in this way. A particularly striking feature of the Hebrew sources for the First Crusade is the negativity with which every single element of the Christian faith is described. To be sure, the negative terms or anti-Christian invectives are not peculiar to the chronicles; they occur regularly in medieval Hebrew liturgical writing and prayers. Most of the invectives find their origin in an ancient Jewish parody of the Gospels, the *Toledoth Yeshu* (History of Jesus) which pilloried the miracles of Jesus's birth, ministry, Passion and Resurrec-tion. According to this parody, which must have been already circulating in an oral form by the second century before appearing in writing in the fourth or fifth, Yeshu's mother was a prostitute. His miracles were based on magic; reports of his Resurrection were fabricated after his death by his loyal followers. Thus we find in the Hebrew chronicles that Jesus is referred to as a 'son of lechery', a 'bastard', 'son of a menstruating woman [conception during a woman's so-called unclean period was thought to produce depraved children]'. He is also called the 'hanged one' or 'the trampled corpse' to reflect the belief that not only was his death dishonourable, it was final. In the *Toledoth Yeshu*, Yeshu's dead body is dragged through the streets of Jerusalem for all to observe that he had died in contrast to what his followers claimed. In keeping with the idea that there was nothing divine about Yeshu and his miracles and also in continuation of other rabbinical material, the Holy Sepulchre is denoted as 'the grave of their idolatry' and churches are described as 'houses of idolatry'. Baptism is called 'stinking water' which 'corrupts' rather than purifies; Christians are depicted as 'uncircumcised' and 'errant' and Christianity as an 'error'; the cross worn by crusaders is called an 'evil sign'. What we see in these invectives is not just a complete Jewish denial of everything Christians in general and those who had taken the cross in particular held sacred; we see a deliberate communal strategy of language which made sure that the message of Jewish negation of Christianity was inculcated into every member of the Jewish community at every possible opportunity. The contrast between this vituperative denial of Christianity and the zeal of Christian spirituality as epitomised in the rhetoric of Christian reform and crusade is breathtaking. It brings out in sharp relief the theological chasm between Christians and Jews, which in some way or other always underlay the relations between them.[13] But the fact that it was thought necessary to deny Christianity through a repetitious mantra of insults against Jesus Christ and the Virgin Mary might also imply that Jewish communities in a strange and paradoxical way could have felt attracted to some of the concepts of personal intercession which these figures offered within Christian theology. As we shall see in a moment, the chronicles do seem to show a remarkable awareness of Christian spirituality, even as they fulminate against it. Just as Christian anti-Judaism was in part fuelled by Christian ambivalence towards the tradition from which it had developed, Jewish anti-Christianity was in part fuelled by the continuing need for Jews to keep themselves from being absorbed into an increasingly Christianising environment. But first we have to explore some of the factors which could have encouraged this verbal denial of Christianity to turn into physical denial with Jews choosing death over submission to the crusaders' swords and/or baptismal water.

Both the Mainz Anonymous and Solomon bar Simson's compilation refer to the martyrdom by Hannah and her seven sons at the time of the Jewish revolt against the Syrian King Antiochus, who had desecrated the Temple (167–160 BCE). Hannah watched as her sons were slaughtered before taking her own life, recalling the binding of Isaac in her final words: 'You erected one altar, I erected seven'. The Hebrew chroniclers constantly cry out to God that in their willingness to sacrifice their children the crusade martyrs have far exceeded Abraham's dedication which involved only one child. The legend of Hannah is found in the second book of Maccabees, the Talmud, post-Talmudic homiletical (midrashic) literature and the tenth-century Hebrew version of Josephus, the so-called *Jossipon*.[14] Avraham Grossman has argued that the Rhineland Jews were particularly attached to aggadic (narrative) traditions such as this legend; the *Jossipon* seems to have been a particular favourite in the eleventh century. This kind of material offered other models of martyrdom which included parents slaughtering their children in the service of God. The most obvious example is the history of the final stand in Masada against the Romans which ended with whole families sacrificing themselves in this way. Scholars have long puzzled over the fact that none of the Hebrew First Crusade chroniclers mentions Masada by name, but Grossman is probably right that the striking similarities between the chronicles' reports of the deaths of the German martyrs and the *Jossipon* report on the martyrdom of those who died in their defiance of Rome must mean that at least the chroniclers were aware of the model.[15] William of Newburgh's report on the martyrdom of the Jews in York during the Third Crusade would corroborate this. William describes the self-martyrdom as an act of 'irrational fury' by 'rational beings'. In order to explain how the York Jews could have acted in this way he writes: 'but whoever reads the *History of the Jewish War* by Josephus understands well enough that madness of this kind, arising from their ancient superstition, has continued down to our own times, whenever any very heavy misfortune fell on them.'[16]

These ideas would have been embedded in the Rhineland communities through the strong influence of sages. Liturgical poetry composed by sages seems to have played a significant role in shaping ideas within these German communities; available *piyyutim* belabour Jewish expectations of speedy messianic redemption, while eschatological passages in the chronicles as well as in the poems repeatedly express the hope that the blood of the martyrs would hasten God's revenge on the enemies of Israel. Grossman also points to the strong affinity which German Jews felt for the land of Israel. By referring explicitly to Abraham's sacrifice of Isaac, the chroniclers put the Rhineland deaths within the framework of the Temple. According to legend Abraham had bound Isaac on Mount Moriah, on the very spot where the future Temple of Jerusalem would stand. The human sacrifice of life is expressed in the language of the Temple sacrifices. To give one example, when the Cologne Jews who had fled to nearby Xanten resolved to kill themselves, they are described as doing so in the context of the evening meal of the Sabbath. The decision is made so as not to be polluted by falling into the hands of the crusaders. The martyrdom is choreographed by a sage who is dubbed high priest. He admonishes the others to turn their table into an altar on which they will transform themselves into the obligatory evening offering of Temple days. By so doing they will enter paradise and gaze upon God in his glory. Marcus, Chazan and others have pointed out that this kind of rhetoric was used deliberately by the martyrs and/or the chroniclers to rob the crusaders of the *raison d'être* of their journey. By performing the Temple sacrifices in the Rhineland, Jerusalem was brought to Ashkenaz; Mainz, in particular, was identified with Jerusalem. Thus the crusaders were deprived of the very place towards which they were marching. The Jews who martyred themselves and their children were performing *Kiddush ha-Shem*; they were true servants of God and not those who mistakenly called themselves soldiers of Christ.[17] Goldin sees the Xanten episode and its later narration as part of an educative process of socialisation of the concept of sacrificing one's life for God. For *Kiddush ha-Shem* could only turn into an effective tool of Jewish resistance if whole communities personally adopted its ethos.[18]

The importance of aggadic traditions, the influence of models of mar-tyrdom in the *Jossipon*, messianic hopes, the prominent position of sages and their influence over the community interacting with a zealous determin-ation to protect their own Jewish identity offer a cogent explanation for the manner in which the deaths of the martyrs were memorialised. Whether these factors were sufficiently powerful for a large number of flesh-and-blood men and women to commit these deeds in this way cannot be answered definitively one way or another. In the final analysis we shall always have to ask ourselves whether the chronicles reflect the views of their authors more accurately than those of their subjects. The novelty of the response makes it more than likely that whatever else they were doing, the chroniclers were also constructing a *post factum* ideology of martyrdom in order to find rationalisations for what had occurred. After all, it was hard enough to interpret *halachah* as allowing self-martyrdom, let alone commanding this kind of sacrifice. The concept of sacrificing one's children for *Kiddush ha-Shem* remained highly contentious and emotionally charged. As we shall see, the chronicles provide plenty of hints that feelings were mixed on these questions.[19] Whatever the case may be, the crusade chronicles and poetry present us with a dramatic Jewish response to persecution. The verbal and physical denial of Christianity makes for a powerful statement of firm Jewish identity. It is hardly surprising that the Hebrew material inspired later generations of Jews in their response to persecution.

The Hebrew accounts of the attacks on the Jews and their response also offer insights into some of the complexities of Jewish interaction with different strata of Christians in Germany at a time when the issues of the struggle between Henry IV and the papacy had not yet been settled. Whatever individual bishops felt about Jews, they did not want their authority challenged or the peace of their towns disrupted by marauding crusaders. Forcing baptism on unwilling Jews, attacking Jews and killing them went against ecclesiastical rules governing Christian relations to Jews. Theory is one thing, reality quite another. As bands of crusaders led by men such as Count Emicho, who used what authority they had to promote violence, rather than curb it, reached these towns, they put immense pressure on existing relations between the bishops and the townsfolk and exposed how fragile relations were between local Christians and between Christians and Jews. In Speyer, Bishop John (1090–1104) stopped crusaders and burghers from massacring Jews as they left their synagogue on the Sabbath on 3 May 1096. Only 10 or 11 Jews were killed; in accordance with the provision of Henry's 1090 charter, the burghers who had been involved in killing Jews had their right hands chopped off. The bishop proceeded to save the remaining Jews of Speyer by hiding them in places of safety nearby. Episcopal authority was weaker in Worms. Bishop Adalbert (1089–1107) was a fierce opponent of the king and had been expelled from his see, and it is not clear who held episcopal authority in 1096. On top of that the attack on the Jews of Worms seems to have been more organised than the attack in Speyer. Although initially Jews had readily received help from their Christians neighbours, the burghers after a while joined forces with the crusaders against the Jews together with people from the surrounding villages. Jews regularly lost local support when Christians were killed in skirmishes. Protecting Jews was one thing, dying for them seemingly quite another. It is at this stage that episcopal authority would break down. By the end of May the Wormser Jews who had stayed in their homes were killed or baptised; those who had taken refuge in the episcopal palace could not in the end hold out against their attackers: they died at the hands of their assailants or martyred themselves and their children.

Much the same happened in Mainz where the Jews were faced by the troops of Emicho of Flonheim. Here too help was offered by Archbishop Ruothard (1088–1109), who at that period was a supporter of the king. The burgrave too gave assistance. The Jews desperately tried to buy Emicho off but were unsuccessful. On 27 May burghers of Mainz unlocked the gates, giving Emicho and his army access to the city. As Emicho laid siege to the episcopal palace, the archbishop's men ran off. Ruothard too fled for his own life. The Jews inside the palace resolved to martyr themselves after their armed resistance had come to nothing. This mass martyrdom is described in particularly haunting tones by the chronicles, which all three stem from Mainz:

> Who has ever witnessed such events?. . . . Were there ever a thousand one hundred sacrifices on one day, all of them like the sacrifice of Isaac the son of Abraham? For one the world shook, when he was offered up on Mount Moriah. . . . What has been done [this time]? . . . when one thousand one hundred holy souls were killed and slaughtered on one day . . .?[20]

The Jews who had sought safety in the palace of the burgrave met with the same fate. In Cologne Archbishop Hartmann (1089–99) tried to save the day by taking the Jews of the city to several neighbouring villages. But at the end of June other crusading bands attacked them there, as we have already seen when we touched on the events in Xanten. In Trier the Jews had been successful in bribing Peter the Hermit's troops to leave them in peace in April. The burghers of Trier, however, started attacking the Jews. At Pentecost on 1 June they were joined by others coming to market. Archbishop Egilbert (1079–1101) did his best to save them by guarding them in his palace, but in the end his own position in the city was too precarious for him to be able to save them as Jews. He was a stranger in Trier and his elevation to his see by Henry IV had been unpopular. The *Gesta* of

Trier record a sermon he preached to the Jews admonishing them to accept baptism. Interestingly, he chided them for blaspheming against the Virgin. This would seem to indicate Christian awareness of Jewish verbal denial of Christianity. The Hebrew sources record that Egilbert and his men prevented the Jews from martyring themselves so that they could be baptised. It was the women they identified as leading others to their deaths. We shall return to this in a moment. In Regensburg the Jewish community was baptised after being herded *en masse* into the Danube or the Vitus brook which was adjacent to the Jewish quarter of the city. It is not clear which crusading army was responsible for this event.[21]

The Hebrew material cites vengeance for the Crucifixion as a clear motive for all of these attacks. As we have seen, Jews knew that some crusaders thought it was folly to go to the East to fight the Muslims without attacking those to whom they assigned the guilt of crucifying Christ. This fits in well with the Latin crusading sources which are replete with the concept of vengeance on the enemies of Christ. As Riley-Smith has explained, medieval ideas of revenge were used by preachers of the crusade to promote the ideas of fighting for Christ against the Muslims. Although revenging Christ on the Jews conflicted with Augustinian ideas about the correct Christian stance towards Jews, it is not difficult to understand how it could have emerged in the minds of zealous crusaders lacking the necessary firm lead to keep them to acceptable ecclesiastical norms. But Riley-Smith has also pointed to the fact that many of the attacks also took place out of the prosaic need for ill-equipped armies to grab the provisions they needed.[22] Greed for Jewish wealth is referred to again and again in both the Hebrew and Latin sources.

But the Hebrew sources of the First Crusade do not only provide us with a programme of Jewish denial and repudiation of Christianity. Bound up in Jewish rejection of Christianity was a considerable knowledge of Christian values. For a start, the chroniclers' rude condemnation of the crusaders' march to the Holy Sepulchre demonstrates that they had a good idea of the basic message of the crusade and the centrality of Christ to it. Their erroneous claim that an indulgence had been proclaimed whereby the sins would be forgiven of anyone who killed a Jew shows that they were aware of the penitential nature of the crusade. The chroniclers refer to the cross with which crusaders had marked their garments.[23] But the manner in which the chronicles portray individual instances of martyrdom moves beyond simple knowledge of Christianity. It betrays the kind of adoption and internalisation of non-Jewish ideas which Ivan Marcus had termed 'inward acculturation'. Inward acculturation does not imply any loss of Jewish identity. On the contrary, Jewish identity is bolstered by internalising Christian values in order to promote Judaism at the cost of Christianity.[24] The language which the chronicles used to conjure up the image of Jerusalem in Ashkenaz, rather than in the East to where the crusaders were marching, is an example of such acculturation. Not only was this a polemical move against the crusading ideal; it also ironically echoed the views of Christian theologians such as Anselm of Canterbury who commanded monks to seek heavenly Jerusalem in their monasteries rather than join the march to earthly Jerusalem.[25] The chroniclers' engagement with the actions and intentions of individual Jewish men and women reveals considerable similarities with current Christian interests in the human condition, which we know so well from contemporary Christian sources. A good example of this is the anguished story of Isaac ben David of Mainz. Isaac had undergone involuntary baptism. He returned to his home and to his children where his wounded mother was confined to her bed. She had escaped baptism. Isaac's wife, Skolaster, had been murdered by the crusaders. Isaac could not cope with the fact that he had allowed himself to be baptised and sought a way to expiate his guilt. Against the express wishes of his mother he took his son and daughter to the synagogue and slaughtered them before the ark 'in sanctification of the great name of God . . . who commanded us . . . to hold fast to his holy Torah with all our heart and with all our soul'. Sprinkling the blood of his children on the ark he proclaimed: 'May this blood cleanse me of all my sins.' He went back to his home to burn it down with his mother locked up inside before returning to the synagogue to burn it down with himself. 'There was burned a blameless, upright, God-fearing man; his soul is interred in the lot of the righteous in the Garden of Eden.' Einbinder has identified the narrator's interest in and exploration of Isaac's tortured behaviour with similar explorations of individuals' internal conflicts in the Romance literature of the time.[26]

Jeremy Cohen, for whom the Hebrew chronicles are literary constructs serving the needs of the survivors, rather than historical records concerning the deceased, has uncovered in this narrative a myriad of conflicting references to biblical and midrashic material which would indicate how troubled the survivors were with this kind of behaviour and how much they had absorbed from Christian culture. Could it really be holy to sacrifice one's children to atone for one's own sins or to burn an unwilling mother to her death? Could the child sacrifice be an oblique reference to Christ's death in expiation for the sins of mankind? After all, for Christians the binding of Isaac prefigured the Passion of Christ. These dichotomies are intensified by the fact that the drama is situated on Thursday 29 May, the night of *Shavuot*, the festival on which Jews celebrate the giving of the Torah. In 1096 this was the Thursday before Christian Pentecost, commemorating the descent of the Holy Spirit in the tongues of fire. Baptisms were traditionally conducted on the eve of Pentecost (and Easter Saturday); the story of the binding of Isaac was part of the liturgy. On this very night Isaac's namesake in Mainz is violently rejecting baptism for the sake of Judaism. In Cohen's reading this narrative radiates profound unease with such extreme forms of Jewish sacrifice.[27]

For Israel Yuval, who reads the Hebrew chronicles more as historical narratives than literary artefacts, the allusions to redemptive sacrifices which are linked to Jerusalem are examples of the messianic nature of these texts. According to his interpretation, Ashkenazi Jews were convinced that God would seek vengeance on those who had spilled Jewish blood. Martyrs, such as Isaac, hoped to bring forward messianic deliverance through bloody acts of *Kiddush ha-Shem*.[28] We have already seen how the chronicles cry out to God to avenge the dead. This reading of the text also includes parallels with current Christian themes. Messianic hope was yet another aspect of crusading fervour; avenging Christ was how many knights of Christ interpreted the business of crusade.

For Shmuel Shepkaru the chronicler's conclusion that Isaac's martyrdom earned him the reward of the righteous in the Garden of Eden is of particular interest. We have already noted that the idea of fellowship between like-minded people and love for other human beings echo current Christian explorations of the human condition and human relationships. But the expectation of Isaac and the other German martyrs of a personal reward for their sacrifice out of their love for God in a well-defined afterlife seems to be an even more striking example of interaction with current Christian ideas. Whereas the aggadic martyrs of the past were not guaranteed a place in a vaguely conceived 'World to Come' by those who memorialised them, the martyrs of Xanten were represented as expecting to come face to face with God and to be adorned with a jewelled crown of gold.[29] The martyrs who were about to be slaughtered in the courtyard of the bishop's palace in Mainz were said to expect to exchange 'a world of darkness . . . for a world of light, a world of pain for a world of happiness, a transitory world for a world that is eternal and everlasting'.[30] Eliezer bar Nathan was sure that the martyrs'

> souls [were] bound in the bond of life in the King's sanctuary. Each of them is garbed in the eight vestments of clouds of glory; each crowned with two diadems, one of precious stones and pearls and one of fine gold; and each bearing eight myrtles in his hand.[31]

For all the biblical and rabbinical imagery, the confluence of the expectations of the Jewish martyrs with the developing ideology of Christian martyrdom is striking. As Shepkaru expresses it so poignantly, the chroniclers were not willing to allow only Christians to enjoy the heavenly fruits of martyrdom. Nor were they willing to concede that Christians were prepared to make greater sacrifices than Jews out of love for God. Jewish heroism in the face of death, with all of its allusions to Christian chivalric literature, proved that the heroes of the day had been the Jewish martyrs, not the crusaders.[32] This brings out sharply a fundamental paradox of Jewish existence in Ashkenaz. However opposed Jews were to the belief system of Christianity, however separate they were from Christians through the observance of Jewish ritual, they shared with their Christian neighbours many basic interests in the human condition and consciously or unconsciously transformed evocative Christian ideas into core markers of their own Jewish identity.

The paradox comes out sharply in the grisly story of Rachel of Mainz inside a chamber of the bishop's palace. Rachel had two girls and two boys whom she was determined to save from baptism. She was particularly concerned that little Aaron should not see his brother Isaac being killed and run away. Aaron did see and hid under a chest. Rachel's two daughters, Bella and Madrona, were more co-operative. They sharpened the knife so that it was ritually fit to slaughter them. Rachel performed the deed and then called for Aaron to come from his hiding place. She had to pull him by the leg to get hold of him. After sacrificing him she placed her children on her lap, two on the left and two on the right. Her sleeves, which must have been long and wide, covered them up. Earlier Bar Simson's compilation had mentioned that Rachel had received Isaac's blood 'in her sleeves instead of in the [Temple] vessel for blood'. The crusaders found her weeping over her children. They assumed she had hidden jewels in her sleeves. When they discovered the children, they beat her to death. As we have seen, the chroniclers compared Rachel's story to the death of Hannah and her sons at the time of the Maccabees. The father of the children then entered the scene. He screamed at the sight of his offspring and fell on his sword to end his own life.[33]

Following Jeremy Cohen, one can see an overlap between the chroniclers' treatment of Rachel with Christian ideas concerning the Virgin Mary as the interceding mother for all mankind. In Jewish tradition the biblical Rachel is the epitome of Jewish motherhood. She was the favourite wife of Jacob, whose name became Israel, and she was considered particularly effective in interceding with God on behalf the children of Israel. In Chapter 31 Jeremiah pictures her weeping over the exile of the children of Israel, i.e. the Jews. The chapter includes a promise from God to return the Jews to their land. This section from Jeremiah is read on the second day of the Jewish New Year to accompany the Torah reading concerning the binding of Isaac. The sobs of Rachel of Mainz evoke all these connotations of the biblical Rachel; her sleeves which were transformed into ritual vessels of blood bring to mind the chalice used in the Christian celebration of the Mass in which Abraham's sacrifice is recalled as prefiguring the Eucharistic sacrifice. The polemical message is loud and clear: Rachel's martyred children were the true sacrifice to God and not Mary's son, Jesus Christ.[34]

Rachel is also an example of powerful independent female behaviour which is another remarkable feature of the Hebrew material of the First Crusade. It is not for nothing that in Trier Christians felt they needed to restrain the women from martyring themselves and encouraging their menfolk to do the same. Was this active female behaviour called forth by the novelty of the situation in which the Rhineland Jews found themselves? Did the chroniclers stress their role to bring out more sharply than ever how unprecedented the Rhineland response to persecution was? After all, the positive response of Christian females to the preaching of the crusade was also unusual. Whatever the case may be, as Einbinder has shown, female martyrs were portrayed much more passively as the twelfth century progressed.[35] On the other hand, little Aaron's reluctance to be killed is just as important. It points to the fact that not everyone hastened to their death during the pogroms. Rachel's husband's late arrival on the scene and his anguish at seeing his dead family makes one ask with David Malkiel whether he would have agreed with his wife that martyrdom really was the very best option. Malkiel suggests, for example, that Skolaster, the wife of Isaac ben David of Mainz, was probably trying to escape when she was overcome by crusaders in a courtyard. He wonders whether, at least originally, Isaac and Skolaster had worked out their separate plans on how to survive rather than to die. The beautiful, young Sarit is another example of a person who was revolted by the killings and tried to escape. She was slaughtered by Judah ben Abraham, whom the chroniclers denote as her father-in-law to be. His reasoning is encapsulated by his words: 'my daughter, since you were not permitted to be wed to my son, Abraham, you will not be wed to any other, to the [Gentile]'. Malkiel also points to episodes where some people only choose to die to fit in. A fascinating example of this is Jacob ben R. Sullam who is described as not coming from a good family and whose mother was not Jewish. As he slaughters himself he 'called out . . . all the days of my life till now, you have despised me'. The value of this kind of appraisal is that it guards us against a too homogenous a view of Jewish Rhineland communities. For all their glorification of *Kiddush ha-Shem*, the chronicles do contain plenty of indications that many participants in the horrible events were terrified and, given the choice, did not want to die and, if they did die, did not die as heroically as posterity would like to think. And, reading between the lines, more conversions must have taken place than the chronicles would have us believe in the first instance.[36]

The Second Crusade

The Second Crusade was called by Pope Eugenius III (r. 1145–53) in December 1145 after the fall of the crusader county of Edessa in 1144. Bernard of Clairvaux was the preacher *par excellence* of this crusade, travelling from region to region in Flanders, the Low Countries, Germany and France in 1146 and 1147. This time the kings of France and Germany were included in the recruitment drive. Conrad III and the German contingents left in spring 1147 for the Holy Land; Louis VII of France left with the French soon afterwards. In the event, Edessa was not regained and the siege of Damascus in July 1148 ended in failure.[37]

The only Hebrew record we have for the Second Crusade comes from the pen of Ephraim of Bonn (1133–after 1196), the author of the *Sefer Zekhirah* ('Book of Remembrance'), which carries on to include reports of many other instances of late-twelfth-century attacks on Jews in Germany, France and England. We shall deal with most of these, which are not crusade-related, in the next chapter. Ephraim spent some years as the head of the rabbinical court in Bonn and composed a considerable number of liturgical poems, some of which are contained in his chronicle. The *Sefer Zekhirah* documents the isolated instances of loss of Jewish life at the hands of crusaders in 1146–7. As Ivan Marcus has shown, the description of the attack on Rabbi Jacob ben Meir at his home in Ramerupt, not far from Troyes, is particularly striking.[38] Jacob was the grandson of Rashi and was known as Rabbenu Tam; he was the leading *Tosafist* of the period. According to Ephraim, Tam's attackers ripped up a Torah scroll in front of his face before taking him outside to a field to argue against the validity of Judaism and enact their revenge on him for the Crucifixion by inflicting five wounds to his head. Tam was rescued by a passing nobleman whom he bribed to save his life. The nobleman had promised to return him to his attackers if he did not convert by the next day. Whether or not Tam was attacked in this way, Ephraim's narrative includes a number of points which echo what we have already discussed with respect to the First Crusade. The attack is said to have occurred on the second day of *Shavuot*, which in 1146 fell on 20 May, the Monday after Pentecost. Once again we have a confrontation on a festival which meant diametrically different things to Jews and Christians. The destruction of a Torah scroll on the day celebrating the giving of the Torah epitomised the seriousness of the anti-Jewish assault. The reference to five wounds obviously refers to the stigmata of Christ. But it also intriguingly resonates with a French crusade song composed between Easter and December 1146 which urged knights to follow King Louis to fight the Muslims in the Holy Land. The fourth couplet of the song starts with '*Deus livrat sun cors a Judeus / Pur metre nus fors de prison; Plaies li firent en cinc lieus, Que mort suffrit e passion.*', i.e. 'God delivered his body to the Jews to get us out of prison. They wounded him in five places so that he endured death and the Passion.' The reference to possible conversion recalls the fact that Pentecost was a liturgical time for conducting baptisms. Rabbenu Tam (Hebrew for 'pure') emerges from the chronicle as the pure, unbaptised counterpoint to the crucified Christ. The

French song promised those who followed Louis that their souls would join the angels in paradise; Ephraim asserted that the martyrs of the Second Crusade received 'eight vestments, like a High Priest, and two crowns'.[39] But it is equally interesting that Tam did not precipitate events by rushing into self-martyrdom. Surviving without undergoing baptism is clearly projected here as a better strategy than killing oneself. The martyrdoms recorded by Ephraim are presented in the language of the First Crusade recalling the binding of Isaac and the sacrifices of the Temple, but almost all of them were 'passive', in the sense that the martyrs were killed, rather than 'active' in the sense that people killed themselves to avoid conversion or death at the hands of Christians. The idealisation of *Kiddush ha-Shem* in the chronicles of the First Crusade meant that the term was applied to both forms of martyrdom, which included Jewish deaths in which the murderers did not offer their victims the choice of conversion.[40]

An important aspect of Ephraim's account of the Second Crusade is his treatment of Bernard of Clairvaux. Ephraim records how Bernard managed to contain the effects of the inflammatory anti-Jewish preaching by the monk Ralph and prevent the kind of bloodshed that had occurred 50 years previously.[41] Two crucial points emerge from this. The first is that Ephraim was not only aware that killing Jews went against ecclesiastical norms. He knew that a proof text for the Christian position came from Psalm 58(9):12: 'Slay them not, lest at any time my people forget.' The second is that Bernard's concerted efforts once again prove how vital the role of leadership was in determining whether or not crusading rhetoric would spill over into anti-Jewish violence. In his letter of 1146 which Bernard sent to various regions to preach the Second Crusade he rejoiced in the crusaders' 'zeal for God', but he went on to stress how important it was that they did not lack the moderation which stemmed from knowledge. Using several verses from Psalm 58(9) he insisted that the Jews were not to be slain. They were the

> *living letters [of Scripture] for Christians, the reminders of Christ's passion. They had been dispersed throughout the world on account of this, so that they would be witnesses to our redemption by suffering just punishment for such a great crime. . . . they had been dispersed and put aside; they undergo harsh captivity under Christian princes. . . . they will convert . . . .*

Bernard had clearly learnt from the events of 1096 how easy it was for crusaders to misconstrue evocative crusading rhetoric as incitement to attack Jews. At the same time, it is noticeable how ambiguous his own language in defence of Jews was. Following his assertions concerning Jewish subservience as a penalty for their role in the Crucifixion, he went on to say that 'where there are no Jews, Christian moneylenders "judaise worse", that is if they can be called Christians rather than baptised Jews'. Once again, Christians are asked to preserve Jews so they can serve them, in this instance by keeping Christians from the sin of usury; but by identifying usury so intrinsically with Jews that the word *judaisare* became tantamount with the practice of usury Bernard was, in fact, adding yet another emotive layer to Christian anti-Jewish rhetoric. It would seem that in this instance Bernard was basing his observations on his French experience. For he did not refer to moneylending in the letter he wrote to the Archbishop of Mainz in which he specifically condemned the actions of Ralph. German Jews were less heavily involved in moneylending than the Jews of northern France in this period. Bernard ended his crusading letter by stating that the rules of Pope Eugenius's crusading encyclical *Quantum praedecessores* whereby crusaders did not have to pay interest on their debts should also apply to Jews, and it seems very likely that he encouraged King Louis to take action on this. Ephraim records Jewish financial losses in this respect.[42]

The Third Crusade

When crusader Jerusalem fell into the hands of Saladin in October 1187 after his victory at the battle of Hattin in July, renewed efforts were made in the West to muster princes and knights to do battle for Christ. Emperor Frederick Barbarossa was able to contain attacks on the Jews in the run-up to the crusade. The leading scholar and pietist Eleazar ben Judah of Worms (d. 1230) recorded how the emperor protected the Jews of Mainz from mob violence in 1187–8. Tragically, Eleazar's wife Dolce and two daughters Bellette and Hannah were murdered by two 'marked' men who stormed into his house on 15 November 1196 in Worms. It is unclear to what extent these men were connected to crusading activity. One of them was caught and brought to justice by the Christian authorities.[43]

In England, Richard the Lionheart left the Jews to their fate; he returned to Normandy directly after his coronation in London in September 1189 to continue his preparations for going on crusade with Philip Augustus of France, leaving for the East in July 1190. Ephraim of Bonn offers details about riots in London against the Jews and the *Kiddush ha-Shem* undertaken by the Jews of York in 1190, but William of Newburgh is far more informative. Riots broke out against the Jews of England at the time of Richard I's coronation. Jews had been excluded from attending the ceremonies. Violence erupted when somehow the surging crowds outside the palace pushed a Jew too far forwards. When a report spread that the king had ordered the death of all Jews, an unruly medley from within and without London set on the Jews of London together with the Jews who had travelled to the city for the occasion. Many Jews were killed. The marauding did not please Richard but he did not seem able or willing to put a halt to it nor to punish the offenders. Rioting spread to King's Lynn, Norwich, Bury, Colchester, Thetford, Ospringe and Lincoln. William was convinced that greed and envy inspired the attacks more than faith. Jews had been drawn to King's Lynn, for example, by the business opportunities it had to offer. William felt that their wealth and numbers, combined with the king's protection, had made the Jews of the town insolent. It was a group of young men entering the port, who may or may not have been crusaders, who attacked the Jews. The local citizenry was afraid to incur royal displeasure. Similar things took place in Stamford, where the crusaders were hardly aided by the local inhabitants. The Jews of Lincoln found safety in the royal castle.

William's treatment of the massacre in York brings out sharply how important the issue of moneylending was in the riots. He focused on the richest Jews of York, Josce and Benedict, and criticised them for living in palatial houses and oppressing the Christians to whom they lent money. Benedict had travelled to London for the coronation and had been forced to convert after being gravely wounded. He died of those wounds after Richard had allowed him to return to Judaism. As far as William was concerned, this meant that he was doubly deserving of hell, once as a Jew and once as an apostate. William records that the attacks on the Jews were masterminded by notables who were indebted to the Jews. They carried with them local people, crusaders looking for plunder and the young men of York but not, as William put it, the 'nobility of the city or the weightier citizens'. The Jews sought safety in Clifford's Tower but the castle itself came under attack. When it became clear to the Jews that there was no way out save baptism, they set fire to the castle and underwent self-martyrdom. William reports that they were led to this by a rabbi from France. We know from Ephraim of Bonn's account and from a contemporary elegy composed by Joseph of Chartres that his name was Yom Tov. This must have been Rabbi Yom Tov of Joigny, who had studied under Rabbi Tam and who had composed an elegy for the Jews who were executed in Blois in 1171. We shall discuss the Blois affair in the next chapter. Tam seems to have ruled that self-martyrdom was permissible if that was the only way baptism could be avoided. According to William, Josce led the way by slaughtering his wife, Anna, and his boys with Yom Tov killing Josce. Besides Yom Tov and Josce, Joseph of Chartres lamented the sacrifice of Moses and Elijah of York. Elijah was also a pupil of Tam. In Joseph of Chartres's words: 'When My sages were gathered [to heaven] and My books rolled up, / The letters were flying and the parchment burned.' The imagery of the letters of the Torah returning to God comes from midrashic material concerning a Jewish martyr who was burnt with a Torah scroll wrapped around him at the time of Hadrian's suppression of the Bar Kokhba revolt. It symbolised the eternal holiness of the words of God and was used by the poet to emphasise the truth of Judaism in opposition to Christianity which had been spurned by the martyrs. From what we have seen earlier, it will come as no surprise that some Jews inside Clifford's Tower tried to avoid death by seeking conversion. To William's dismay these Jews were cut down by the crowds as they emerged from the castle. After the killings those responsible for attacking the Jews made their way to York Minster to destroy the bonds recording their debts. This underlines how significant the role of moneylending was in these events.[44]

The crusade massacres in England reinforce what we have said earlier in connection with the First and Second Crusades. Crucial to the events was the absence of the king whose attention was on his pending crusade rather than on 'his' Jews. Crucial was the fact that all of this happened at the start of a new reign of a king who was going on crusade with the King of France who had expelled 'his' Jews at the start of *his* reign. As we have seen, it is plausible that there was some expectation that something similar was bound to take place in England.[45] But most telling of all is how, once again, the violent atmosphere of the crusade brought out into the open some of the ambiguities governing the relations between Christians and Jews. By the end of the 1180s the Jews of England were serving their king well enough through their moneylending activities. But did their royal service befit the theological kind of service they were supposed to be playing in Christian society? William of Newburgh had no doubt that it did not. This is clear from his observations that God had used the violence, which had been perpetrated by misguided, greedy people, to teach the Jews a lesson for being above themselves.

Later crusades and conclusion

Crusading violence continued into the thirteenth and fourteenth centuries on its own or, more often than not, in combination with other kinds of anti-Jewish sentiments. But with some very notable exceptions such as the Shepherds' Crusade of 1320, authorities were usually capable of reining in widespread attacks on the Jews. But the persecutions of the crusades of the late eleventh and twelfth centuries exposed in the most uncompromising fashion both irrevocable differences and startling similarities between developing ideas of Christian and Jewish identities. An important legacy must have been the powerful message of Jewish rejection of baptism. Not only did many Jews choose to die rather than be baptised, not only did some Jewish parents kill their children rather than expose them to baptism, those who succumbed to baptism to save their lives returned to Judaism as soon as they were allowed to. Bar Simson's compilation concerning the First Crusade went to great pains to emphasise that the forced converts did everything they could to live as Jews even while nominally Christian.[46] This kind of rejection of what in the atmosphere of Christianising Europe was the most precious gift imaginable can only have had a detrimental effect on Christian perception of Jews.[47] It is not for nothing that the concept of deliberate Jewish disbelief became an important issue in twelfth- and thirteenth-century polemical material. Israel Yuval has argued that the Jewish martyrdom of 1096 had a very particular effect on Christian–Jewish relations. Yuval asserts that Jewish self-martyrdom profoundly shocked Christians and that it led them to reason that if Jews were willing to sacrifice their own children, they would be all the more ready to take the life of Christian children.[48] This takes us to the next chapter which concerns accusations of ritual murder and the increasing number of instances of judicial violence against Jews in the twelfth and thirteenth centuries.

Notes and references

1 Uta-Renate Blumenthal, *The Investiture Controversy. Church and Monarchy from the Ninth to the Twelfth Century* (Philadelphia, PA, 1988); I.S. Robinson, *Henry IV of Germany, 1056–1106* (Cambridge, 1999), 36, 38–41, 194–201, 211–35; Giles Constable, *The Reformation of the Twelfth Century* (Cambridge, 1996); H.E.J. Cowdrey, *Pope Gregory VII, 1073–1085* (Oxford, 1998), 559–60; Richard W. Southern, *Saint Anselm. A Portrait in a Landscape* (Cambridge, 1990), 268–9; Elizabeth M. Hallam and Judith Everard, *Capetian France, 987–1328*, 2nd edn (Harlow, 2001), 100–1.

2 Christopher Tyerman, *God's War. A New History of the Crusades* (London, 2006), 58–76, 90–1; Jonathan Riley-Smith, *The First Crusaders, 1095–1131* (Cambridge, 1997), 53–80.

3 Tyerman, *God's War*, 76–89; Alan V. Murray, *The Crusades. An Encyclopedia*, 4 vols (Santa Barbara, CA, 2006), q.v.

4 Translation *JLSEMA*, 452–3; Simonsohn, no. 37, pp. 35–6; Shlomo Simonsohn, *The Apostolic See and the Jews: History*. Pontifical Institute of Mediaeval Studies: Studies and Texts, 109 (Toronto, 1991), 12–13; Kenneth Stow, *Alienated Minority. The Jews of Medieval Latin Europe* (Cambridge, MA, 1992), 243.

5 Rudolph Hiestand, 'Juden und Christen in der Kreuzzugspropaganda und bei den Kreuzzugspredigen', in Alfred Haverkamp (ed.), *Juden und Christen zur Zeit der Kreuzzüge* (Sigmaringen, 1999), 158–9. There might have been some trouble in Monieux in Provence, but the evidence is unclear.

6 Guibert de Nogent, *Autobiographie*, ed. and trans. Edmond-René Labande. Les Classiques de l'histoire de France au moyen âge, 34 (Paris, 1981), xv–xvi, 246–52; *Self and Society in Medieval France. The Memoirs of Abbot Guibert of Nogent (1064?–c. 1125)*, ed. John F. Benton, trans. C.C. Swinton Bland (New York, 1970), 134–7, 237.

7 Labande, 248.

8 Eadmer, *Historia novorum in Anglia*, II, ed. Martin Rule, RS, 81 (London, 1884), 99.

9 Hiestand, 'Juden', 201, 203; *HB*, 1, 8, 258–9; *EJ*, 225.

10 *HB*, 231. See also Anna Sapir Abulafia, 'The Interrelationship between the Hebrew Chronicles on the First Crusade', in idem, *Christians and Jews in Dispute. Disputational Literature and the Rise of Anti-Judaism in the West (c. 1000–1150)* (Aldershot, 1998), XVIII and *HC*.

11 On the vexed question of earlier persecutions and on Jewish responses to them see Avraham Grossman, 'The Cultural and Social Background of Jewish Martyrdom in Germany in 1096', in A. Haverkamp, *Juden und Christen,*

74–5; Jeremy Cohen, *Sanctifying the Name of God. Jewish Martyrs and Jewish Memories of the First Crusade* (Philadelphia, PA, 2004), 21; *EJ*, 35–7; Stow, *Alienated Minority*, 94–6; but for a different take see Schmuel Shepkaru, *Jewish Martyrs in the Pagan and Christian Worlds* (Cambridge, 2006), 141–65.

12 *HB*, 9, 13, 17–20; Grossman, 'The Cultural and Social Background', 73–4; see also David Malkiel, 'Destruction and Conversion. Intention and Reaction, Crusaders and Jews, in 1096', *Jewish History* 15 (2001), 257–80.

13 Anna Sapir Abulafia, 'Invectives against Christianity in the Hebrew Chronicles of the First Crusade', in idem, *Christians and Jews in Dispute*. XVII.

14 *HB*, 358–9 and for example, 336, 16–17 n. 75.

15 Grossman, 'The Cultural and Social Background', 80–3.

16 *The History of William of Newburgh*, in *Chronicles of the Reigns of Stephen, Henry II and Richard I*, ed. R. Howlett, RS, 82,1, 320; trans. Joseph Stevenson (*The Church Historians of England*, vol. 4.2, London, 1856), ed. Scott McLetchie (1999): http://www.fordham.edu/halsall/basis/williamofnewburgh-intro.html.

17 Grossman, 'The Cultural and Social Background', 83–6; *HB*, 432–43, 7; Robert Chazan, *God, Humanity and History. The Hebrew First Crusade Narratives* (Berkeley, CA, 2000), 163–74, 201–15; Ivan G. Marcus, 'From Politics to Martyrdom: Shifting Paradigms in the Hebrew Narratives of the 1096 Crusade Riots', in J. Cohen (ed.), *Essential Papers on Judaism and Christianity in Conflict. From Late Antiquity to the Reformation*, (New York, 1991), 469–83.

18 Simha Goldin, 'The Socialisation for *Kiddush ha-Shem* among Medieval Jews', *JMH* 23 (1997), 117–38; see also his *The Ways of Jewish Martyrdom*, trans. Yigdal Levin, trans. ed. C. Michael Copeland (Turnhout, 2008).

19 Grossman, 'The Cultural and Social Background', 75–6; Haym Soloveitchik, 'Religious Law and Change: The Medieval Ashkenazic Example', *Association for Jewish Studies Review* 12 (1987) 205–21; J. Cohen, 'The Hebrew Crusade Chronicles in Their Christian Cultural Context', in A. Haverkamp, *Juden und Christen*, 17–34.

20 Translation, *EJ*, 256.

21 *HB*, 3–9, 34–45, 262–481; *EJ*, 225–97; Friedrich Lotter, '*Tod oder Taufe*. Das Problem der Zwangtaufen während des Ersten Kreuzzugs' and Eva Haverkamp, '*Persecutio* oder *Gezerah* in Trier während des Ersten Kreuzzugs', in A. Haverkamp, *Juden und Christen*, 127–34; 35–71; Chazan, *God, Humanity and History*, 134–5; G. Waitz (ed.), *Gesta Treverorum*, in MGH *Scriptores*, VIII (Hanover, 1848), 190.

22 Jonathan Riley-Smith, 'The First Crusade and the Persecution of the Jews', in W.J. Sheils (ed.), *Persecution and Toleration*, Studies in Church History, 21 (Oxford, 1984), 51–72.

23 *HB*, 11–2, 250–3, 260; *EJ*, 225–6, 243–4.

24 Ivan G. Marcus, *Rituals of Childhood in Medieval Europe* (New Haven, CT, 1984), 8–13; Idem, 'A Jewish–Christian Symbiosis: The Culture of Early Ashkenaz', in David Biale (ed.), *Cultures of the Jews. A New History* (New York, 2002), 461–72.

25 James A. Brundage, 'St Anselm, Ivo of Chartres and the Ideology of the First Crusade', in *The Crusades, Holy War and Canon Law* (Aldershot, 1991) IX, 177–8.

26 Susan Einbinder, 'Signs of Romance: Hebrew Prose and the Twelfth-century Renaissance', in Michael A. Signer and John Van Engen (eds), *Jews and Christians in Twelfth-century Europe* (Notre Dame, IN, 2001), 222–3; *HB*, 374–80; translations taken from Cohen, *Sanctifying*, 92–3; see also Chazan, *God, Humanity and History*, 203–15.

27 Cohen, *Sanctifying the Name*, 91–105.

28 Israel J. Yuval, *Two Nations in Your Womb. Perceptions of Jews and Christians in Late Antiquity and the Middle Ages*, trans. B. Harshav and J. Chipman (Berkeley, CA, 2006), 144–54.

29 *HB*, 434–7; *EJ*, 281.

30 *HB*, 326–7, 330–1; translations from *EJ*, 254.

31 *HB*, 468–9; translation from *HC*, 93; some of the imagery used here comes from the vestments of the High Priest.

32 Shepkaru, *Jewish Martyrs*, 161–210; see also Elliot R. Wolfson, 'Martyrdom, Eroticism, and Asceticism in Twelfth-century Ashkenazi Piety', in Signer and Van Engen, *Jews and Christians*, 177–83; idem, 'From after Death to Afterlife: Martyrdom and Its Recompense', *American Jewish Studies Review* 24 (1999), 31–44; Susan B. Edgington, 'Christian Martyrdom', in Murray, *The Crusades*, vol. 3, 804–5.

33 *HB*, 354–9; translation from *EJ*, 258–60 (Bar Simson's compilation with greater detail than 238–9 (Mainz Anonymous)).

34 Cohen, *Sanctifying*, 106–29.

35 Einbinder, 'Signs of Romance', 225–8; idem, 'Jewish Women Martyrs: Changing Models of Representation', *Exemplaria* 12 (2000), 109–10; Shepkaru, *Jewish Martyrs*, 177–84.

36 David Malkiel, 'Vestiges of Conflict in the Hebrew Crusade Chronicles', *Journal of Jewish Studies* 52 (2001), 323–39; *HB*, 366–7, 430–1; translation

EJ, 261, 279; on Sarit see also Einbinder, 'Signs of Romance', 226–7 and Cohen, *Sanctifying*, 142–58.

37 Jonathan Phillips, 'Second Crusade (1147–1149)', in Murray, *The Crusades*, vol. 4, 1084–90.

38 Ivan G. Marcus, 'Jews and Christians Imagining the Other in Medieval Europe', *Prooftexts* 15 (1995), 211–15.

39 Habermann, *Gezerot*, 121, 123; *HC*, 117–19, 130–1, 132; 'Chevalier, mult estes guariz' in Joseph Bédier and Pierre Auby (eds), *Les Chansons de Croisade* (Paris, 1909), 3–16, lines on pp. 8–9, translation, pp. 11–12.

40 Shepkaru, *Jewish Martyrs*, 215–56.

41 Habermann, *Gezerot*, 116; *HC*, 122.

42 Letter 363 (preaching the crusade) and letter 365 (condemning Ralph's preaching) in *Sancti Bernardi opera*, ed. Jean Leclercq and Henri Rochais, 8 (Rome, 1977), 311–17 and 320–2; Habermann, *Gezerot*, 121; *HC*, 131; Much has been written on Bernard and the Jews, see for example David Berger, 'The Attitude of St. Bernard of Clairvaux toward the Jews', *Proceedings of the American Academy for Jewish Research* 40 (1972), 89–108; Jeremy Cohen, ' "Witnesses of Our Redemption": The Jews in the Crusading Theology of Bernard of Clairvaux', in Bat-Sheva Albert (ed.), *Medieval Studies in Honour of Avrom Saltman* a.o. (Ramat Gan, 1995), 67–81 and my 'The Intellectual and Spiritual Quest for Christ and Central Medieval Persecution of Jews', in Anna Sapir Abulafia, *Religious Violence between Christians and Jews. Medieval Roots, Modern Perspectives* (Basingstoke, 2002), 72–5; Stow, *Alienated Minority*, 113–14, 223.

43 Helen J. Nicholson, 'Third Crusade (1189–1192)', in Murray (ed.), *The Crusades*, vol. 4, 1184–90; Habermann, *Gezerot*, 161–4; trans. *CSJMA*, 117–22; Judith R. Baskin, 'Dulce of Worms: The Lives and Deaths of an Exemplary Medieval Jewish Woman and Her Daughters', in Lawrence Fine (ed.), *Judaism in Practice: From the Middle Ages through the Early Modern Period* (Princeton, NJ, 2001), 429–37.

44 William of Newburgh, RS 82.1, 280, 293–322. Trans. Joseph Stevenson (*The Church Historians of England*, vol. 4.2, London, 1856), ed. Scott McLetchie (1999): http://www.fordham.edu/halsall/basis/williamofnewburgh-intro.html; Joseph Jacobs (ed.), *The Jews of Angevin England* (New York, 1893; repr. New York, 1977), 107–8, 130–1; Habermann, *Gezerot*, 127; Cecil Roth, 'A Hebrew Elegy on the York Martyrs of 1190', *Transactions of the Jewish Historical Society of England*, vol. 16 (1945–1951), 213–20; Shepkaru, *Jewish Martyrs*, 233–42; Susan L. Einbinder, *Beautiful Death. Jewish Poetry and Martyrdom in Medieval France* (Princeton, NJ, 2002), 167–8 (quoted translation from Joseph of Chartres on p. 168); R.B. Dobson, *The Jews of*

Medieval York and the Massacre of March 1190, Borthwick Papers 45, York, 1974.

45 Robert C. Stacey, 'Crusades, Martyrdoms, and the Jews of Norman England, 1096–1190', in A. Haverkamp, *Juden und Christen*, 243–51.

46 *HB*, 482–3; *EJ*, 294.

47 Kenneth Stow makes much of this in 'Conversion, Apostasy, and Apprehensiveness: Emicho of Flonheim and the Fear of Jews in the Twelfth Century', *Speculum* 76 (2001), 911–33; see also Goldin, 'Socialisation', 134–6.

48 Yuval, 'Vengeance and Damnation, Blood and Defamation. From Jewish Martyrdom to Blood Libel Accusations', *Zion*, n.s. 58 (1993), 33–92 [Hebrew]; 135–204; Yuval, *Two Nations in Your Womb*, 135–204.

chapter 8

Anti-Jewish libels

One of the most curious and disturbing aspects of twelfth-century Christian–Jewish relations is that from time to time Christians accused Jews of bizarre and inhuman conduct. At the core of these accusations lay the idea that Jews would regularly conspire to kidnap a Christian child (usually a boy) and torture it to death. The process of the killing was often described as a sacrilegious attempt to mimic the Crucifixion. In this way the accusation of murder ironically went side by side with the even-more-serious accusation of deliberately mocking the suffering of Jesus Christ. Other embellishments of the core accusation concerned the alleged victim's blood and the supposed use his killers made of it. Another variation of the accusation, which emerged at the end of the thirteenth century, had Jews stealing the consecrated host and torturing it to re-enact the Passion. Bizarrely, this accusation seemed to assume that, regardless of what they said, Jews in their hearts did believe that the consecrated host was the Christ-child; their ill-treatment of it was therefore as much an act of deliberate disbelief as the alleged participation of their forefathers in the Crucifixion had been an act of deliberate deicide. From these few words it should be obvious that the ritual murder accusations, blood libels and host-desecration accusations were polemical tools which contained numerous interlinking layers of theological ideas combined with various elements of popular myths. Different scholars have studied different aspects of the accusatory tales. What unites their often very different conclusions is the fact that the stories consistently reveal more about the religious, cultural and indeed socio-economic or political realities of the accusers than the realties of the accused. What was the genesis of these strange tales and why did they emerge in the twelfth century?

Antiquity

The first time Jews stood accused of expressing their hatred of the Other by conspiring ritually to kill a non-Jew and eating bits of his body was in the second century BCE. The Greek scholar Posidonius claimed that he had discovered a Greek prisoner in the Temple in Jerusalem when it was captured by Antiochus in 168 BCE who told him that the Jews did this every seven years with a Greek. As Langmuir has demonstrated, this literary fabrication was repeated by others and picked up by the Alexandrian scholar Apion (d. 45–8 CE), an outspoken critic of the Jews. Apion amended the story to say that Jews conspired in this way to kill a Greek once a year. Josephus took on Apion and his anti-Jewish litany in his *Contra Apion*. Among the many topics he addressed was this story and, ironically, it was through Josephus's refutation of it that it survived. Having said that, Josephus's *Treatise against Apion* was not nearly as widely read as his historical writings, the *War of the Jews* and the *Jewish Antiquities*. Langmuir has argued convincingly that it is extremely unlikely that twelfth-century Christians derived the idea of accusing Jews of ritual murder from the *Contra Apion*.[1] The second pre-medieval accusation comes from the early fifth century when exception was taken to the way that Jews celebrated Purim. Part of the boisterous activities seems to have been the burning of a model of Haman, the Persian arch-enemy of the Jewish people. At some point Jews were accused of using an effigy of Jesus rather than of Haman and turning their ceremony into a mocking of the Crucifixion. In 408 Emperor Theodosius II prohibited Jews from doing this. In 415 the Jews of the Syrian town of Inmestar were accused of using their re-enactment of the hanging of Haman to string up and kill a Christian child on the cross they were using as Haman's gallows. The accusation was recounted in the *Ecclesiastical History* of Socrates (d. *c.* 450), who continued the work of Eusebius. Socrates's work was known to the West but, again, Langmuir has demonstrated that medieval authors seem not to have picked up on his account. As far as the event itself is concerned, Simon and Parkes, for example, assume that the Jews were drunk when the child was killed. Others such as Langmuir take account of the possibility that the accusation was, in fact, a fabrication. All of this means that we cannot simply assume that twelfth-century Christians drew on accusations from the distant past when they formulated their own.[2] This does not, however, mean that Langmuir was correct to denote the ritual-murder accusation as the brain-child of Thomas of Monmouth, the author of the *Life of William of Norwich*.

William of Norwich

The body of little William was found in Thorpe Wood in 1144. His biographer Thomas of Monmouth says the discovery occurred on 25 March, which is the Feast of the Annunciation of the Virgin; in 1144 this coincided with Easter Saturday and 19 Nisan, the fifth day of Passover. The bare facts of the case which can be distilled from Thomas's account are that it was William's family who started spreading the idea that he was killed by the Jews. His uncle, Godwin Sturt, brought charges against the Jews at the diocesan synod convened a fortnight after Easter. The bishop and his court wished to pursue the matter and called the Jews to give an account of themselves. Relying on the sheriff, whose job it was to give them the king's protection, they refused. The Jews 'belonged' to the king, not the bishop. When they eventually did appear under duress, the sheriff came with them. They refused to undergo an ordeal and sought safety in the Norman castle of Norwich, until King Stephen sent word to leave them at peace.

Thomas of Monmouth was the first to pen a full-blown ritual-murder story, but as John McCulloh has argued, he cannot have been responsible for inventing the idea of ritual crucifixion from scratch. McCulloh has shown that before Thomas started his opus around 1154–5, a notice had appeared in a Bavarian martyrology that a boy named William had been crucified by the Jews in England. References to William's alleged crucifixion by the Jews in other continental sources and, indeed, also in English sources seem not to have derived from Thomas's *Life*. It is not impossible that rumours about William had reached Würzburg in February 1147, where Jews were murdered when they were accused of being responsible for the mutilated corpse of a man (it remains unclear whether there was a ritual component to this accusation). The incident occurred a week after Purim and coincided with preparations for the Second Crusade. All of this indicates that Thomas was not the 'creator of the ritual-murder accusation' as Langmuir has claimed. This is also borne out by the brevity with which sources mention William's crucifixion. It is as if readers would immediately grasp what was happening without any further explanation. For all his additional details about how Jews met once a year in Narbonne to decide which town to target for ritual murder, Thomas too seemed to be recording the occurrence of ritual crucifixion as if it were a matter of fact.[3] This is puzzling. On the one hand it indicates that for some reason the idea of ritual murder seems to have been, as it were, in the air. On the other, the idea seems to have been less universally shocking than one might expect. After all, in Norwich no Jews fell victim to the charge. The same is true for many other instances of the charge in England, where, one should add, most of the documented ritual-murder accusations took place until 1235, the year when the Jews of Fulda in Germany were accused of murdering a Christian child and using his blood. Many Jews lost their lives in that instance due to popular violence.

Much is always made of the importance of the confluence of Lent/ Easter and Purim/Passover for the ideas underlying ritual-murder accusations and blood libels. For one thing, the carnival nature of Purim jarred with the solemnity of Lent; for another, the Jewish celebration of Passover was seen as a negation of Christ's Resurrection. On top of that loomed the role New Testament Jews were seen to have played in Jesus's suffering on the cross.[4] However, other elements of the tales should be taken into account. Rules concerning the calculation of Easter meant that the earliest Easter could fall was 22 March and the latest 25 April. This means that in all years in which Easter fell in March, the Feast of the Annunciation of the Virgin either coincided with Easter or fell in Holy Week or in the week immediately after Easter. We have already seen that William died around 25 March; his feast day was put on 24 March, the eve of Lady Day. Other supposed martyrs such as Harold of Gloucester, Richard of Pontoise and Robert of Bury were later given Lady Day itself.[5] Thomas of Monmouth recorded two visions in his *Life of William* where William is in heaven in the entourage of the Virgin Mary and her son. In a third the Virgin came to Norwich to bestow a crown of flowers on William. It is almost as if the twelve-year-old William represented the child who Jesus once was to his virginal mother.[6] Such an idea would fit well into the developing interest in the miracle stories of the Virgin Mary in twelfth-century England.

Marian miracle stories

Tales concerning the miracles of the Virgin had circulated throughout Christendom for centuries. What matters to us here is that it was in late eleventh- and twelfth-century England that the first collections of general stories concerning the Virgin were assembled, namely stories which were not tied to a particular local shrine. Drawing on earlier collections, William of Malmesbury put together his *De Laudibus et Miraculis Sanctae Mariae* by 1141.[7] As Jennifer Shea has pointed out, William included a number of evocative tales which concern Jews.[8] The most famous among these was the 'Jewish Boy' story. The tale, which was first recorded in the sixth century, concerns a Jewish boy who partook of the Eucharist with his Christian playmates. When his father discovered what he had done he threw him into the burning oven. When his mother obtained help from their Christian neighbours, they managed to get into the oven and discovered the boy intact. He informed everyone that he had been shielded from the flames by the Virgin and her son, whose image he had seen on the altar in the church. The father was then thrown into the oven and burnt. The lad and his mother together with many other Jews converted. William of Malmesbury added a number of interesting details in his telling of the tale. He had the Jewish boy describe the Virgin, saying 'that beautiful woman whom I saw sitting on a throne, and whose son was divided among the people, was with me in the burning oven'. It is clear that William used the tale to advocate belief in the real Eucharistic change of the bread during the celebration of the Mass. After all, the Jewish boy had been able to see with his own eyes what Christians were expected to take on faith. We have concrete evidence that this story was known in Norwich, at least in Norman clerical circles. Herbert Losinga, who reigned as bishop between 1091 and 1119, used this story in a sermon which he preached at Christmas in Norwich. In his version the Jewish mother was the one who instigated the crime, although she had a change of heart once her child was thrown into the fire by her husband. She then obtained help from her Christian neighbours. As Miri Rubin points out, the Jewish child was very much on his own, with only the Virgin and her child, the child she bore on Christmas Day, to protect him.[9]

This tale provides a disturbing and strikingly contradictory vignette of Christian–Jewish relations in the abstract. On the one hand, Jews and Christians are pictured as freely intermingling. How otherwise could the

Jewish boy have taken communion with his friends? The priest celebrating communion had no idea he was a Jew. The Jewish mother had Christian friends who came running when she needed them. At the same time, the Jewish father (in some versions the Jewish mother) was envisaged as an unfeeling monster who would burn his own flesh and blood alive. In the end the 'good' Jews converted; the evil Jew was killed. Clearly, on a straightforward level the story was meant to re-enact alleged Jewish perfidy against Jesus, but at the same time it seemed to emphasise two different things. On the one hand, Jews and Christians lived cheek by jowl; on the other, Jews (especially Jewish men) did terrible things. But if Christians really believed Jews acted in this way, would they have interacted so closely with them in the first place? It is almost as if the story provided a shocking corrective to Christians as to just where the boundaries had to be drawn between themselves and their Jewish neighbours. It was as if to remind them that Jews were only to be tolerated within Christian society so that they could serve Christians until they saw the light and converted. In this tale the Jewish boy served Christians by 'proving' the truth of transubstantiation, a tenet many Christians struggled with. In other words, Jews were being used here for Christian purposes and, as we have seen, Christians could manipulate the tale in the way which best suited them. The underlying ambiguities governing Christian–Jewish relations remained as potent as ever.[10]

One of the ways this story was disseminated was through the vernacular versions of the Marian tales which also started appearing in the twelfth century. The oldest is the Anglo-Norman *Le Gracial* collection by William Adgar of *c.* 1165. William Adgar served as a canon at St Paul's before becoming the chaplain of St Mary Magdalene in London in 1162. More widely disseminated was the French vernacular collection by Gautier de Coincy of around 1218. Shea has demonstrated how the vernacular translations of Marian tales concerning Jews tended to sharpen the image of Jews to make Jewish treachery against the Virgin even more explicit than in the original Latin settings. She has argued that the vernacular versions were meant for courtly audiences and that the language of courtly romances was used by the authors to convince their audiences of Jewish perfidy.[11] A hugely popular version of the miracles was the *Cantigas de Santa Maria*, associated with Alfonso the Wise.

Another relevant Marian miracle story for our purposes concerned a waxen image of Christ in Toledo. On 15 August, the Feast of the Assumption of the Virgin, the Virgin interrupted the Mass being said in the cathedral by complaining that Jews were insulting her son. When the knights of Toledo searched the Jewry they found Jews re-enacting the Crucifixion on a waxen image of Jesus in the synagogue. The Jews were killed. Adgar had the tale as did the *Cantigas*, Gautier referred to it.[12] The similarity between this story and the idea that Jews used a waxen image of Jesus in their Purim festivities seems obvious; the similarity with the idea that Jews might crucify a Christian child is uncanny.

Another important story, which went back to at least the seventh century, concerned an image of the Virgin which a Jew in Constantinople wilfully attempted to defile by casting it into a latrine. Needless to say the image could not be sullied. This story appeared in Adgar and Gautier and in the *Cantigas*. Adgar exacerbated the emphasis William of Malmesbury had already put on the wilful desire Jews seemed to have to calumniate the Virgin in order to bring dishonour to the Christian faith. The treacherous Jew was linked to the devil; his despicable act was denoted by the word *felunie* which would have been understood particularly well by a courtly audience which sought to overcome felony by *courtoisie* and *vaillance*. Adgar even added a prologue to the story in which he celebrated the defeat of the Jews by Vespasian and Titus as due punishment for Jewish blasphemy against Christ and the role they played in his death.[13] Many sources accused Jews of desecrating ecclesiastical objects with the aim of deriding Christianity. Peter the Venerable, Abbot of Cluny (r. 1122–56) wrote to Louis VII that Jews mishandled the ecclesiastical pawns they had in their possession.[14] Rigord said much the same in his biography of Philip Augustus.[15] In his *Chronica Majora* Matthew Paris (d. 1259) accused Abraham of Berkhamsted, an important Jewish moneylender, of setting up a statue of the Virgin suckling the Christ-child in his latrine and murdering his wife for her efforts to keep the statue clean.[16]

The miracle story concerning the archdeacon Theophilus who used a Jew as an intermediary to gain access to the devil to get back the ecclesiastic position he had lost was widely disseminated in Latin and vernacular versions. The story emphasised the link between the Jews and the devil; in Adgar's version the devil is the Jewish protagonist's feudal lord. Equally important is the idea that Jews posed a danger to Christian society because they led Christians astray. A sense of binary allegiances was created with wicked Jews serving the devil and good Christians serving God, with the

Virgin giving succour to those who had crossed the boundary line between the two.[17]

Gautier de Coincy's collection of Marian miracle stories and the *Cantigas de Santa Maria* included the story of a Jew murdering a little chorister, who sang the *Gaude Maria* particularly beautifully, and hiding his body in a cellar. The lad's mother is led to it by the miraculous sound of his *Gaude Maria*.[18] The accusation which emerged in Saragossa in 1250 was strikingly similar to this story. According to rumours a seven-year-old chorister had been crucified by the Jews. It is unclear to what extent Alfonso believed the accusation.[19] But, as we have noted in Chapter 6, he did refer to the rumours in the *Siete Partidas*.

As the language used in the Jewish Marian stories grew harsher and as it belaboured the theme of Jewish treachery against the Virgin in particular and Christians and Christendom in general and as the tales disseminated more widely through their rhymed vernacular forms to the courtly laity, the tales would have increased the likelihood that they could be manipulated to the detriment of Jews if that meshed with local circumstances.[20] It would seem to me that it is very likely that the increased interest in the Virgin and the availability of tales which pitted Jewish protagonists against all that was most precious to Christians would be one of the reasons why ritual murder was, as it were, in the air by the second half of the twelfth century. Interest in Mary and her son would have been intensified through preaching crusade against the enemies of Christ. Additional contributory factors would have been contemporary Christian searching for greater understanding of the Eucharistic change. What happened when the priest consecrated the host? We know from sources of the period that the consecrated host was sometimes seen as the baby Jesus. In some instances the baby appeared to be suffering from wounds. It is probable that images such as these contributed to ideas of young boys being sacrificed by Jews as little Jesuses.[21] Another possible contributing factor might have been the knowledge that in Ashkenaz Jews had chosen to martyr themselves and *their children* rather than fall into the hands of crusaders and be forced to accept baptism. Israel Yuval has made a very great deal of this idea.[22] I am not at all convinced that Jewish martyrdom was a contributory factor in the genesis of ritual-murder accusations; it seems to me that Christians had plenty of material of their own making for that. But, it is certainly possible that the image of Jews as being unreasonable and cruel was confirmed in the minds of Christians as they became increasingly aware of more cases of Jewish martyrdom.

Norwich, Bury, Gloucester

Just as the Marian miracle stories could be manipulated, so could the ritual murder accusations themselves and the narratives which recorded them for posterity. Jeffrey Cohen reads into Thomas of Monmouth's *Life of William* an attempt to forge some kind of cohesion within the disparate lay and ecclesiastical sections of the Christian community of Norwich. Seen in this light, Thomas would have picked up on the ritual-murder allegations he encountered when he came to Norwich and fashioned his tale to promote a potentially lucrative shrine for his religious home. In so doing, he would have used the Jews, the one component of Norwich which in medieval terms was unassimilable, to put flesh to a story which would attract Norman and Anglo-Saxon alike across the social scale. In the final resort, the story concerned Christians far more than Jews. As on so many other fronts, Jews were being used for Christian purposes. Ironically, Thomas gave the game away when he put into the mouths of the Jews of Norwich the absurd words:

> *You ought to be very much obliged to us, for we have made a saint and martyr for you. Verily we have done you a great deal of good, and a good which you retort upon us as a crime. Aye! We have done for you what you could not do for yourselves.*[23]

Jews in the abstract had indeed served Christians by performing treacherous acts which were supposed to inspire greater religious and ethical cohesion among Christians.

Bale has suggested that Thomas of Monmouth and the Bishop of Norwich hoped that William's cult would deflect interest from the cult of St Edmund in neighbouring Bury. Bury retaliated by inventing and promoting the cult of Robert of Bury in 1181. As we have seen, the monastery was heavily indebted to Christian and Jewish moneylenders by this time. We know very little of Robert because the *Life* which Jocelin of Brakelond penned of him is no longer extant. Jocelin briefly mentioned the boy was martyred in his chronicle, but he gives no further details. Gervase of

Canterbury (d. *c.* 1205) claimed the boy was martyred at Easter.[24] It is worth mentioning that Anselm the Younger, the nephew of Anselm of Canterbury, who was Abbot of Bury between 1122 and 1148, was a great devotee of the Virgin and an early collector of her miracle tales.[25] Once again, we notice convergence between attested interest in the Virgin and indebtedness to Jews and ideas concerning Christian martyrdom at the hands of Jews.

In Gloucester Harold's cult (1168?) was actively, if not terribly success-fully, promoted by the Benedictines of St Peter's. In the chronicle of their monastery we see how the monks tried to turn the discovery of a drowned child's body on 18 March to their advantage. Claims were made that the child had been spirited away by the Jews on 21 February for them to torture him to death on the night of 16 March. Jews from the whole of England had gathered in Gloucester as if to celebrate a circumcision. Signs of the tortures inflicted on the child were supposed to be burns, a crown of thorns and traces of wax on his face and in his eyes. It is difficult to say whether this event should be dated to 1167 or 1168 because the days of the week indicated in the chronicle match the calendar of 1167, and 21 February suitably fell on Shrove Tuesday in that year. But 17 and 18 March fell around Passion Sunday in 1168. In 1168 Purim fell on 25 February; in 1167 it fell on 7 March. It is very likely that we are witnessing here a botched attempt to force dates to refer to evocative moments in the Christian liturgical calendar. It is equally possible that confusion concern-ing the year of the supposed event arose when the chronicle of St Peter's was compiled at the end of the fourteenth or start of the fifteenth century.[26] The crucial element of this story is the reference to circumcision, a Jewish ritual involving the drawing of blood from a baby boy, which so powerfully and so physically expressed the demarcation between Christians and Jews. In Christian theological terms, the rite of circumcision was seen as a con-tinual deliberate Jewish denial of Christ. For Jews circumcision marked and celebrated the continual covenant between God and his people. In other words, a circumcision feast in Gloucester, to which many Jews from outside Gloucester would have come, would have meant diametrically different things to the Jews and Christians of that city. One can see how the narrative of ritual murder might have been used at such a time by monks to create a shrine of their own which would evocatively expose what they would have seen as the fault lines of Christian–Jewish relations. The crowds of Christians accompanying the body of little Harold into the church of

St Peter's could be imagined as a suitable counterweight to the well-attended Jewish circumcision celebration. Again, it is important to emphasise that no Jews in Gloucester met with any physical harm.

Richard of Devizes

The ritual-murder trope was, however, not only used in an attempt to promote Christian cohesion through the creation of evocative new shrines. It could also be used as a literary expression of an author's view of the intricacies and ambiguities of Christian–Jewish relations in his town. This seems to be the case at Winchester, where Jews had not been harmed in the 1189–90 crusade riots, but soon thereafter seem to have become implicated in an accusation of ritual murder. Our record for this is the chronicle of Richard of Devizes, a monk at St Swithun's in Winchester, which covers the early part of King Richard's reign until October 1192. Richard of Devizes concocted an elaborate tale of ritual murder around a mysterious case involving the Jews of Winchester in 1192, as recorded in the Pipe Rolls of 1193. With his usual cutting satire Richard narrated how a Christian French orphan boy had been sent by a French Jew to serve in a Jewish household in Winchester. The boy travelled with a companion. On Good Friday 'near the Pasch, a holy day of the Jews' (in 1192 Good Friday fell on 3 April which was the fourth day of the Jewish Passover), the boy disappeared and after a few days his friend accused his Jewish master of crucifying him. In the *mêlée* that followed he accused the Jew of having 'torn the heart out of my breast; this man has cut the throat of my only friend, and I presume he has eaten him too'. The Christian wet-nurse in the Jewish household claimed she saw her Jewish master take the boy down to the cellar. In the end the case came to nothing: the wet-nurse could not testify in court because she was in breach of canon law which forbade Christians to suckle Jewish children and the boy's friend was under age. In any case the Jew bribed the court. What do we make of this? Bale interprets it as a literary fiction which wove together Benedictine ideas about Jewish ritual murder with more general religious concepts of the iconic image of a small boy. Crucially, he links the tale to a mid-twelfth-century Marian miracle story involving a Jewish lad travelling from France to Winchester who was saved from robbers by the Virgin Mary. The boy converted. Richard's aversion to everything French and his disgust for Jews are clear. In his words on the absence of anti-Jewish riots in 1190 he called the Jews 'bloodsuckers'; the citizens of Winchester in their wisdom 'did not want partially to vomit forth the undigested mass violently . . . they hid it in their bowels . . . dissimulating their disgust . . . till . . . they could cast out all the morbid matter once and for all'. But he also claimed that Winchester is full of liars and a haven for the spread of false rumours. Was it Richard's intention to poke fun at rumours of ritual murder which surfaced in Winchester around 1192 by satirising the kind of stories put about by his fellow Benedictines in Norwich, Gloucester and Bury? Or is it more likely that he used the opportunity to express forcefully his unease about the social and religious realities of the presence of Jews in Winchester? For his tale offered no solutions. Jews continued to celebrate Passover at the time of Easter; Christian women continued to contravene ecclesiastical rules and wet-nurse Jewish babies; and Jews continued to bribe the courts so that no official action could be taken against them.[27] Whatever the case may be, similar rumours came to the fore in Winchester in 1225 which had to be dropped when the alleged victim turned out to be alive and well. A more serious charge was made in 1232 when a body of a strangled one-year-old was discovered. Claims were made that the boy had been castrated and that his eyes and heart had been cut out. Notwithstanding the fact that it was the boy's mother who took to her heels, the finger was pointed at Abraham of the successful Pinche family of moneylenders. Feelings ran high and the sheriff had to protect Winchester Jewry by putting them into the prison. In the end they were ransomed for 20 marks and the boy's murder was pinned on his mother. Abraham was later executed for allegedly stealing some money six years earlier.[28]

Early suggestions of cannabalism

In Richard of Devizes's account of ritual murder the Jew was not just accused of crucifying a Christian child, he was presumed to have eaten his victim. Some have seen this preposterous claim as further evidence of the fanciful nature of Richard's report. But it cannot be as simple as that. For one thing the alleged victim in the 1232 ritual-murder accusation was said to have had his heart cut out. To be sure, cutting out someone's heart is not the same as eating it; but boundaries between charges of mutilating bodies and hints of cannibalism can be fuzzy. This is borne out by the development of reports of ritual murder in France. The incident concerns Richard of Pontoise, who was supposed to have been crucified by Jews on Good Friday, 22 March in 1163, which coincided with the second day of Passover. A shrine for the boy was erected in the Church of the Holy Innocents in Paris where many miracles took place. In the course of discussing the case of Richard of Pontoise, Rigord informs us that when Philip Augustus was growing up in the palace he had often heard from his playmates that the Jews of Paris cut the throat of a Christian every year on Maundy Thursday or another day in Holy Week as a kind of sacrifice. They did this while they were hiding in subterranean tunnels. The idea of cannibalism creeps into William the Breton's reworking of Rigord, which took place before 1215. Immediately preceding his reference to Richard of Pontoise's crucifixion, William claimed that the Jews not only annually sacrificed '*immolabant*' a Christian, they '*ejus corde se communicabant*' ('shared his heart amongst themselves' or 'took communion with his heart'). We have here, in other words, not just an accusation of cannibalism; we have the idea of a Jewish inversion of the Christian celebration of the Eucharist with the alleged victim not just playing the part of the crucified Jesus, but also the part of Jesus, whose body and blood are consumed by the faithful by means of the Eucharist.[29]

All of this points to the fluid nature of the sordid details of ritual-murder accusations. Langmuir's sharp distinctions between accusations of murder, ritual murder and blood libel, in which Jews were accused of using their victims' blood and of which he cites the case of Fulda in 1235 as the first example, seem on reflection too artificial. As we have seen, the body of a drowned child was enough to spark rumours of ritual murder. Ideas of cannibalism were already mooted around 1200. In a cultural setting where allegory was freely, if not indiscriminately, used to make sense of difficult texts or unsettling natural phenomena, the basic components of a story, which was manipulated to express the conundrums of Christian–Jewish relations, could be moulded at will to suit time, place and circumstance. William the Breton was writing in praise of his king who had decided at the start of his reign to expel the Jews from his royal lands. Most of these Jews were living in close proximity to the royal palace on the Île-de-la-Cité. The idea of Jews subverting Christian society in the bowels of Paris by inverting the celebration of the Mass could be seen as an interpretative gloss on his decision to expel the Jews. Again, it is worth emphasising that seizure of goods and expulsion would hardly have been the only actions Philip would have taken if he had really believed what his biographers claimed Jews did. Evidence of this is his brutal response to the execution of one of his men at the behest of Jews in 1192.

Bray or Brie

Whether the location was Bray-sur-Seine (in the County of Champagne), as some claim or Brie-Comte-Robert (owned by the Count of Dreux), as Jordan argues, matters little to us. What matters to us is that Rigord claims that Philip sprang into action when the news reached him on 18 March 1192 that the Jews of Bray/Brie had with the countess's permission shamefully put a Christian to death. Our Hebrew source is Ephraim of Bonn, who tells us that the Christian was an *eved*, that is to say, a man in some kind of position of service to the king. This explains why what had happened in Bray/Brie was Philip's concern. Ephraim claims that the Christian had murdered a Jew in Bray/Brie and that his family had asked the [dowager] countess for justice: 'they gave her money to hang the murderer. They hanged him on Purim' [1 March 1192]. William the Breton's poetic elaboration of the affair, which he composed after his prose continuation of Rigord, claimed that the Jews in question were moneylenders and that the Christian could not pay his debts. Again, it is interesting how both Rigord and William manipulated the case into a narrative of ritual murder. Both described the Christian as a martyr suffering crucifixion at the hands of the Jews after having been crowned with a crown of thorns and chased through the town. Rigord summed up the affair by quoting John 18:31, where the Jews responded to Pilate that 'it is not lawful for us to put any man to death'. The inference was, of course, that just as much as the Jews of the New Testament were responsible for the death of Jesus Christ, even though the Romans did the actual killing, the Jews of Bray/Brie were responsible for this Christian's death. This would, in fact, indicate that, notwithstanding his embellishments, Rigord recognised that the man was executed at the behest of the Jews and not by their own hands in the preposterous way he himself had suggested. Ephraim is astonishingly vague about who exactly performed the hanging. Astonishing too is his statement that the hanging occurred on Purim. This could, of course, have actually been the case and for the Jewish community of Bray/Brie receiving justice on the day that they celebrated past victory over the likes of Haman would have been a fortuitous happenstance. There are scholars who assume that the Jews did actually execute the Christian as part of their Purim festivities.[30] To me, however, it is inconceivable that Jews in Zarfat would have incurred such risks within a decade of the expulsion from the Île-de-France. It seems to me much more likely that Ephraim was engaged in his own embellishments. The mention of Purim adds special pathos to his account because the theme of biblical deliverance by way of Esther's beneficial intervention with the mighty Ahasverus was in such stark contrast with what happened in the brutal reality of 1192: the 'evil' king came and burnt the Jews of Bray/Brie. More than 80 Jews seem to have lost their lives; in this instance the children were spared. Rigord and William have one Christ-like martyr; Ephraim has the great and the good of the Jewish community of Bray/Brie who according to Ephraim chose to be burnt rather than to betray the Jewish concept of the oneness of God through accepting baptism. But allusion to Purim also evoked the hope of future deliverance and revenge on the persecutors of Israel: 'All this I have seen in my brief span of time (Ecclesiastes 7:15). I am disgusted with life (Job 10:1). May our Creator exact vengeance on our behalf and speedily bring our messiah.'[31]

Two things are remarkable: first it is striking that Ephraim did not shy away from supplying a detail which might have added grist to Christian accusations of ritual murder; second it seems clear to me that Jews were murdered in retaliation for the death of a Christian which originally had nothing to do with ritual murder. This would seem to indicate once again that at least in the second half of the twelfth century the concept of ritual murder was a trope which was used to define and restore proper relations between Christians and Jews. In this case Rigord and William used it to deliver the vivid message that on no account should a Christian lose his life on account of Jews. Christian princes should not re-enact the role of Pilate; they should emulate the conduct of Philip Augustus. As for Ephraim, he was responding to the real-life killing of Jews rather than to fancy tropes with which his Christian counterparts interpreted what had happened. His response and the responses of other Hebrew sources consisted of a counter trope which transformed Jewish deaths in cases like these into human sacrifices which physically nullified the tenets of Christianity. These sacrifices were thought to be the most effective way to call on divine assistance to turn the tables on the persecutors of Israel. It was only when ritual-murder accusations began to take on the guise of blood libels and, moreover, began to move out of the literary sphere into the real world that we have some examples of specific and unequivocal Jewish engagement with the accusation itself. The clearest example is in the *Nizzahon Vetus* ('Old Polemic'), a handbook containing a wealth of French and German arguments to counter Christian arguments against Judaism. The work was compiled in Germany and dates from the end of the thirteenth or beginning of the fourteenth century. The blood libel is described there as a fabrication Christians used so as to have an excuse to murder Jews. Arguments are put forward to prove that Jews were not permitted by the Torah to kill non-Jews and emphasis is placed on the prohibition of consuming any kind of blood. Although there are a few allusions to this type of argumentation in passages of Hebrew poetry from as early as 1220, the overriding Jewish response to the idea that Jews created Christian martyrs was to build up a rival polemic of martyrdom to combat Christianity.[32]

Blois

We can trace this clearly in the extensive Jewish reports on the (ritual-) murder accusation in Blois in 1171 which led to the burning of about 30 Jews by the Count of Blois. We owe the idea that a ritual crucifixion might have occurred in Blois to the reporting of Robert of Torigni (d. 1186). He lumped what allegedly happened in Blois together with the cases of William of Norwich, Harold of Gloucester and Richard of Pontoise and stated that Jews crucify Christian infants at Easter time whenever they get the chance.[33] But this is clearly yet another instance of the trope of ritual murder being attached to a case – in this instance trumped up – of child murder. The facts seem to be these. At dusk, on Maundy Thursday, which in 1171 not only coincided with Lady Day but also coincided with the third day of Passover, a Christian servant watering his master's horse came across a Jew doing the same with his. The Jew seems to have been holding a number of rolls of untanned leather. When the Christian's horse bolted at the whiteness of the leather, which must have gleamed in the approaching night, the Christian took fright, and rode back into town claiming that the Jew had thrown a dead child into the river. No child was missing and no body was ever found. The servant's lord took the matter to Count Theobald who threw the Jews of Blois into prison. The backdrop of this action and what happened next seems to have been that the servant's lord and Theobald himself had financial ties with a female Jewish moneylender in Blois named Pucellina. The lord in question and the Countess of Blois, Alix, who was the daughter of King Louis VII by his first marriage to Eleanor of Aquitaine, seem to have both detested this Pucellina. Pucellina's relations with the count may also have been of a sexual nature. As for the count, it seems as if he was planning to use the accusation as a ruse to exact a large sum of money from 'his' Jews. Things got out of hand when, for whatever reason, the initial financial offer made on behalf of the Jews was considered too low. The count then was swayed by a priest to test the veracity of the Christian servant's claim by making him undergo an ordeal. When the servant was deemed to have passed the test and the Jews were thus deemed to be guilty of killing a child and dumping it in the river, ransom money was no longer considered an option. The only way out for the Jews was baptism. When they refused to abandon their faith, they were burnt on 26 May. In Ephraim's account, which he based on letters which appeared just after the event, the death of these Jews was as an act of martyrdom; the burnt bodies of the Jews were comparable to Temple offerings to God. And as they were burnt the martyrs were heard to be singing *Alenu leshabeach* to the sweetest of melodies.[34]

Alenu leshabeach is a Jewish prayer which thanks God for choosing Israel to serve him before going on to express the prophetic hope that in the future all peoples will come under the rule of God. Originally the prayer was used in the liturgy of the Jewish New Year (*Rosh ha-Shanah*) but in the course of the twelfth and thirteenth centuries the prayer became the standard closing prayer of the three main daily services in the Jewish liturgy. The prayer begins with

> *It is our duty to praise the Lord of all . . . for He has not made us like the nations of the lands . . . for they prostrate themselves before vanity and folly, and pray to a god who does not save. . . . But we bow down and prostrate ourselves before the King of the Kings of Kings, the Holy One, blessed be He!*[35]

The Hebrew for 'a god who does not save' is *el lo yoshia*, which could easily evoke the word *Yeshu*, which is the Hebrew for Jesus, and could thus be considered as maligning Christianity. Whether the victims at Blois sang *Alenu* or not, the report that they did is another example of the Jewish response to the (ritual-) murder accusation. A counter history of martyr-dom was created which revolved around a vociferous denial of Christianity. The attention the incident received in Hebrew sources reveals the great alarm Jews felt as they experienced for the first time that the lord who was supposed to protect them in exchange for their service was the instigator of official violence against them. A number of Hebrew intercommunal letters attest to the efforts undertaken by the Jews of the Île-de-France and Champagne to intercede with King Louis and Count Henry to make sure they would not follow Theobald's example. A spate of Hebrew poems picked up on the themes of martyrdom expressed in the two Hebrew prose accounts already mentioned.[36]

Germany

In Germany a pattern of non-ritual murder accusations eliciting vengeful violence occurred in Boppard in 1179, Vienna in 1181, Speyer in 1195, Neuss in 1197, Erfurt in 1199 and again in 1221, and Lauda in January 1235 and Wolfhagen in November 1235. Some of these outbreaks carried a hint of ritual murder, as in Würzburg in 1147; most did not. The concept of ritual murder must, however, have been in the air, because already in 1187 the Jews of Mainz were made to swear to the Bishop of Mainz that they did not kill Christians at Easter.[37] The striking difference with France was that these outbreaks of violence were popular. For a large part this must have been due to the fact that by the end of the twelfth century the German emperor had much less control over 'his' Jews than the king of England or the king and princes of France. Another factor must have been the history of popular crusading violence against Jews which dated from 1096. The backdrop for the outbreak of violence in the thirteenth century was the frequency with which crusades had been preached and the vigour with which heresy had been hunted down. The favoured agent of Pope Gregory IX in this endeavour was Conrad of Marburg, who had been single-minded in his pursuit of heretics between 1231 and 1234. Conrad helped circulate ideas that heretics were engaged in nightly feasts of un-bridled lust involving the devil, mishandling of the host and acts of canni-balism. Marburg lay within a radius of 50 miles from Fulda.[38]

On Christmas Eve 1235 a mill in Fulda burnt down, killing the five sons of the miller and his wife who were attending Christmas Mass. Almost immediately two Jews were accused of murdering the children and collecting their blood in wax-coated sacks. The purpose of this was the alleged need Jews had for Christian blood for ritual or magical purposes. On 28 December more than 30 Jews, primarily women and children, were murdered by the citizens of Fulda and/or crusaders travelling through the town. Gregory IX had called for a crusade at the end of 1234. The citizens of Fulda proceeded 150 miles to the emperor in Hagenau with the dead bodies and with their account of what had happened to them. In the meantime, in much the same way as the Jews of France had done in 1171, the Jews of Germany turned to Frederick for assistance. He decided to settle the matter once and for all by proper legal procedures. When the temporal and ecclesiastical lords could not come to a verdict, a commission of a number of trusted Jewish converts was established to settle the matter. The outcome of this was the unequivocal statement that there was absolutely no evidence in the Old or New Testament that Jews needed Christian blood; indeed, the Law of Moses and the Talmud even forbade the consumption of animal blood. In his 1236 charter Frederick declared that the Jews of Fulda had been innocent and forbade the spreading of the blood-libel accusations.[39]

Notwithstanding the emperor's efforts, the accusation spread, with nine more cases occurring in Germany before the end of the thirteenth century. In 1247 in Valréas, which came under imperial rule, the collection of blood was linked to the accusation of crucifixion. Popular outrage amidst preparations for yet another crusade, together with the active involvement of two Franciscans led to a complicated judicial process in which Jews were tortured until they confessed to crucifying a little girl and collecting her blood. Many Jews were executed and Jewish children baptised; lords in the region seem to have used the occasion to confiscate Jewish property. Pope Innocent IV became involved in the case when Jews turned to him for help. In a number of letters he reiterated the principle that Jews should be protected from violence. The Pope declared that Jews did not 'share the heart of a murdered child' (*se corde pueri communicant interfecti*) and that they should not be accused of doing so whenever the body of a dead child was found. Innocent's words echo the accusation which William the Breton had voiced at the turn of the century (*ejus corde se communicabant* ['took communion with his heart']), and this reinforces the idea that the concept of Jewish cannibalism predated Fulda.[40]

Neither imperial nor papal strictures could prevent the recurrence of blood libels in Germany. In 1267 the Jews of Pforzheim in Baden were under attack. Thomas of Cantimpré (d. 1272), the active Dominican preacher and confessor, who so prodigiously collected moral stories, wrote in comment on the affair that Jews thought they needed Christian blood to release them from the curse they had brought upon themselves when they had said to Pilate: 'Let his blood be upon us.' According to Thomas, the curse had manifested itself in male Jews as a bloody flux. They thought they could cure their affliction with Christian blood, while in reality it could only be cured if they converted to Christianity and partook of Christ's salvific blood. Accusations of this nature continued, culminating in the 1287 case of Good Werner, who had supposedly been crucified by the Jews. Crucifixion rather than blood was emphasised in this instance and Germany obtained its first shrine in Oberwesel. The accusation led to the death of about 500 Jews in a large number of neighbouring towns in the region of the Middle Rhine. Local authorities proved unwilling and/or incapable of protecting the Jews living in their lands. This was also crystal clear when around 5,000 Jews were killed in the so-called Rintfleisch massacres, which were unleashed in 1298 in Franconia and the surrounding area. More than 150 places were affected. By this time a new libel had been introduced, that of the desecration of the host. But before we discuss that we need briefly to revisit England and France to see how ritual-murder accusations had developed there in the thirteenth century.[41]

Hugh of Lincoln

In 1255 it was Lincoln's turn to vie for a shrine. We have come to the case of little Hugh of Lincoln, one of the best-known putative victims of ritual murder. Once again we have the ingredients we have come to suspect: a dead child, a group of Jews coming together to celebrate a feast, this time a wedding, a bishop and his clergy eager for a shrine and a champion for the story in the shape of John of Lexington, the bishop's brother and a trusted administrator of the king. Exceptionally, the events were placed in July and August rather than in spring around the time of Easter. Completely new was the contribution of Henry III, who at least for a time decided to take the accusation seriously. Henry had the Jew Copin, who had been coerced into confessing ritual crucifixion, executed and he imprisoned some 90 Jews and sent them to London for trial, 18 of whom were executed when they refused to be tried by an all-Christian court. The others were later released, even though they had been found guilty as charged. The vital point in this case is Henry's endorsement, albeit brief, of the accusation, which lent lasting legitimacy to the charge. The fanciful account of the case by Matthew Paris and the wildly popular rendition of it in an Anglo-Norman ballad meant that the tale was not forgotten. Edward I added royal approval to Hugh's cult by building him a shrine shortly after he expelled the Jews from England in 1290.[42]

Troyes

In France in Troyes the trope of (ritual) murder seemed once again to have been used to explain away the death of a Christian. By this stage Champagne had just come under royal authority after the marriage of Philip IV (r. 1285–1314) with the heiress of Champagne in 1284. Most of our information derives from five Jewish liturgical laments which celebrate the martyrdom of the 13 Jews who were burnt at the stake on 24 April 1288. Two of these are Hebrew and Old French versions of each other. A dead body had been placed in the house of one of the Jews on Good Friday, 26 March, which coincided with the seventh day of Passover. The Jewish sources allude to active engagement by some kind of mendicants in the proceedings. The burnings were perpetrated by the bailiff of Troyes without royal consent. That did not stop Philip from expropriating the Jewish property that had been confiscated. Striking in the Jewish material is the image of the martyrs steadfastly refusing to convert and willing to become burnt offerings to God. The volume of the material attests to the alarm the Jews clearly felt at the turn of events. A poignant counterpoint to this observation is the evidence presented in the Jewish poetry of just how much intercultural activity there was between Christians and Jews. Besides the use of Champenois French, the poetry betrays many literary elements of Christian romantic literature. Engagement is sought with personal details of the deaths of individual martyrs. In the French poem familiar words are used to the opposite effect from Christian usage. The sobriquet 'felon' is used for the tormentors of Jewish heroes who receive the labels 'prodome' and 'home de valor'.[43]

Accusations of host-desecration

Notions of Jewish treachery reached new heights in Paris in Easter 1290, which fell on 2 April and coincided with the sixth day of Passover. A Jew was accused of desecrating the host which an old woman had procured for him to buy off a loan she could not repay. With the accusation of host-desecration we have come full circle. Ideas of Jews creating little 'Jesuses' through crucifying Christian children, of Jews parodying communion with the heart of a child, of Jews nefariously using Christian blood, of Jews desecrating images of the Virgin and crucifying waxen figures of Jesus, all these ideas somehow blended together to culminate in the accusation that Jews would torment the Eucharistic host to deride everything that Christians held holy. Once again, Jews were made to serve a very Christian purpose, in this instance the substantiation of the belief concerning the real presence of Christ in the consecrated communion wafer. The Feast of Corpus Christi, which had been established in the 1260s, was also meant to inculcate Christians with a deeper understanding of and love for the Eucharist. It is possible that this charge was easier to believe than the charge of ritual murder because, as we have seen, there was a tradition of accusing Jews of mistreating ecclesiastical objects which, notwithstanding stiff ordinances to the contrary, had been left as pawns in their care. And the scenario of this accusation did not require a dead body. Be that as it may, in Paris the accused Jew was burnt while holding a copy of the Talmud, which he thought would safeguard him from the flames; his family and other Jews were converted. A chapel was built for the host to which Philip IV contributed property. It was sanctioned by Pope Boniface VIII. The new charge spread from Paris and similar charges emerged in Germany. We have already mentioned how it was used against Jews in Franconia in the Rintfleisch massacres of 1298. A contemporary Jewish poem lamented the accusation. In so doing it accused Christians of conspiring against Jews and vigorously denied everything their attackers were trying so hard to prove about the host by using Jews in this terrible way.[44]

The narrative of ritual murder, shocking as it was, did not of itself produce violence. In twelfth-century England, where the story developed and was particularly explicit, the libel did not provoke murderous attacks on the Jews. That does not mean that the narrative did not harbour explosive possibilities of violence in certain circumstances. In France we see how the narrative was used to explain instances of judicial violence against Jews. In thirteenth-century Germany we see how the explosive narrative flourished particularly well in the diffuse power structures of the empire. A vicious circle developed with violence begetting violence; the narrative itself evolved from performing an explanatory role to becoming the very medium for evoking retributive violence against Jews. The similarities between the Marian miracle literature and ritual murder and host-desecration libels do not just help us understand the genesis of those libels. The diffusion of the Marian miracle tales in courtly circles and beyond makes it easier for us to comprehend how the libels could become such gruesome real-life enactments of supposed Jewish treachery against Christian religious and lay values. One of the many tragedies of medieval Christian–Jewish relations is how the image of the felonious Jew killing Christian children and torturing the host continued well beyond the thirteenth century, even in places like England whence Jews had been expelled in 1290. The stories of Robert of Bury and Hugh of Lincoln continued to make their mark in literature and art. The late medieval Croxton *Play of the Sacrament* impressed on people that Jews desecrated the Eucharistic host. Probably the best-known version of the tale of the chorister murdered by a Jew is the Prioress's tale in Chaucer's *Canterbury Tales*. And the tale's closing lines call on 'yonge Hugh of Lincoln, slain also / With cursed Jewes' to 'Preye eek for us'.[45] Another of the tragedies of medieval Christian–Jewish relations is that the Jewish ideological response of martyrdom to this violence did nothing to stem Christian ideas about innate Jewish cruelty. Although it seems highly unlikely that Jewish martyrdom at the time of the First Crusade had anything at all to do with the development of the trope of ritual murder, it could well have influenced the way the trope was used and developed, especially in thirteenth-century Germany. As far as German Jewry was concerned, the Good Werner and Rintfleisch pogroms struck a vicious blow to the cultural and intellectual flowering of German Jewry. Although in contrast to England and France, Jews continued to live in some areas of Germany for much of the Middle Ages, centres of Ashkenazi creativity shifted to eastern and central Europe or joined forces with other forms of Jewish life in Italy and Spain.[46]

Notes and references

1 Gavin I. Langmuir, 'Thomas of Monmouth', in idem, *Toward a Definition of Antisemitism* (Berkeley, CA, 1990), 212–14.

2 M. Simon, *Verus Israel. A Study of the Relations between Christians and Jews in the Roman Empire AD 135–425*, trans. H. McKeating (Oxford, 1986), 130; Schreckenberg, 376; Langmuir, 'Thomas of Monmouth', 214–16.

3 John M. McCulloh, 'Jewish Ritual Murder: William of Norwich, Thomas of Monmouth, and the Early Disseminations of the Myth', *Speculum* 72 (1997), 698–740; Israel J. Yuval, *Two Nations in Your Womb. Perceptions of Jews and Christians in Late Antiquity and the Middle Ages*, trans. B. Harshav and J. Chipman (Berkeley, CA, 2006), 168–9.

4 On Purim see Cecil Roth, 'The Feast of Purim and the Origins of the Blood Accusations', *Speculum* 8 (1933), 520–6; Gerd Mentgen, 'Über den Ursprung der Ritualmordfabel', *Aschkenas* (1994), 405–6 and Elliott Horowitz, *Reckless Rites. Purim and the Legacy of Jewish Violence* (Princeton, NJ, 2006).

5 William Chester Jordan, *The French Monarchy and the Jews from Philip Augustus to the Last Capetians* (Philadelphia, PA, 1989), 18. These feast days were sometimes assigned at a later date.

6 August Jessopp and Montague Rhodes James (ed. and trans.) *The Life and Miracles of St. William of Norwich* (Cambridge, 1896), 67–70, 74–7, 129–32; McCulloh 'Jewish Ritual Murder', 720–2.

7 Miri Rubin, *Gentile Tales. The Narrative Assault on Late Medieval Jews* (New Haven, CT, 1999), 10.

8 My pupil, Jennifer A. Shea, 'The Influence of the Cult of the Virgin Mary on Christian Perceptions of Jews, with Particular Reference to the Role of Marian Stories in England and France, *c.* 1050–*c.* 1300 (Cambridge University PhD, 2004).

9 Miri Rubin, *Gentile Tales*, 8, 10, quotation p. 10; Shea, PhD, 88; McCulloh, 'Jewish Ritual Murder', 737–8.

10 Robert C. Stacey, 'From Ritual Crucifixion to Host-desecration: Jews and the Body of Christ, *Jewish History* 12 (1998), 15 says in this article perceptively that 'Ritual crucifixion tales are not . . . dramas of vengeance. Christ, through his Church, overcomes the Jews' attack upon the Christian community, but the threat itself is not removed . . . the Jews remain, unconverted and malevolent, within the Christian body politic'; see also Anthony Bale, 'Fictions of Judaism in England before 1290', in Patricia Skinner (ed.), *Jews in Medieval Britain* (Woodbridge, 2003), 129. See also the references to David Nirenberg's ideas in Chapter 9.

11 Jennifer A. Shea, 'Adgar's *Gracial* and Christian Images of Jews in Twelfth-century Vernacular Literature', *JMH* 33 (2007), 181–96; PhD, 152, 109. See also Jordan, *French Monarchy*, 45–6 and his 'Marian Devotion and the Talmud Trial of 1240', in *Religionsgespräche im Mittelalter*, ed. Friedrich Niewöhner. Wolfenbütteler Mittelalter-Studien, 4 (Wiesbaden, 1992), 69–76.

12 Shea, 'Adgar', 186–8; PhD, 86–8, 139–46.

13 Shea, 'Adgar', 185, 193–5; Shea, PhD, 89–91, 131.

14 G. Constable (ed.), *The Letters of Peter the Venerable*, vol. 1 (Cambridge, MA, 1967), 327–30; see also Ivan G. Marcus, 'A Jewish–Christian Symbiosis: The Culture of Early Ashkenaz', in David Biale (ed.), *Cultures of the Jews. A New History* (New York, 2002), 478–84.

15 Rigord, *Histoire de Philippe Auguste*, ed. and trans. Élisabeth Carpentier, Georges Pon and Yves Chauvin. Sources d'Histoire Médiévale, 33 (Paris, 2006), 146–7.

16 Bale, 'Fictions of Judaism', 136–8.

17 Shea, 'Adgar', 188–91.

18 Shea, PhD, 156; the online Oxford *Cantigas de Santa Maria* database.

19 Deborah Jo Miller, 'The Development of the Ritual Murder Accusation in the Twelfth and Thirteenth Centuries and its Relationship to the Changing Attitudes of Christians to Jews' (MPhil, Cambridge University, 1991), 46; Yitzhak Baer, *A History of the Jews in Christian Spain*. Volume 1: *From the Age of Reconquest to the Fourteenth Century*, trans. Louis Schoffman with an introduction by Benjamin R. Gampel (Philadelphia, PA, 1992), 116, 149.

20 Shea, 'Adgar', 181–96.

21 Benedicta Ward, *Miracles and the Medieval Mind. Theory, Record and Event 1000–1215* (Trowbridge, 1987), 14–17; cf. Bale, 'Fictions', 132.

22 Israel J., 'Vengeance and Damnation, Blood, and Defamation: From Jewish Martyrdom to Blood Libel Accusations', *Zion* 58 (1993), 33–90 [in Hebrew].

23 Jeffrey J. Cohen, 'The Flow of Blood in Medieval Norwich', *Speculum* 79 (2004), 26–65; Marjorie Chibnall, ' "Racial" Minorities in the Anglo-Norman Realm', in Susan J. Ridyard and R.G. Benson (eds), *Minorities and Barbarians in Medieval Life and Thought* (Sewanee, 1996), 49–50; Jessopp and James, *The Life and Miracles of St. William of Norwich*, 95.

24 Bale, 'Fictions', 130–2; Anthony Bale, *The Jew in the Medieval Book. English Antisemitism, 1350–1500* (Cambridge, 2006), 16–17, 107–10.

25 Shea, PhD, 42–3.

26 *Historia et Cartularium Monasterii Sancti Petri Gloucestriae*, ed. William H. Hart, RS 33, 1 (1971 repr.), 20–1; J. Jacobs (ed.), *The Jews of Angevin*

England (New York, 1893; repr. 1977), 45–7; Joe Hillaby, 'The Ritual-Child-Murder Accusation: Its Dissemination and Harold of Gloucester', *Transactions of the Jewish Historical Society of England* 34 (1996), 74–85; Bale, 'Fictions', 130–2; Bale, *The Jew*, 16–17, 109.

27 *The Chronicle of Richard of Devizes of the Time of King Richard the First*, ed. John T. Appleby (London, 1963), 64–8; Jacobs, 146–52; Anthony P. Bale, 'Richard of Devizes and fictions of Judaism', *Jewish Culture and History* 3 (2000), 55–72; Bale, 'Fictions', 133–5; Robert Levine, 'Why Praise Jews: Satire and History in the Middle Ages', *Journal of Medieval History* 12 (1986), 291–6; Kennedy, 'Faith in the One God', 143; Nancy F. Partner, *Serious Entertainments. The Writing of History in Twelfth-century England* (Chicago, IL, 1977), 175–9.

28 N.C. Vincent, 'Jews, Poitevins, and the Bishop of Winchester, 1231–1234', in Diana Wood (ed.), *Christianity and Judaism* (Oxford, 1992), 128–9.

29 Friedrich Lotter, '*Innocens Virgo et Martyr*. Thomas von Monmouth und die Verbreitung der Ritualmordlegende im Hochmittelalter', in Erb Rainer (ed.), *Die Legende vom Ritualmord. Zur Geschichte der Blutbeschuldigung gegen Juden* (Berlin, 1993), 49–50; Rigord, *Histoire de Philippe Auguste*, 130–3; *Oeuvres de Rigord et de Guillaume le Breton, Historiens de Philippe Auguste*, vol. 2 (Paris, 1885), 179–80; Kenneth Stow, *Jewish Dogs. An Image and Its Interpreters* (Stanford, CA, 2006), 86–7, 91, 108–9, 179–80 (I remain unconvinced by Stow's redating of the Pontoise case).

30 Roth, 'The Feast', 521–2; Mentgen, 'Über den Ursprung', 410; Horowitz, *Reckless Rites*, 258–65.

31 Rigord, *Histoire*, 310–11; *Oeuvres de Rigord*, vol. 2, 194, 37; Ephraim of Bonn, *Sefer Zekhirah*, ed. A.M. Habermann, *Sefer Gezerot Ashkenaz ve-Zarfat* (Jerusalem, 1945), 128; cf. Robert Chazan, 'The Bray Incident of 1192: *Realpolitik* and Folk Slander', *Proceedings of the American Academy for Jewish Research* 37 (1969), 1–14; Jordan, *French Monarchy*, 35–7, 270–1, 286; trans. from Robert Chazan, 'Ephraim ben Jacob's Compilation of Twelfth-century Persecutions', *Jewish Quarterly Review* 84 (1994), 405.

32 Israel Jacob Yuval, ' "They Tell Lies: You Ate the Man": Jewish Reactions to Ritual Murder Accusations', in Anna Sapir Abulafia (ed.), *Religious Violence between Christians and Jews. Medieval Roots, Modern Perspectives*, (London, 2002), 86–106; David Berger (ed.), *The Jewish–Christian Debate in the High Middle Ages. A Critical Edition of the* Nizzahon Vetus (Philadelphia, PA, 1979), nos 16 and 244, p. 54 [Hebrew, pp. 14–15], 229–30 [Hebrew, p. 163], 342–3.

33 *Chronica Roberti de Torigneio* in *Chronicles of the Reigns of Stephen, Henry II and Richard I*, ed. Richard Howlett, RS 82.4 (London, 1889), 250–1.

34 Ephraim of Bonn, *Sefer Zekhirah*, ed. Habermann, 124–6; Susan Einbinder, 'The Jewish Martyrs of Blois', in Thomas Head (ed.), *Medieval Hagiography. An Anthology* (New York, 2000), 537–60.

35 *Encyclopaedia Judaica*, vol. 2 (Jerusalem, [1971–2]), 557–8.

36 Susan L. Einbinder, *Beautiful Death. Jewish Poetry and Martyrdom in Medieval France* (Princeton, NJ, 2002), 45–69; *CSJMA*, 114–17; Yuval, *Two Nations*, 171–2, 192–5. See also Stow, *Jewish Dogs*, 99–118; 198–202. I remain unpersuaded that the multiple instances of irony in the Hebrew letters concerning Blois indicate that they were composed with Philip Augustus in mind rather than Louis VII.

37 Yuval, 'They Tell Lies', 88–9; Miller, 'The Development', 25–7; Lotter, '*Innocens Virgo et Martyr*', 53–4; Habermann, *Gezerot*, 161; trans. *CSJMA*, 118. Shortly afterwards trouble occurs for the Jews of Mainz on account of the build-up to the Third Crusade, see above.

38 Gavin I. Langmuir, 'Ritual Cannibalism', *Toward a Definition of Antisemitism*, 271–6.

39 Langmuir, 'Ritual Cannibalism', 276–81; Lotter, '*Innocens Virgo et Martyr*', 54–7; *CSJMA*, 124–6.

40 Lotter, '*Innocens Virgo et Martyr*', 58–62; Jordan, *French Monarchy*, 146–7; Stow, *Jewish Dogs*, 86–7, 249–50 n. 42; Grayzel I, no. 116, pp. 268–71; Simonsohn, no. 185, pp. 194–5.

41 Lotter, '*Innocens Virgo et Martyr*', 64–70; Friedrich Lotter, 'The Scope and Effectiveness of Imperial Jewry Law in the High Middle Ages', *Jewish History* 4 (1989), 47.

42 Langmuir, 'The Knight's Tale of Young Hugh of Lincoln', in *Toward a Definition*, 237–62; Bale, *The Jew*, 137–8.

43 Jordan, *French Monarchy*, 190–1; Einbinder, *Beautiful Death*, 126–54; Einbinder, 'The Troyes Laments: Jewish Martyrology in Hebrew and Old French', *Viator* 30 (1999), 201–30.

44 Jordan, *French Monarchy*, 191–4; Miri Rubin, *Gentile Tales*, 40–51; Stow, *Jewish Dogs*, 86–7.

45 Bale, *The Jew*, 55–143, 169–72.

46 Haym Soloveitchik, 'Catastrophe and Halakhic Creativity: Ashkenaz – 1096, 1242, 1306 and 1298', *Jewish History* 12 (1998), 71–85.

chapter 9

Conclusion: Jewish service in encounters between Christians and Jews

The cover of this book shows a stained glass window of Chartres Cathedral from *c.* 1220–30 depicting the apostle Matthew sitting on the shoulders of the prophet Isaiah. Apostles were frequently featured in this way in medieval art. By placing one on top of the other artists graphically portrayed the service the prophets of the Hebrew Bible were thought to have rendered to the apostles through their prophecies concerning Christ.[1] A fourteenth-century manuscript from Rouen contains a play for 1 January, the day on which the Feast of Fools was traditionally celebrated. On that day ecclesiastical decorum was set aside. The play was called the Procession of Asses or the Procession of the Prophets and took place in the nave of the church before Mass. The text derived from a pseudo-Augustinian sermon against the Jews, Pagans and Arians, which was dramatised in eleventh-century Limoges; it was turned into a play in Laon in the thirteenth century. The play vividly brought to life the idea that the Old Testament prefigured the New by having one costumed actor after another act out the main prophets and deliver their prophecies of Christ. The proceedings were livened up by an actor playing Balaam's donkey who was stopped in his tracks by an angel telling him not to heed Balak (Numbers 22:21ff). A furnace was lit on stage to re-enact how Nebuchadnezzar threw Shadrach, Meshach and Abednego into a furnace because they refused to worship an idol. The actors praise God from within the furnace and Nebuchadnezzar points to a fourth unscathed man in the furnace representing Christ (Daniel 3:92 in the Vulgate).[2]

Jewish service

In late-twelfth-century Paris, Peter the Chanter included the term *Jews* in his *Summa Abel*, a collection of vignettes known as distinctions in aid of preachers. This is the first rubric of his entry for the topic:

> *The lives of Jews are preserved* (servantur) *on account of God's justice so that punishment is manifest in them and dispersion, on account of the death of Christ, because they said: 'His blood be upon us and upon our children' (Matthew 27:25), on account of confirmation and service* (confirmationem et obsequium) *so that they, as it were, testify on our behalf against the Gentiles, because they are our book carriers* (capsarii). *For the testimony of an enemy is precious; whence: 'the elder [Esau] shall serve the younger [Jacob]' (Genesis 25:23, Romans 9:13), on account of the fulfilling of God's promise who says: 'If the number of the children of Israel be as the sand of the sea, a remnant shall be saved' (Romans 9:27, cf. Isaiah 10:22), on account of their conversion which [will] happen through distress, whence 'Fill their faces with shame [and they shall seek thy name, O Lord]' (Psalm 82[3]:17).*

In his commentary on Psalm 58(9):12 Peter wrote:

> *'slay them not'* . . . . *For [the Jews] are our book carriers and the bearers of our texts and the witnesses to Christ's Passion, they must clean the streets of Christendom rather than be rich and they must perform public service to Christian society* (publici servi Ecclesie).

Peter's pupil, Thomas of Chobham, added the following observation to his interpretation of 'slay them not':

> *If they wish to live at peace under the yoke of our servitude and refrain from impugning our faith or attacking our persons, they are to be preserved among us and allocated work of a base sort so that they cannot exalt themselves over Christians. And so indeed are Jews to be especially sustained among us because they are our book carriers and bear the witness of the Law against themselves and for us.*

The connection which Peter the Chanter made between the preservation of the Jews and their service makes it crystal clear that for him the *raison d'être* of Jews was to serve as witnesses to the truth of Christianity by way of their texts and their downtrodden circumstances and to give body to the promise of future conversion. His words put to mind Augustine's reference in *The City of God* to a Roman idea that the Latin word for slave, *servus*, stemmed from the fact that the lives of prisoners of war were often preserved (*servabantur*) so that they could become slaves. In other words, Jews are preserved to serve. Augustine linked slavery to sin and pointed out that Noah was the first person to use the word in the Bible when he punished his middle son, Ham, for his sin against him.[3]

Following Augustine, Isidore of Seville identified Ham, the middle son of Noah, with the unbelieving Jews. The narrative in Genesis (9:20–9) narrates how after the flood Noah got drunk on the wine he produced from the vines he had planted. In his stupor he lay naked in his dwelling to be chanced upon by Ham. In Augustine and Isidore's reading Noah prefigured Christ as he hung naked on the cross. Noah's dwelling prefigured the Jewish people whence Christ came. Just as Ham had seen the nakedness of his drunken father, the Jews had consented to the murder of Christ; just as Ham had announced Noah's nakedness to his brothers, they exhibited and made known what was hidden in prophecy; just as Ham became a servant to his brothers, the Jewish people were 'the desks for Christians, carrying the law and the prophets as witness to the Church's assertion that we honour by sacrament what they announce through the letter'.[4]

One of the stories included by William of Malmesbury in his twelfth-century collection of Marian miracles recounts how in early-twelfth-century Toulouse a Jew made fun of Christ on Good Friday by saying that Christians 'who adore Jesus and his witnesses worship dead men, ashes and those lying in the dust of the grave'. He was struck dead by a Christian in response. The Jews sought justice from the Count of Toulouse. Resisting their attempts to bribe him, he decided that every year a Jew would be struck on the neck by a Christian to teach them how foolish they were to mock Christ. The story must be connected to the custom in Toulouse of delivering a ritual blow to a Jew on Good Friday. The first clear description we have of this rite of 'colaphisation' dates to 1020 from the hand of Adémar of Chabannes, an eleventh-century monk whose vivid imagination coloured much of his historical output. Anonymous legend projected the

Toulouse custom back to the Carolingian period amidst fears of Jewish connivance with Saracen invaders. From other sources we know that some kind of ritual violence against Jews occurred in Béziers too before it was stopped in 1161. David Nirenberg has analysed similar rituals for Spain, which included the stoning of the Jewish section of town, in the fourteenth century. He has stressed that both Christians and Jews knew the rules of these ritual games and that usually no one got hurt. The violence was ritual, giving Christians the opportunity to let off steam, while Jews were being put to Augustinian service by helping the Christian participants remember their dominant role in Christian–Jewish relations.[5] As we have stressed many times before, the crucial problem remains whether the sinister undertones of such customs fuelled anti-Jewish sentiments and, even more crucially, to what extent they could be contained in times of communal tension and/or lack of public authority. Or to put it differently, this kind of ritual violence vividly embodied the many ambiguities governing the concept of Jewish service in Christian society.

The preservation of Jews is premised on theological memories of the past and hopes for the future. The concept of Jewish service, whether through witnessing to the truth of Christianity, or through reminding Christians of the Passion, or through epitomising divine punishment for rejecting Christ, made Jews, for good or for ill, an integral part of Christian thought and society. That is why Christian–Jewish relations never left the Christian agenda altogether. As we have seen, in its positive guise the concept of Jewish service gave theoretical underpinning to the concrete existence of flesh-and-blood Jews in Christian lands, guaranteeing them at least a modicum of physical security to live their lives as Jews. We have seen expressions of this in Pope Alexander's bull protecting Jews of Spain in 1063 against Christian knightly fervour and we have seen how Bernard of Clairvaux used the concept to quash anti-Jewish violence during the preaching of the Second Crusade. We have also observed how William of Newburgh used the concept of Jewish service to condemn the violence perpetrated against the Jews of England in the run-up to the Third Crusade. In its negative guise, however, the concept of Jewish service embedded in Christian consciousness the idea of Jewish inferiority. Jews existed for the sake of Christendom and not independently in their own right as Jews. The punitive aspect of the theory of Jewish service also fuelled ideas that it should be as demeaning as possible in practice: Jews had to be kept in their place because of their rejection of Christianity in the past and refusal to convert in the present. Bernard himself said of Jewish service: 'There is no servitude more repulsive or oppressive than that of the Jews which they drag after them wherever they go. They offend their masters everywhere.'[6] Rupert of Deutz (d. 1129), a prolific Benedictine theologian and staunch supporter of papal reform, hoped the burden of Jewish service would induce Jews to seek an escape through conversion. Even if they were insincere converts, their offspring would be faithful Christians.[7] Innocent III's *Etsi Iudeos* bull of 1205 raged against reports that French Jews had required their Christian wet-nurses to express their milk into the latrine for three days after receiving the Eucharist at Easter, and stated that Jews had brought perpetual servitude upon themselves through crucifying Christ. One of the most important canon lawyers of the thirteenth century, Hostiensis (d. 1271), encapsulated the inherent paradox of Jewish service by stating: 'Although Jews are enemies of our faith, they are our *servi* [they serve us] and are tolerated and defended by us'; a gloss on the *Sicut Iudeis* entry in the *Decretals* of Gregory IX stated more simply: 'Jews indeed are not to be considered our enemies, although they are enemies of our faith.'[8]

Jewish responses

But the French Jews, who seemed to be worried that their babies would be corrupted by the consecrated host their wet-nurses had received at Easter, clearly did *not* regard themselves as servants to Christians. On the contrary, as we have seen in our discussion of the Hebrew crusade chronicles, insulting language against every aspect of Christian belief was embedded in medieval Jewish vocabulary. We have also looked at *Alenu*, one of the most important prayers in the Jewish liturgy, and noted how the prayer emphasised God's special selection of the Jewish people above those who 'prostrate themselves before vanity and folly, and pray to a god who does not save'. The words which are ascribed to a Jew in the Toulouse story, are, in fact, remarkably similar to twelfth- and thirteenth-century French and English versions of the *Alenu* prayer which expanded this section to state

for they bow to vanity and emptiness and pray to a god who cannot save –
man, ash, blood, bile, stinking flesh, maggot, defiled men and women,
adulterers and adulteresses, dying in their iniquity and rotting in their

Jew's responding with own aggression

wickedness, worn-out dust, rot of maggot [and worm] – and pray to a god who cannot save.

As the Jews of Ashkenaz began to use different versions of the *Alenu* prayer to round off their three chief services of the liturgical day during the twelfth and thirteenth centuries, they would have had yet another constant reminder of Jewish belief in the religious superiority of Judaism over Christianity.[9] It is not for nothing that Christian censors regularly eradicated this part of the *Alenu* prayer from Jewish prayer-books.

Another bane for Christian officials was the so-called 'benediction of the *minim*' of the *Amidah*, the central section of the three daily services which comprised 19 benedictions (seven on the Sabbath and festivals). The *Amidah* commenced with blessings praising God as the God of Abraham, Isaac and Jacob and lauding his might to raise the dead (known as the blessings of the 'Fathers' and 'Might'). It concludes with a benediction pleading for peace. The twelfth benediction is the most controversial one because it effectively calls for God to destroy the *minim* and overthrow the enemies of Israel. The vexed question is who these *minim* might have been when the prayer was devised and, from our point of view the far more interesting question, who medieval Jews were thinking about when they recited the blessing day in and day out. Broadly speaking, modern consensus has it that the prayer predated the emergence of Christianity in so far as it referred to the oppressors of Israel. In the early period of Jewish–Christian rivalry when the lines of division between Christians and Jews were still so very permeable, the curse of the *minim* was added. The Hebrew means 'heretics' and the term was probably meant to denote Jewish Christians who were regarded as a particular threat to the Jewish community. Rome would have been seen as the oppressor of Israel. It would seem likely that in our period the term had broadened out as a catch-all for Christians. In the second century, Justin Martyr was already complaining in his anti-Jewish polemic, *Dialogue with the Jew Trypho*, that Jews cursed Christians. The version of the benediction in the late-thirteenth-century religious compendium of Rabbi Jacob of London, the *Etz Hayyim*, reads:

May there be no hope for the apostates and may the heretics perish in an instant, may all the enemies of your people, the house of Israel, be quickly rooted out, and may you quickly root out the kingdom of wickedness and shatter it to pieces and cast it down and subdue it and humble all our enemies speedily in our days. Blessed art thou Lord who shatters the enemies and humbles the wicked.[10]

It would seem disingenuous not to conclude that this prayer was an expression of frustration about Jewish conversion to Christianity and the perilous position of Jews under medieval Christian rule.

Our next example comes from the *Seder*, the ritual evening meal held in Jewish households at the start of Passover. During the *Seder* four glasses of wine are drunk. The fourth represents the cup of deliverance. By retelling the story of how the ancient Israelites were liberated by God from slavery in Egypt, medieval Jews replenished their hopes for deliverance in the future from their existence in the diaspora. And so, in the preliminaries to the fourth glass a passage was recited, calling on God to come in aid of the Jewish people against those who oppress them. The first instance of this happening comes from the late-eleventh-century *Machzor Vitry* from the school of Rashi. The standard text used from then on in Ashkenaz comes from Psalm 78(9):6–7, which is paraphrased in Jeremiah 10:25: 'Pour out thy wrath upon the nations that know thee not, and upon the kingdoms that call not upon thy name. For they have devoured Jacob, and laid waste his dwelling place'; Psalm 68(9):25: 'let the fierceness of thine anger overtake them' and Lamentations 3:66: 'destroy them in anger from under the heavens of the Lord'. The biblical texts concern the ancient enemies of Israel, but it is hard not to imagine that medieval Jews might have had more immediate matters in mind when they recited these words. This is reinforced by the *Etz Hayyim* version of the *Seder*, which English Jews shared with the Jews of Normandy, in which at this point numerous additional biblical quotations are woven into the text which call for God's retribution: 'Add iniquity upon their iniquity and let them not come into thy righteousness (Psalm 68(9):28)', 'Their swords shall enter into their own heart . . . (Psalm 36(7):15)', 'Give them, O Lord, whatsoever thou wilt give; give them a miscarrying womb and dry breasts (Hosea 9:14)' etc. Some of these verses pertain to the Babylonian exile after the destruction of the First Temple by Nebuchadnezzar, while others are taken from Psalms in which evil-doers were vilified and deliverance sought for Israel; the excerpt from Hosea was, in fact, aimed at sinful Israelites. Put together, the texts give off the impression of an evil world in turmoil in which the

Children of Israel are certainly not without fault. God's corrective actions are needed to usher in the messianic period which was so keenly awaited. Israel Yuval sees in these curses yet another example of how medieval Jews wove together their hopes for messianic deliverance with the expectation that God would revenge their sufferings on those who had perpetrated them. His interpretation would seem to be supported by the fact that Rabbi Yom Tov of Joigny, who would lead the Jews of York into self-martyrdom, used 'Lord, pour out your wrath' as the opening words of his elegy for the Jews murdered at Blois in 1171. And we recall that those martyrs sang *Alenu* as they burned to death, at least according to Ephraim of Bonn and others who later eulogised their deaths. We have seen how Jewish texts like these and the texts commemorating those who lost their lives during the crusades fervently and repeatedly called out for God's vengeance.[11]

Yuval has read into these and similar utterances an Ashkenazi cult of messianic vengeance which was premised on the idea that each Jewish death would hasten God's redemptive actions. As we have noted in a previous chapter, he has even suggested a connection between the violence of Jewish self-martyrdom and Christian anti-Jewish libels of ritual murder. I have argued that Christians had more than enough material to construct these libels from within their own consciousness. Furthermore, I wonder whether it would not be more fruitful to apply to Jewish ideas and language of vengeance against Christians some of the categories Nirenberg has used to analyse Christian ritual violence against Jews. Just as Christians, in Nirenberg's reading, were letting off steam by ritually striking Jews during Holy Week or by stoning Jewish quarters in late-medieval Spain, so also medieval Jews were letting off their pent-up frustrations against the pressures of their lives under Christian hegemony by anti-Christian language and rituals. As Nirenberg emphasises throughout his important study, the Middle Ages were intrinsically violent and it would be a mistake to judge Jewish or Christian language and ritual by the politically correct standards of our modern, sanitised Western world.[12] The crucial difference between medieval Christian and Jewish expressions of violence was, of course, that official violence remained the prerogative of Christians, not Jews. The interplay between Christian expressions of anti-Judaism and actual Christian violence against Jews in a judicial or non-judicial setting continues to puzzle students of Christian–Jewish relations. Keeping the lid on Jewish violence was a far simpler matter than containing Christian violence.

An interesting insight is gained from a passage in the *Sefer Hasidim* in which Pietists are offered practical advice on how to resist temptation. When something tempting presents itself they are encouraged to reflect how they would muster the courage to resist baptism, if it were forced on them, and choose to be killed for the sake of the Unity of God (*Kiddush ha-Shem*) rather than be baptised. Anyone with the strength to resist baptism should be able to resist anything else.[13] We see here not only how Christianity is pictured as the worst temptation imaginable, but also how resistance to Christianity is being used as a tool to perfect Jewish behaviour. Christianity is serving Judaism here and not the other way around. Equally, we realise that at times resisting baptism was anything but easy for Jews.

Our final example comes from the *Nizzahon Vetus* where the Christian assertion of Jewish service is taken head on: 'they bark their assertion that it is improper for the uncircumcised and impure [Christians] to serve Jews'. We see how anti-Christian invectives are used to discredit the assertion even before the first counter-argument is presented. Biblical texts from Genesis (25:23) and Isaiah (60:1, 61:5) are used to prove that Gentiles are meant to serve Israel. Christians serve Jews by buying meat from them which Jews cannot use for their own consumption because they have been deemed to be ritually unsuitable. Christians serve Jews on a day-to-day basis. The practical example in the passage is fascinating. Jewish selling of meat to Christians was a thorn in the ecclesiastical flesh and many a council condemned the practice as, for example, in 1267 in Vienna, when it was stated that Christians were not to purchase meat or other foodstuffs from Jews, 'lest Jews perhaps defraud Christians, whom they think of as enemies'. The ruling appeared together with rulings against sexual relations between Jews and Christians, Christians partaking in Jewish celebrations, Christians and Jews eating and drinking together and Jews employing Christian servants, including wet-nurses.[14] None of these activities accorded with the theological ideas of Jewish service; all of these indicated that Jews and Christians in practice seemed to have kept ignoring the myriad of rules and regulations which were trying to keep them apart.

Of all the examples given so far only two stem from works which were consciously written as Christian–Jewish or Jewish–Christian polemics, Justin Martyr's dialogue and the *Nizzahon Vetus*. Rivalry between Jews and Christians was not confined to the genre of disputations. It permeated both communities and was expressed in everyday language, biblical exegesis and liturgy, literature, art, theological tracts and legal texts. These expressions are the windows through which we can glimpse how both communities viewed each other, how they continued to give their own shape to the many features they had in common and how they at times internalised their opponents' ideals and adapted them to make them their own. A good example of shared material which had profoundly different meanings and connotations for both communities was the use made of the vision of Isaiah, in which he saw God sitting on his throne around which the six-winged seraphim proclaim his glory: 'Holy, holy, holy, the Lord God of hosts, all the earth is full of his glory.' In Christian–Jewish disputations, Isaiah 6:3 was a standard text with which Christian polemicists attempted to prove that the Hebrew Bible bore witness to the Trinity. The thrice-voiced *sanctus* could only refer to the Father, Son and Holy Spirit. In the liturgy of the Mass the *Sanctus* was used to call the faithful to join the angels in praising God and in affirming the Trinity.

Sanctifying God lay at the heart of the third blessing of the Jewish *Amidah*, which is called 'the Sanctification of the Name': 'Thou art holy and holy is your name, the holy praise you every day, selah. Blessed art thou Lord the holy God.' The full text of Isaiah 6:3 was pronounced when the third blessing was expanded during the repetition of the *Amidah* during communal prayers. The expanded text is known as the *Kedushah* (Sanctification) and it comprises one of the most solemn moments of the liturgy in which the congregation is engaged in responses sanctifying God. The significance of the third blessing comes out beautifully in the words of Judah Halevi in his twelfth-century polemic in defence of Judaism, the *Kuzari*:

> *After one affirms the blessings of 'Fathers' and 'Might' [the first two blessings of the* Amidah *], which impress the concept that God is integrated with this physical world, he will then exalt, sanctify and elevate God to impress the point that no experience of a physical nature could ever be ascribed to God's holiness. This is expressed in the third blessing of 'You are holy'. During this blessing, one should internalize in his heart all that the philosophers described about God's holiness and loftiness . . .*

Although Judah Halevi went on to stress the difference between the Jewish concept of a personal God who created the universe and the philosophical concept of an impersonal God in a universe which existed eternally, the care he took to state that it was unimaginable to connect anything physical to God brings to mind Jewish rejection of the Christian doctrine of the Incarnation. Finally, the rabbis actually used the term *Kiddush ha-Shem* to describe the communal recitation of the *Kedushah*. This brings to mind the physical sanctification of the Name, also called *Kiddush ha-Shem*, which so many Jews endured at their own hands or at the hands of their attackers during the crusade pogroms and other assaults connected with anti-Jewish libels. Isaiah 6:3 was not just a random verse in the Bible. For both Christians and Jews the words touched the core of what made them who they were.[15]

Christian learning

But before we go any further we have to outline the context in which the cultural encounters between Jews and Christians were taking place. In our discussions on the position of Jews in the different polities of Latin Europe we have touched on some of the most significant expressions of Jewish intellectual creativity. In the previous two chapters we have explored aspects of the late-eleventh- and twelfth-century Reform Movement which impacted on the crusades. We have also examined how increased Christian interest in the Virgin Mary and Jesus Christ contributed to the development of anti-Jewish libels in the twelfth and thirteenth centuries. And we have drawn many examples from contemporaneous Hebrew works of prose and poetry. At this point it is important to sketch the development of Christian intellectual endeavours in general and the genre of Christian–Jewish disputations in particular. For although these disputations are not the sole repository of religious polemical material, they do teach us a very great deal about Christian engagement with Judaism. Jewish–Christian polemics for their part will give us additional material about Jewish responses to Christianity.

The *Decretals* of Gregory IX pulled together the efforts canonists such as Burchard of Worms and Ivo of Chartres in the eleventh and especially Gratian in the twelfth centuries had been undertaking in compiling ecclesiastical rulings. The advances in collecting, systematising, refining and codifying canon law were intimately connected to the renewed interest in the study of Roman law in Bologna in the late-eleventh century. The rediscovery of Justinian's Code in the late-eleventh and twelfth centuries allowed scholars to build on what they knew of Roman law through, for example, the abridgement of the Theodosian Code in the *Breviarium*, the *Roman Law of the Visigoths* of 506.[16] Parallel to these important developments in Roman and canon law was the burst of intellectual activity in the budding schools of late-eleventh- and twelfth-century northern Europe.

Learning was, of course, not a discovery of the eleventh century. Thus we see that already in the Carolingian ninth century there was a concerted effort to improve monastic schooling by reviving the classical curriculum of the *trivium* consisting of grammar, which concerned the structure of language, rhetoric, which concerned the art of persuasive formulation, and dialectic, which concerned the study of logic. By the second half of the eleventh century studies in monastic schools and, especially, in cathedral schools were re-energised by the renewed deployment of Aristotle's logical works *Categories* and *On Meaning*, which took the study of dialectic to new levels. Renewed interest in Plato's cosmology fostered scientific thought, which included the study of the *quadrivium*, mathematics, astronomy, music and geometry. The *trivium* and the *quadrivium* made up the classical seven liberal arts. Ciceronian texts improved scholars' rhetorical skills and aroused their interest in human reason and the benefits of political communities. These interests expanded exponentially throughout the twelfth and thirteenth centuries as the whole gamut of Aristotelian texts on logic, metaphysics, science, ethics and politics steadily made its way to the North through Latin translations from Arabic translations or the original Greek. We have discussed how Christians and Jews collaborated on many of these translations in Spain. As more classical material became available, studies started to emancipate themselves from a purely devotional framework. Cathedral schools began to support masters who attracted students from far afield to engage in broader studies. Theology, law, philosophy and medicine began to emerge as special areas of study beyond the liberal-arts curriculum. Cathedral schools, which had the intellectual and physical elasticity to host a diverse group of masters, had the scope to develop into universities. Paris is the prime example of this. By the thirteenth century its different schools had come together as a university of masters and scholars divided among the Faculty of the Arts, which comprised the liberal arts and philosophy (which included physics, metaphysics and ethics) and the Faculties of Theology, Medicine and Law. Paris's great forte lay in the field of theology; Bologna retained its lead in law; the universities of Padua and

Montpellier excelled in medicine; Oxford gained a particular reputation for the advances made in science. In Paris theologians such as Peter the Chanter and his pupils applied the insights they gained from their studies to arrive at practical answers to all kinds of pressing socio-economic and ethical questions of the day. As we have seen earlier on in this book, Peter's circle held distinct views on the problem of usury.

One of the characteristics of twelfth-century thought was the tension scholars experienced between the dictates of reason and the demands of faith. Reason was seen as the innate, God-given faculty humans possessed to uncover truths about the world and their place in it. Reason was what separated man from animal. Reason in conjunction with the tools of grammar, rhetoric and dialectic enabled human beings to make sense of conflicting data and allowed them to organise, systematise and augment the learning they were discovering in their classical sources. The challenge in all of this was to make sure that this learning did not come into conflict with the teachings of faith. The Christian scholars of this period were working within the general framework of the institutional Church; many of them held ecclesiastical positions of authority. Universities which had developed from cathedral schools were ecclesiastical foundations. In the twelfth century there was a surge of confidence in the powers of reason to confirm the teachings of faith. After all, if reason ultimately came from God, it should be able to lead humans to understand God better, as long as reason was used correctly. Thus Peter Abelard (d. *c.* 1142) could argue that reason and faith were parallel routes to the Trinity. And John of Salisbury (d. 1180) could argue for the intrinsic values of a political community, while at the same time propounding the synergy between the prince of that community and its ecclesiastical components. As scholars gained cognisance of more and more Aristotelian texts, a greater understanding developed between the different remits of reason and faith. It was not for nothing that when Aquinas composed his overview of theology, the *Summa Theologica*, in the late 1260s and early 1270s, he devoted its first book to the relationship between faith and reason, the two-part second book to reason and the third to matters of faith. As far as Aquinas was concerned, human reason could work out that God existed and that God was one; but faith was needed to know about the Trinity and the Incarnation. Once faith had opened the way to the special Christian understanding of God, reason could help Christians probe Christian doctrines about God even further.

Christian–Jewish disputations

A remarkable feature of the cultural boom which began in the late eleventh century was the burst in the production of Christian–Jewish disputations. In the tradition of Justin Martyr, whom we have just mentioned, Augustine and Isidore of Seville, late-eleventh-, twelfth- and thirteenth-century scholars composed polemics through which they explored the relationship between Christianity and Judaism. From the 1060s polemics were penned by Peter Damian (d. 1072), who played a major role in the Reform Movement, Gilbert Crispin (d. 1117) Abbot of Westminster, Peter Alfonsi, Guibert of Nogent, Rupert of Deutz, Peter Abelard, Peter the Venerable, Walter of Châtillon (1202–3), a renowned poet and poetic rival to another outstanding twelfth-century poet, Alan of Lille (d. 1202–3), who was also a distinguished theologian and philosopher, Joachim of Fiore (d. 1202), the great apocalyptic thinker, Archbishop Rodrigo Jiménez de Rada of Toledo, and many others. And as we have seen, public investigations were initiated against Judaism in Paris in 1240 and in Barcelona in 1263. Why? Why were so many leading theologians, scholars and poets so interested in Judaism that they took the trouble to write a refutation of it? It would seem that the religious renewal of the period combined with the revival of classical studies raised questions about Christian doctrines that touched on the very essence of Christian beliefs and identity. And as we have seen, an integral part of that essence was Christianity's relationship with Judaism.[17]

An excellent example of the need for Jewish service in this context can be found in Joachim of Fiore's *Adversus Iudeos* ('[Treatise] against the Jews'). Joachim was an ascetic monk who founded the Florensian order which offered a rule that was even stricter than the Cistercian one. Writing in Calabria towards the end of the twelfth century, Joachim translated the visions which he had experienced of the Trinity into a highly complex system outlining the course of history. In his view history progressed from the age or status of God the Father to the status of God the Son to the status of God the Holy Spirit. The final status would come just before the apocalyptic end of time. It would be marked by intense spiritual understanding of the Bible disseminated by the preaching of spiritual men. Through this preaching almost everyone would convert to Christ. The few stragglers remaining behind would join forces with Antichrist, but they together with Antichrist would be overcome by the power of the Holy Spirit and the Pauline conversion of *all* Gentiles and Jews would finally take place. Joachim was confident that this final apocalyptic conversion would take place by 1260. Joachim's apocalyptic programme hinged on a complete concordance between the Old and New Testaments. And that is where he needed the Jews. It was essential to Joachim to convince Jews to convert as the age of the Holy Spirit approached. Jewish conversion would not just hasten the coming of the status; it would validate Joachim's programme. Thus we see in his treatise how he embraces Jewish objections to Christianity in a remarkable attempt to draw Jews in by explaining how very close Judaism and Christianity are. Of all the Christian–Jewish polemics of the twelfth century this must be the most positive one. But Joachim's positive attitude towards Judaism is premised on his conviction that Jews were about to perform their service to Christianity, which was to convert, i.e. cease being Jews in a Jewish sense. Joachim's repudiation for any Jew, or for that matter any Christian, who gave precedence to a literal reading of biblical texts over a spiritual one was fierce. A crucial example of Jewish service was introduced in his *Exposition on the Apocalypse*, which he wrote after his anti-Jewish treatise. There Joachim built on the explanation Peter Alfonsi had given of the Tetragrammaton, the four letters denoting the name of God in the Hebrew Bible. Following Alfonsi, Joachim used the fact that of the four letters, *yod, heh, vav, heh,* the *heh* was repeated to prove the Christian understanding of God as being one and at the same time comprising three persons. For Jews the four letters of the name of God were ineffable. They were not linked together to form a word; replacement words like *Adonai* ('my Lord') or simply *Shem* ('Name') were used. Only the High Priest in Temple days would utter the Name once a year on the Day of Atonement. This is the Name Jewish martyrs sanctified when they performed *Kiddush ha-Shem.* Joachim was deeply moved by the confluence he saw between the profound mystery of the Trinity and the Jewish mystery of the inexpressible Name of God. His pictorial representation of the different letters of the Name of God in three intersecting circles was an essential component of his apocalyptic thinking.[18]

Some three or four generations earlier Rupert of Deutz had also used the Trinity as his paradigm for the unfolding of history. His vast exegetical output was premised on the idea that the Bible had to be understood in terms of the salvific work of God the Father, God the Son and God the

Holy Spirit. At the centre of this understanding lay the blindness of the Jews to the true meaning of Scripture. Jews served Rupert as a witness to Christian truth and a foil for proper biblical understanding. In Rupert's view Jewish blindness was caused by their envy and particularism which fuelled their desire to reserve God's blessing for themselves to the exclusion of the Gentiles. They espoused circumcision in contrast to the Church's universal invitation to come to Christ's table. Like the resentful elder son in the parable of the prodigal son of Luke 15, Jews begrudged anyone else partaking of their father's table. Rupert, like Joachim after him, pleaded with Jews to understand and accept their serving role which had opened the way for Gentiles to partake of salvation. As we have just seen, Rupert hoped that the hard hand of their Christian masters would encourage Jews to perform their theological service and convert.[19]

As Christian scholars flexed their intellectual muscles to engage more fully with Christian truths using the tools of reason, they were stimulated to use those same tools further to explore the relationship between Christianity and Judaism. And so, as Amos Funkenstein has demonstrated, reason became an integral component of twelfth-century Christian–Jewish disputations.[20] An excellent example is how Odo of Cambrai (d. 1113) made the Jewish interlocutor in his *Disputation with the Jew, Leo, Concerning the Advent of Christ, Son of God* ask the following provocative question:

> *In one thing especially we laugh at you and think that you are crazy.*
> *You say that God was conceived within his mother's womb, surrounded by*
> *a vile fluid, and suffered enclosure within this foul prison for nine months*
> *when finally, in the tenth month, he emerged from her private parts (who*
> *is not embarrassed by such a scene!). Thus you attribute to God what is*
> *unbecoming, which we would not do without great embarrassment.*

This question opened the way for Odo to explain how rational Christians were as they used their reason to look beyond the smutty details of a woman's anatomy to fathom the mystery of the Son of God assuming flesh from the Virgin Mary. Jews, on the other hand, were much more animal-like. Lacking reason they could only judge by their senses.[21] Odo's rhetorical Jew served him well as an irrational foil for the brilliant rationality of new Christian scholarship. Animal-like Jews were a recurrent theme in Peter the Venerable's diatribe against Judaism. According to the Abbot of Cluny Jewish reason was prevented from functioning properly by the diabolical contents of the Talmud. In an intellectual climate where possession of reason and its effective use were considered the very hallmark of what it meant to be human, accusations of irrationality mattered. What drove the stakes even higher was the fact that Jews did ridicule the doctrine of the Incarnation and Virgin Birth because to their minds it was totally incompatible with reason. Around 1170 in Narbonne the Jewish exegete of the Bible and expert in grammar, Joseph Kimhi, for example, used his *Book of the Covenant* to demonstrate how irrational Christian faith in the Incarnation was. He declared that his reason did not permit him to 'diminish the greatness of God' by imagining that God 'needlessly entered the womb of a woman, the filthy, foul bowels of a female, compelling the living God to be born of a woman'.[22] The overlap between Christian questions concerning the rationality of the Incarnation and Jewish objections makes us realise just how much was at stake when Christian scholars sought rational explanations for the doctrines of their faith. As David Timmer has intimated, it was more than ironic that Jews involuntarily served Christian scholars by stimulating them ever more to further investigation of their faith.[23]

The Talmud

It was Peter Alfonsi who was the first to introduce the Talmud properly to Christian scholars of north-western Europe. Peter used the myriad of anecdotes of the Talmud to prove that Judaism was less rational than Christianity and Islam. Much of this had, of course, to do with his own need to justify his conversion to Christianity. Alfonsi, as Peter the Venerable would do after him, used Talmudic stories in which God was described anthropomorphically as, for instance, crying over the misfortunes of the Jews or ceding an argument to rabbis debating the finer points of law, to demonstrate that Jews blasphemed against God by describing him in human terms. We can see here how Christian polemicists turned Jewish objections against the Incarnation inside out to accuse Jews of precisely what Jews accused Christians of: demeaning God by making him too much like a man. A great deal has been written about the impact of the Talmud on Christian–Jewish relations. Christians were shocked at the existence of such an extensive corpus of Jewish post-biblical material. This would seem to give the lie to the Augustinian idea of Jews bearing witness to Christianity by carrying the books of the Hebrew Bible. Christians were confronted with the fact that Jews were not the Augustinian 'milestones' they had imagined them to be. Far from remaining 'senseless and unmoving' they had fashioned for themselves authoritative texts which not only went beyond the letter of the Bible but also contained material which seemed to ridicule the Virgin Mary and Jesus Christ. As Jeremy Cohen has argued so forcefully, all of this seemed to negate the principle which had secured a place for Jews in Christian society. As we know the Talmud was actually put on trial for blasphemy in Paris in 1240 at the behest of Pope Gregory IX and with the co-operation of King Louis IX. Yehiel of Paris was given the unrewarding task of defending the Talmud against the allegations brought against it. But by the time the Talmud was put on trial in 1263 in Barcelona at the court of King James I something had changed. Sections of the Talmud were now being used to prove the truth of Christianity, in this case that the Messiah had come and that he was Jesus Christ. These arguments were put forward by the Jewish convert Paul, who had entered the Dominican order and who was hell-bent on converting as many of his former co-religionists as he could. His private agenda meshed well with the wide-ranging missionary aims of the Dominican order of the second half of the thirteenth century which trained its preachers in Hebrew and Arabic so that they could engage with Jews and Muslims, as it were, on their own ground. The spokesman for the Jewish community was Nachmanides. As Chazan has argued, Barcelona was in many ways a practice run for the Dominicans to see what they could achieve by using the Talmud in support of Christian truths. This led among other things to the production of the *Pugio Fidei* by the Dominican Ramon Martí around 1278, which marshalled a myriad of texts from the Hebrew Bible, the Talmud and rabbinical material to prove to Jews the truth of Christianity. This kind of argument was incorporated into the mendicant sermons Jews were forced to attend in their synagogues as part of the mendicant programme of conversion. Nachmanides's report of the Barcelona affair was in large part designed to arm Jews against Christian use of the Talmud and other rabbinical material. A contemporary of Nachmanides and fellow rabbi in Barcelona was Solomon ibn Adret. Rabbi Solomon's writings aimed, among other things, to arm Jews against the use Christians were making of Jewish material. The prolific Catalan missionary Ramon Llull (d. 1315–16) was someone who was very taken with the new conversion programme. His approach to Judaism, in so far as it could serve his passion for conversion, was, in fact, refreshingly positive. He freely availed himself of Jewish thought, in particular the mystical ruminations of contemporaries such as Solomon ibn Adret, to fashion a comprehensive 'art' which was designed to convert all unbelievers to Christianity.[24]

For Jews the official attacks on the Talmud were profoundly disturbing. It was as if the powers-that-be were reneging on their service contract that had effectively been in place for centuries. The basic assumption underlying the Jewish presence in Christian society had been that as long as Jews stuck to the boundaries which had been set for them by Christians, in the interests of Christians, and as long as Jews did not try to deviate from what they had always been doing, they would be left alone to follow the dictates of their faith. Christian ignorance of the rich material of the Talmud and Christian speculation whether contemporary Jews were Jewish heretics because they adhered to the Talmud did not make the Talmud a novelty. And for all the condemnation of the Talmud and the continuing instances of censorship of passages which were considered to be insulting to Christianity, the papacy, for its part, was, in the final analysis, reluctant to deprive Jews altogether of the texts which they needed to practise their religion.[25] In the context of our investigation it is, indeed, striking how quickly the Talmud was pressed into Christian service, becoming a new and threatening tool in the hands of Christian missionary preachers. Considering the Talmud debate from the perspective of Jewish service allows us to move away from the narrow constraints of judging Christian–Jewish relations solely on the basis of Augustine's theory of witness. We need to remember that witnessing to the truth of Christianity through the books of the Hebrew Bible was only one of the many types of service Jews were thought to provide to Christian society. We need to recall that Gregory the Great did not refer to Jewish witness in his legislation concerning Jews. The impact of Christian knowledge of the Talmud should be seen in the context of increased Christian knowledge of contemporary Jewish exegesis and other forms of Jewish intellectual activity. The crux of the matter was that Christian churchmen were forced to come to terms with the fact that their flesh-and-blood Jewish neighbours and the theoretical Jews of their theological ruminations were the same people. This led to ever-more-searching questions as to whether the role these real Jews played in Christian society accorded with theological ideas of Jewish service. This brings us neatly to the vexed question of Jewish usury.

Usury

As we have seen, the issue of usury or moneylending was a veritable breed-
ing ground for troubled Christian–Jewish relations. Antipathy to charging
interest on loans ultimately went back to the Bible, in particular
Deuteronomy 23: 19–20:

> *Thou shalt not lend to thy brother money to usury, nor corn, nor any other*
> *thing: But to the stranger. To thy brother thou shalt lend that which he*
> *wanteth, without usury: that the Lord thy God may bless thee in all thy*
> *works in the land, which thou shalt go in to possess.*

Any interest on loans was thus considered to be 'shameful gain' (*turpe
lucrum*). By the second half of the eleventh century this gain was not just
regarded as being shameful, it was considered to be nothing short of theft.
Rather than doing any real work, usurers made their money through the
passage of time. In effect then they sold time which was not theirs to sell,
for time belonged to God. To Guibert of Nogent's mind Christian and
Jewish usurers were thieves who fed off the needs of the poor. Peter
Lombard's *Sentences* of the mid-twelfth century categorised usury among
the crimes of fraud, rapine and theft. The Third Lateran Council of 1179
stipulated that open usurers should be excommunicated and not given a
Christian burial. Peter the Chanter's circle waxed hotly against the evils of
Christian and Jewish usury with Fulk of Neuilly undertaking an anti-usury
preaching tour in northern France between 1195 and *c.* 1200 and Robert
of Courson fulminating against it in the early thirteenth century. Gratian's
Decretum and Gregory IX's *Decretals* contain numerous texts condemning
usury. By the thirteenth century Aristotle's vilification of usury joined
biblical strictures of it. The context of the whole debate about the propriety
of profiting from loans was the developing economy of the central Middle
Ages. What Christian theologians, churchmen and, indeed, princes found
themselves having to do was to work out how economic ideas which had
emerged in a period dominated by a gift economy should be applied to
their own era which increasingly transformed itself into a profit economy.[26]

Bernard seemed prepared to countenance Jewish usury, if only to
remind Christians of Jewish service in this respect so as to prevent violence
against Jews at a time of crisis. But this did not mean he did not abhor the
practice of usury and Jewish involvement in it. We can see this clearly in his

vicious attacks on Anacletus II, the rival Pope to Innocent II in the 1130s. Anacletus was Petrus Pierleoni, the grandson of a Jewish convert. Jews might serve Christians but to Bernard's mind no one of recent Jewish descent from a family of (Christian) bankers engaged in usury was suitable to become the *servus servorum* ('servant of servants'), i.e. the Pope.[27] The complicating factor in all of these discussions about usury was that Jewish, and Christian, moneylending was needed to supply capital to the burgeoning economy. And princes profited from Jewish moneylending through taxation. As we have noted, the problem was exacerbated by the fact that Christian borrowers were indirectly put under pressure when princes made monetary demands on 'their' Jews. In England William of Newburgh felt that Jewish lenders were lording over Christian borrowers instead of serving them as a reminder of Christ's Passion. Robert Grosseteste warned the Countess of Winchester not to benefit from Jewish usury in the early 1230s; in his view Jews should live a life of toil from the land as their just punishment for the Crucifixion. The lords whom they served should benefit from their hard work, rather than the Jews themselves. Usury to his mind was a cruel practice because it took advantage of those who were vulnerable. And although Deuteronomy seemed to permit Jews to charge Christians interest, Psalm 14(5):5 ('he that hath not put out his money to usury') and Ezekiel 18:8 ('Hath not lent upon usury, nor taken any increase') did not. In other words Jewish usury should not be tolerated. Thomas Aquinas and John Peckham voiced views on Jewish usury in 1270 in their responses to questions which had been sent to them by Margaret, the daughter of Louis IX, who had married Duke John I of Brabant earlier that year. Margaret wanted to know to what extent it might be permissible to benefit from Jewish taxes when Jews earned their money through the practice of usury. Aquinas responded by saying that princes could not freely expend the money they collected from Jews engaged in usury. As far as possible the money had to be used to make restitution to those who had been made to pay interest. For the rest it had to be used for pious purposes. Peckham went further in his advice that rulers should force Jews to live by the toil of their hands or from trade. Jews should be kept on an as short as possible a string to encourage them to convert. Although there is no indication that Aquinas's and Peckham's words had any effect on the Jews of Brabant, Peckham had considerable influence on the fate of the Jews in England when he became Archbishop of Canterbury in 1279.[28] For these theologians Christian society should not avail itself of the service of Jewish usury.

As Kenneth Stow has demonstrated, it is ironic that papal rulings on Jewish usury were, in fact, more lenient than the opinions of theologians and the stipulations by canonists. The first item of papal legislation on Jewish usury was Innocent III's letter of 1198 to the Archbishop of Narbonne in which Jews (and Christians) were forbidden to charge interest to crusaders. The relevant canon of the Fourth Lateran Council ruled that repayment of these debts and payment of interest accrued on them had to be put off until the crusaders had returned home. Another canon from the same council ruled against Jews charging *immoderate* interest. Implicit in the ruling was that a moderate rate of interest fitted within the parameters of Jewish service. For canonists this went too far. In their influential commentaries in the *Decretals* Ramon of Penyafort (d. 1275) and Hostiensis interpreted Innocent's rulings as meaning that any interest was forbidden.[29]

Jews were equally troubled about charging interest on loans. But in Jewish circles these discussions were not just held against the backdrop of the developing money economy; they touched on the stark realities of Jewish economic survival. Thus Rabbi Tam allowed Jews to engage in moneylending because he recognised that this was the only way they could make the money they needed to pay their taxes and feed their children. But he did more than that. As Haym Soloveitchik has demonstrated so poignantly, he encouraged his *Tosafist* followers, who were inclined to go beyond even the most meticulous observance of the law, to avail themselves of a loophole in the law which made loans between Jews possible by using non-Jewish middlemen or strawmen to create the fiction that the loans were not being arranged between Jews. Tam's words brokered no misunderstanding: 'I have dwelt on this arrangement at length so that everyone should know it is fully permissible.'[30]

Ideas that the practice of usury corrupted society were dangerous for Jews. As moneylending steadily became the staple activity of Jews in England and northern France by the end of the twelfth century, these attacks threatened their livelihood and the very essence of the service they provided to princes which ensured them the right to live in their lands. As theologians raged against the evils of usury, princes were compelled to find a balance between allowing Jews to perform an unsavoury service which was useful to them and being seen to profit from an evil which was deemed to corrupt Christian society. We have seen how princes such as Louis IX of France and Henry III and Edward I of England internalised rhetoric against Jewish usury and began to put increasing pressures on Jews and strictures on Jewish moneylending; Jewish moneylending became more and more dishonourable and less and less profitable. The question which then loomed was how distasteful and dishonourable this aspect of Jewish service could become before it was deemed to outweigh the benefits other aspects of Jewish service were supposed to provide to Christendom.

At the same time Jewish polemicists railed against Christian attacks on Jewish usury and the idea that Jews were corrupting Christian society. Joseph Kimhi, for example, insisted that Jews were not only meticulous about not charging fellow Jews interest, they, unlike Christians, did not make profits from selling their coreligionists commodities such as wheat or wine on credit. He was adamant that the tenor of Psalm 14(5): 5 did not differ from Deuteronomy 23:21. According to Kimhi, Jews were morally superior to Christians in that there was less thieving and oppression among Jews than among Christians. Children were raised better, Jewish women did not prostitute themselves; Jews freely offered each other hospitality and sustained the poor in their communities. Nor was Kimhi overly impressed by holy Christians who separated themselves from the world. Pious Christians were in an acute minority and, as far as Kimhi was concerned, it was a well-known fact that unmarried priests and bishops were not as continent as they should be. Rabbi Meir ben Simeon made the point that where there were no Jewish moneylenders, Christian moneylenders stepped in who charged higher rates of interest. Even Grosseteste compared Jewish moneylenders favourably to the Cahorsins, the Christian usurers from Cahors.[31] Bernard's words regarding the usefulness of Jewish moneylenders ring in our ears.

Alleged Jewish violence

Peter the Chanter was not just interested in usury. He, as Peter Lombard before him and others after him, was keen to come to grips with the exact nature of Jewish guilt for the Crucifixion. Did the Jews of the New Testament know what they were doing when they clamoured for Jesus's death? Did they know he was God; did they know he was the Messiah? And why were they so keen for Jesus to be killed?[32] What we have here is

Christian scholars, in effect, working out the precise nature of the service Jews were thought to have rendered Christianity through their participation in the Crucifixion and the intention behind it. This aspect of Jewish service was, of course, by far the most complicated and the most emotive one of all. Without the Crucifixion, there would have been no salvific Resurrection. At the same time, serving Christianity through the act of deliberate or unwitting or wilfully ignorant deicide was hardly a recommendation for good relations between Christians and Jews. In the course of the twelfth century deliberate deicide, rather than unwitting deicide, was added to the repertoire of Jewish service. Jewish disbelief in Jesus and his teaching was deemed to have been deliberate. This was thought to have been caused by their pride, envy and malice.[33] As with the case of usury, language like this begged the question of how much vituperation the concept of Jewish service could bear before its demerits seemed to outweigh the benefits it was supposed to render.

The same milieu which racked its brains about the rationale of the Incarnation, the Virgin Birth and the intentions of the participants in the Crucifixion also produced the ritual-murder accusations, blood libels and host-desecration accusations we have discussed at length in the previous chapter. In these bizarre accusations we can also see how Jews were made to serve Christians. Through their (deliberate) disbelief, Jews served to bring out in sharp relief Christian belief; through their treacherous acts Jews functioned as useful foils voicing unspeakable doubts so that these could be quelled through the miracles of Christ and the Virgin, bringing Christians closer to their God. And throughout these stories clear demarcations were made between Christians and Jews. Once again the emotive and brutally negative nature of this kind of service could lead to Christians wanting to rid themselves of Jewish service altogether.

The *Song of Songs*

Demarcations were also made by using Jews as foils for bad behaviour as a preaching aid to improve Christian society. A good example of this can be found in the cycle of commentaries on the *Song of Songs* by Bernard of Clairvaux, Gilbert of Hoyland (d. 1172) and John of Ford (d. 1214). These sermons were an integral part of the Cistercian quest for God and it is striking how often Jews were mentioned. References to the expectation of Jewish conversion at the end of time could be positive enough. But usually Jewish beliefs and alleged Jewish behaviour were presented as errant and despicable. Bernard's anti-Jewish language in his *Song of Songs* sermons has been studied by David Berger. Striking is the way Bernard used Jews as a foil to lampoon the ills he wished to eradicate from Christian society. The commentaries of Gilbert of Hoyland and John of Ford revealed both men's interest in Jews. In sermon 31 of John of Ford, for example, John combined a fervent desire for Israel to convert with chilling language of abuse because they had not already done so.

> *But how tragic is your lot, house of Israel! You have set up in your heart, like twin doorposts, a complete refusal to feel fear or sorrow at the shedding of such great blood, and for a lintel, you have laid down a defiant rejection of the sense of shame . . . . Yet even to this day, the blood of his only Son cries out to the Father from the gateway of this house. There is nowhere for the sons of Israel to turn aside, they cannot go in or out, without this blood forcing itself on their attention, their accuser and their judge, but* also their deliverer.

He felt that there is something truly terrible about Jewish wickedness which did not fear Jesus as God or even respect him as a man and he drew a negative comparison with Pontius Pilate's regard for Jesus.[34] The ambiguity towards Jews and their service is palpable in these works as was the use these Cistercians made of Jews and Judaism in their interpretation of the *Song of Songs*.

Like Isaiah's vision of God's throne, the *Song of Songs* was used by Christians and Jews for diametrically opposed purposes. Both Jews and Christians had to make sense of the unusually erotic contents of this particular component of the biblical canon. For Jews the *Song* celebrated the love between God and his people Israel; for Christians it was the celebration of the marriage between Christ and his Church, or for an increasing number of Christian exegetes from the twelfth century onwards, the Virgin Mary, who intriguingly took on the role of the bride of Christ together with her role as his mother. In all of this the ultimate conversion of Jews was an essential component and this aspect of Jewish service could be assigned a positive role, as for example, in commentaries on the *Song* of Honorius Augustodunensis (d. *c.* 1140), which bring to mind the positive ratiocinations of Joachim of Fiore.[35] This is Jewish service in its most honourable guise and this brings us to a special area in Christian–Jewish relations in which Jewish service played a much more positive role than in others: Christian Hebraism.

Christian Hebraism

By the twelfth century a number of Christians showed genuine awareness of how much they needed to learn from Jews about the language of the Hebrew Bible and several layers of its meaning. An early example of the awareness of the need for Hebrew in Christian–Jewish polemics comes from the work of someone called Odo who wrote a theological compendium, the *Ysagoge in Theologiam*, in England in the 1140s. Odo was strongly influenced by the work of Jerome, who had used Hebrew extensively in the production of the Vulgate translation of the Hebrew Bible in the fourth century. Following Jerome, Odo felt that all kinds of Christian truth were embedded in the original language of Hebrew. Recent analysis of Odo's Hebrew texts reveals that his knowledge of that language and, indeed, biblical Aramaic was impressive.[36]

Other Christians such as the Cistercian Abbot Stephen Harding (1109–34) called in the help of Jews to make sure the Latin version of the Old Testament was as accurate as possible. Canons of the Parisian School of St Victor consulted Jews to gain insight into Jewish biblical commentaries in their search for the historical meaning of the biblical text. Interestingly enough, Andrew of St Victor (d. 1175) did not always feel compelled to refute Jewish exegesis where it clashed with Christian interpretations. His colleague Richard of St Victor reproached Andrew for judaising, but Andrew, following in the footsteps of his teacher Hugh of St Victor (d. 1141), was using Jewish material to acquire a solid basis for subsequent spiritual interpretations. Peter Comestor (d. 1187), the author of the hugely influential *Historia scholastica* ('Scholastic History') which was a retelling of the Bible, and Peter the Chanter made much use of Andrew's work.[37]

Particularly striking is the knowledge of Hebrew of one of John of Salisbury's close associates, Herbert of Bosham, who served with John in the household of Thomas Becket. Herbert had a special interest in the Psalms. He took the trouble to pull together his master Peter Lombard's commentaries on the Gallican Psalter. But spiritual exegesis was not his first love. It was the literal understanding of the Psalms that he craved. To this end he not only went back to Jerome's translation of the Psalms, the so-called *Hebraica*, he made extensive use of Rashi's exegesis on the texts. But remarkable as Herbert's use of Rashi was, we need to remember that as far as he was concerned a sounder understanding of the letter served to reach a more profound spiritual sense of the text. Nor did Herbert fail to castigate Rashi when he rejected the messianic reading of Psalms such as Psalm 2 and Psalm 21(22), which were pivotal for Christology.[38]

In the thirteenth century exegetes such as Alexander Neckam (d. 1217) consulted Jews; a Hebrew grammar was put together by Roger Bacon (d. 1292).[39] For Christian Hebraists Jews had to be more than Augustine's mute and unchanging 'milestones'. But this did not take away their interest in Jewish service. However great their regard was for Hebrew and for the ability of their Jewish contemporaries to introduce them to a world of unknown intellectual treasures, the fundamental purpose of their foray into what we might nowadays call Jewish Studies was *not* to build a bridge to Judaism. It was to gain the expertise they needed to secure ever-more professionally the underpinnings of Christian exegesis. And for some it made them more effective in their attempt to convince Jews to convert.

Conclusion

Increased knowledge of Hebrew which allowed Christian exegetes to explore the Hebrew Bible on their own and greater concentration on the power of rational arguments might have caused Christians to wonder whether they needed Jewish witness to Christian truth as much as Augustine thought they did. In my earlier publications I concluded that these developments helped create an atmosphere in which there was increasingly less room for Jews in Christian society. But witness was only one type of service Jews were expected to render to Christianity; Jews continued to perform many other forms of service such as functioning as foils for Christian behaviour, as proving Jewish guilt for the Crucifixion and as typifying the kind of punishment God was supposed to mete out to non-Christians. 'Service' is, in fact, a much better marker for the role Jews were meant to play within Christian–Jewish relations than 'witness'. Theoretically, their service was meant to delineate the correct relationship between those following the Old Law and those following the law of the

Gospels. The neutrality of the term makes it possible for the concept of service to cover the full range of ambiguities underlying Christian attitudes to Judaism. In practical terms, the concept of service covers all the ways that Jews could prove beneficial to those who protected them. The determining factor for the position of Jews in Christian polities was the way in which temporal authority managed to steer a course between concepts of dishonourable and honourable types of Jewish service and create a sustainable role for flesh-and-blood Jews. A perennial problem in Christian–Jewish relations was that of containment. Fierce language and rituals castigating Jews in order to let off steam, shocking legends in order to demarcate Christian from Jew and bolster Christianity, condemnation of Jews as a tool to perfect Christian society, all this could take place in an atmosphere of give and take between Christians and Jews in the same way that Jews had their own vituperative arsenal of words and rituals aimed at Christianity. It was up to temporal authority to make sure that any verbal abuse remained verbal and did not become physical. It was up to princes to ensure that negative views concerning Jews did not impinge on Jewish survival.

We have seen throughout this book that some princes were far more effective than others in this respect and that others deliberately used negative imagery of Jews in pursuit of their own particular interests. We have noted the importance of the nature of Jewish economic service in this context. However useful moneylending was to the economy of Latin Christendom in this period, it carried with it theological and social opprobrium. We have seen the negative impact on Jews where their economic activity was primarily limited to moneylending, as in England and Zarfat, in contrast to Jewish economic diversity in the Latin Mediterranean and to a certain extent in Ashkenaz. The ruthless exploitation by English kings of Jewish moneylenders provoked anti-Jewish feeling among their hard-pressed Christian debtors and in the end the Jews themselves had little left with which to serve their royal masters. In France kings seem to have internalised negative ecclesiastical views about Jews as one of the many tools to expand their own authority at expense of the barons. Greater economic diversity is one of the reasons why the Jews of Ashkenaz could integrate as well as they did in the cities of Germany. Indeed it is striking how the German emperors availed themselves of an increasingly constrictive vocabulary of Jewish protection as they lost ever more ground in their competition for power to princes and cities. This helps us understand better how in Germany Jews could be deemed to be *servi* of the royal chamber while at the same time functioning as citizens in a number of important cities.

The concept of service also helps us to recognise that there was no fundamental difference between Christian attitudes towards Jews in Ashkenaz, Zarfat and Sefarad. The positive approach of the Christian kings of eleventh-, twelfth- and thirteenth-century Iberia was not derived from their rejection of negative ecclesiastical views about Jews. As we have seen, they functioned within the same broad framework of Christian theological views as did everyone else in Christian society. The difference in Iberia was that those views had to compete with a centuries-old Muslim tradition of *convivencia* which was far less diffident about the role of Jews in contemporary polities than traditional Christian ones. But at least as important were the exigencies of the conquests of the twelfth and thirteenth centuries which meant that pragmatism had to count for a lot more than theology. In the circumstances, it makes sense that well into the thirteenth century the monarchs of the peninsula were not as bothered by the ambiguities presented to them by Christian thinking about Jews as their counterparts in the north, since these monarchs used Jewish service to consolidate their royal authority. The developments in Iberian approaches to Jews in the course of the fourteenth and fifteenth centuries take us far beyond the framework of this study, but it is worth mentioning that in the wake of persecutions in 1391 in Castile, Aragon, Valencia and Majorca, the problem of forced conversion once again raised its ugly head in Iberia, bringing in its wake all of the predictable suspicions of false Jewish converts threatening the fabric of Christian society. Pragmatic use of Jewish service in one period was no guarantee for pragmatism in another. At any particular time, princes throughout Latin Christendom had to consider to what extent they continued to benefit from concrete Jewish service. When the nature of practical Jewish service began to suffer from theological ideas about the need of Jewish service to epitomise Jewish subjection to Christianity, princes had to consider whether it was worth their while to continue to give Jews a space in their body politic. As we have seen, in France and England princes divested themselves of Jewish service when it seemed more beneficial for them to do so, notwithstanding any theoretical theological service Jews were thought to perform by ecclesiastical norms. Ironically, it was the institutional Church which never lost the idea that for all its vituperation of Jews there was room for Jews in Christendom. The many canons of Lateran IV which circumscribed Jewish activities and behaviour were not meant to excise Jews from Christendom. On the contrary, it was a way of making sure that Jews would occupy the 'right' kind of place in Christian society. And for all the restrictions inflicted upon them, Jews managed to maintain a presence in papal Avignon and Comtat-Venaissin after Jews had been expelled from every other part of what now is France. Of all cities in Latin Christendom, Rome is the city with the oldest continuous Jewish community.

As for Jews, they, of course, knew full well that their security hinged on how useful they could be to the princes who offered them protection. We have seen how in the early fourteenth century Asher ben Yehiel made it very plain that in his view Jews were preserved on account of the revenue they paid to the powers-that-be. But that does not mean Jews accepted the parameters Christians attached to their service. Rashi flatly rejected Christian notions that the Hebrew Bible prefigured Christ. We have seen how Jewish thinkers such as Joseph Kimhi, Judah ben Isaac of Paris, Meir of Rothenburg and Meir ben Simeon of Narbonne railed against lords who restricted Jewish freedom of movement or seized Jewish property. It is fitting to end with the statement by Yehiel of Paris in his defence of the Talmud in 1240 in which he is reported to have said: 'our bodies lie within your power, not our souls'.[40] For however much Jews were deemed to be in the service of Latin Christendom, the exegetical, liturgical, legal, philosophical and literary achievements of the scholars of medieval Zarfat, Ashkenaz and Sefarad continue to serve Jewish cultural life to this very day.

Notes and references

1 Photograph courtesy of The Art Gallery Collection/Alamy; Schreckenberg, 426; Heinz Schreckenberg, *The Jews in Christian Art* (London, 1996), plates 3, 8 (cf. cover), 12, pp. 67, 70, 72.

2 T.P. Campbell, 'Liturgical Drama and Community Discourse', in *The Liturgy of the Medieval Church*, 635–7; K. Young, *The Drama of the Medieval Church*, vol. 2 (Oxford, 1933), 125–71 (text, 154–65); E.K. Chambers, *The Mediaeval Stage* (Oxford, 1903), 52–6; G. Dahan, 'L'Interprétation de

l'Ancien Testament dans les drames réligieux (xie–xiiie siècles)', *Romania* 100 (1979), 71–103.

3 Gilbert Dahan, 'L'Article *Iudei* de la *Summa Abel* de Pierre le Chantre', *Revue des Études Augustiniennes* 27 (1981), 106–7, 125–6; John Watt, 'Parisian Theologians and the Jews: Peter Lombard and Peter Cantor', in P. Biller and B. Dobson (eds), *The Medieval Church: Universities, Heresy, and the Religious Life. Essays in Honour of Gordon Leff* (Woodbridge, 1999), 72–4, trans. of Chobham on pp. 73–4; Thomas of Chobham, *Summa Confessorum*, Art. 7. 4.6.11, in Frederick Broomfield (ed.), *Analecta Mediaevalia Namurcensia*, 25 (Louvain, 1968), 434; Augustine, *De Civitate Dei*, 19.15, ed. Bernhard Dombart and Alfons Kalb, CCSL 48 (Turnhout, 1955), 682; trans. R.W. Dyson (Cambridge, 1998), 942–3.

4 Isidore, *Quaestiones in Vetus Testamentum*, in *Genesin*, Chapter 8, PL 83, 235–6; Augustine, *Contra Faustum*, XII.23, trans. Richard Stothert in Philip Schaff (ed.), *A Select Library of the Nicene and Post-Nicene Fathers of the Christian Church*, vol. 4: *St. Augustin: The Writings against the Manichaeans and against the Donatists* (Grand Rapids, MI, repr. 1974), 190–1; Jeremy Cohen, *Living Letters of the Law. Ideas of the Jew in Medieval Christianity* (Berkeley, CA, 1999), 29.

5 Jennifer A. Shea, 'The Influence of the Cult of the Virgin Mary on Christian Perceptions of Jews, with Particular Reference to the Role of Marian Stories in England and France, *c.* 1050–*c.* 1300 (Cambridge University PhD, 2004), 93; José M. Canal (ed.), *El Libro "De Laudibus et Miraculis Sanctae Mariae" de Guillermo de Malmesbury, OSB (+c. 1143)* (Rome, 1968), 74–6; Bernhard Blumenkranz, *Juifs et Chrétiens dans le monde occidental, 430–1096* (Paris, 1960), 382–3; *Ademari Cabannensis Chronicon*, III, 52, ed. P. Bourgain with R. Landes and G. Pon, CCCM, 129 (Turnhout, 1999), 171; David Nirenberg, *Communities of Violence. Persecution of Minorities in the Middle Ages* (Princeton, NJ, 1996), 200–30.

6 Bernard of Clairvaux, *De Consideratione* I, III.4, in *Sancti Bernardi opera*, ed. Jean Leclercq and Henri Rochais, 3 (Rome, 1963), 398, translation taken from *Five Books on Consideration*, trans. John D. Anderson and Elizabeth T. Kennan, Cistercian Fathers Series, 27 (Kalamazoo, MI, 1976), 30.

7 In *Genesim*, IX, 4, in *Ruperti Tuitiensis de sacra Trinitatis et operibus eius*, ed. Hrabanus Haacke, CCCM 21 (Turnhout, 1971), 536.

8 Grayzel I, no. 18, 114–17; John A. Watt, 'Jews and Christians in the Gregorian *Decretals*', in Diana Wood (ed.), *Christianity and Judaism*, Studies in Church History, 29 (Oxford, 1992), 103–5; translations from p. 105.

9 See Chapter 8; text in M. Halamish, 'An Early Version of "Alenu le-Shabeah"', *Sinai* 110 (1992), 263; trans. taken from I.J. Yuval, *Two Nations in Your Womb. Perceptions of Jews and Christians in Late Antiquity and the*

Middle Ages, trans. B. Harshav and J. Chipman (Berkeley, CA, 2006), 119, see also pp. 193–6.

10 Rabbi Jacob ben Jehuda Hazan of London, *The Etz Hayyim*, ed. I. Brodie, vol. 1 (Jerusalem, 1962), 90; D.J. van der Sluis *et al.* (eds), *Elke Morgen Nieuw* (Neukirchen-Vluyn, 1978), 257–66, 393–6.

11 *Etz Hayyim*, vol. 1, 329–30; Yuval, *Two Nations*, 92–134; Susan Einbinder, 'The Jewish Martyrs of Blois', in Thomas Head (ed.), *Medieval Hagiography. An Anthology* (New York, 2000), 554–5; I.J. Yuval, 'Passover in the Middle Ages', in Paul F. Bradshaw and Lawrence A. Hoffman (eds), *Passover and Easter. Origin and History to Modern Times* (Notre Dame, IN, 1999), 127–60.

12 Yuval, *Two Nations*; Nirenberg, *Communities of Violence*.

13 Sholom A. Singer, *Medieval Jewish Mysticism: Book of the Pious* [partial translation of *Sefer Hasidim*](Wheeling, IL, 1971), 35.

14 David Berger (ed.), *The Jewish–Christian Debate in the High Middle Ages. A Critical Edition of the Nizzahon Vetus* (Philadelphia, PA, 1979), no. 212, p. 207 [Hebrew, p. 145], 329; Grayzel II, 246–8.

15 Anna Sapir Abulafia, 'The Bible in Jewish–Christian Dialogue', in Richard Marsden and E. Ann Matter (eds), *The New Cambridge History of the Bible*, forthcoming; Yehuda HaLevi, *The Kuzari. In Defense of the Despised Faith*, trans. and annotated by N. Daniel Korobkin (Northvale, NJ, 1998), 150; Van der Sluis, *Elke Morgen Nieuw*, 167–76. The idea of reciprocal engagement of medieval Jews and Christians with each other in all manner of social and religious encounters lies at the heart of Yuval's *Two Nations*.

16 *JLSEMA*, 217; R.N. Swanson, *The Twelfth-century Renaissance* (Manchester, 1999), 69–70.

17 Anna Sapir Abulafia, *Christians and Jews in the Twelfth-century Renaissance* (London, 1995); idem, 'Intellectual and Cultural Creativity', in Daniel Power (ed.), *The Central Middle Ages* (Oxford, 2006), 149–77; Marcia L. Colish, *Medieval Foundations of the Western Intellectual Tradition, 400–1400* (New Haven, CT, 1997).

18 Anna Sapir Abulafia, 'The Conquest of Jerusalem: Joachim of Fiore and the Jews', in Marcus Bull and Norman Housley (eds), *The Experience of Crusading*, vol. 1. *Western Approaches* (Cambridge, 2003), 135–7; Beatrice Hirsch-Reich, 'Joachim von Fiore und das Judentum', in P. Wilpert (ed.), *Judentum im Mittelalter. Beiträge zum christlich-jüdischen Gespräch* (Berlin, 1966), 228–63; Bernard McGinn, *The Calabrian Abbot: Joachim of Fiore in the History of Western Thought* (New York, 1985), 161–203; Robert E. Lerner, *The Feast of Saint Abraham. Medieval Millenarians and the Jews* (Philadelphia, PA, 2001).

19 Anna Sapir Abulafia, 'The Ideology of Reform and Changing Ideas Concerning Jews in the Works of Rupert of Deutz and Hermannus Quondam Iudeus', in idem, *Christians and Jews in Dispute. Disputational Literature and the Rise of Anti-Judaism in the West (c. 1000–1150)* (Aldershot, 1998), XV; David E. Timmer 'The Religious Significance of Judaism for Twelfth-century Monastic Exegesis: A Study in the Thought of Rupert of Deutz, *c.* 1070–1129' (Notre Dame PhD, 1983) and 'Biblical Exegesis and the Jewish–Christian Controversy in the Early Twelfth Century', *Church History* 58 (1989), 309–21.

20 Amos Funkenstein, 'Basic Types of Christian Anti-Jewish Polemics', *Viator* 2 (1971), 373–82.

21 Translation from Odo of Tournai, *On Original Sin, and A Disputation with the Jew, Leo, Concerning the Advent of Christ, Son of God: Two Theological Treatises*, trans. I.M. Resnick (Philadelphia, PA, 1994), 95; Anna Sapir Abulafia, 'Christian Imagery of Jews in the Twelfth Century: A Look at Odo of Cambrai and Guibert of Nogent,' in idem, *Christians and Jews in Dispute*, X.

22 Frank Talmage (trans.), *The Book of the Covenant* (Toronto, 1972), 36–7; Hannah Trautner-Kromann, *Shield and Sword* (Tübingen, 1993), 69–71; Robert Chazan, *Fashioning Jewish Identity in Medieval Western Christendom* (Cambridge, 2004), 254–8.

23 Timmer, 'The Religious Significance', 209.

24 Jeremy Cohen, *The Friars and the Jews. The Evolution of Medieval Anti-Judaism* (Ithaca, NY, 1982); Robert Chazan, *Daggers of Faith. Thirteenth-century Christian Missionizing and Jewish Response* (Berkeley, CA, 1989) and *Barcelona and Beyond. The Disputation of 1263 and Its Aftermath* (Berkeley, CA, 1992); Harvey J. Hames, *The Art of Conversion. Christianity and Kabbalah in the Thirteenth Century* (Leiden, 2000).

25 Kenneth R. Stow, *Alienated Minority. The Jews of Medieval Latin Europe* (Cambridge, MA, 1992), 251–9.

26 Anna Sapir Abulafia, *Christians and Jews*, 60–2, with references to the literature on p. 152 notes 32–7.

27 Anna Sapir Abulafia, 'The Intellectual and Spiritual Quest for Christ and Central Medieval Persecution of Jews', in *Religious Violence between Christians and Jews: Medieval Roots, Modern Perspectives* (Houndmills, 2002), 73–5.

28 John A. Watt, 'Grosseteste and the Jews: A Commentary on Letter V', in M. O'Carroll (ed.), *Robert Grosseteste and the Beginnings of a British Theological Tradition. Papers Delivered at the* Grosseteste Colloquium *Held at Greyfriars, Oxford on 3rd July 2002* (Rome, 2003), 201–16; Christoph

Cluse, *Studien zur Geschichte der Juden in den mittelalterichen Niederlanden* (Hanover, 2000), 174–85.

29 Kenneth R. Stow, 'Papal and Royal Attitudes toward Jewish Lending in the Thirteenth Century', *Association for Jewish Studies Review* 6 (1981), 161–83.

30 Haym Soloveitchik, 'Religious Law and Change: The Medieval Ashkenazic Example', *Association for Jewish Studies Review* 12 (1987), 219; idem, 'Pawnbroking: A Study in *Ribbit* and of the Halakah in Exile', *Proceedings of the American Academy for Jewish Research* 38–9 (1970–1), 203–68.

31 Talmage, *The Book of the Covenant*, 32–5; Trautner-Kromann, *Shield and Sword*, 65–9; Chazan, *Fashioning Jewish Identity*, 298–304, 105–6; Joseph Shatzmiller, *Shylock Reconsidered. Jews, Moneylending, and Medieval Society* (Berkeley, CA, 1990), 80–1, 97–8.

32 Watt, 'Parisian Theologians', 55–68.

33 Jeremy Cohen, 'The Jews as the Killers of Christ in the Latin Tradition, from Augustine to the Friars', *Traditio* 39 (1983), 1–27 and his *Christ Killers. The Jews and the Passion from the Bible to the Screen* (Oxford, 2007).

34 Quotations from Wendy Beckett (trans.), *John of Ford, Sermons on the Final Verses of the Song of Songs*, vol. 3, Christian Fathers series, 43 (Kalamazoo, MI, 1982), 30–1 (my italics).

35 Jeremy Cohen, 'Synagoga conversa: Honorius Augustodunensis, the Song of Songs, and Christianity's "Eschatalogical Jew"', *Speculum* 79 (2004), 309–40; E. Ann Matter, *The Voice of My Beloved. The Song of Songs in Western Medieval Christianity* (Philadelphia, PA, 1990).

36 Anna Sapir Abulafia, 'Jewish Carnality in Twelfth-century Renaissance Thought', in idem, *Christians and Jews in Dispute*, XII; Hans-Georg von Mutius, *Die Hebräischen Bibelzitate beim Englischen Scholastiker Odo. Versuch einer Revaluation*, Judentum und Umwelt, 78 (Frankfurt am Main, 2006).

37 Beryl Smalley, *The Study of the Bible in the Middle Ages*, 3rd edn (Oxford, 1983), Chapters 3, 4 and 5; Signer, 'Thirteenth-century Christian Hebraism: The *Expositio* on Canticles in MS. VAT. Lat. 1053', in D. Blumenthal (ed.), *Approaches to Judaism in Medieval Times*, vol. 3 (Atlanta, GA, 1988), 91–3; Signer, 'Introduction', *Andreae de Sancto Victore Opera, vi, Expositionem in Ezekielem*, ed. M.A. Signer, CCCM 53E (Turnhout, 1991), ix–xxxvii; Deborah Goodwin, *'Take Hold of the Robe of a Jew'. Herbert of Bosham's Christian Hebraism* (Leiden, 2006), 95–127; Gilbert Dahan, *L'Exégèse chrétienne de la Bible en occident médiévale, XIIe–XIVe siècle* (Paris, 1999), 376–83.

38 Goodwin, *'Take Hold of the Robe of a Jew'*, but also Eva de Visscher, 'The Jewish–Christian Dialogue in Twelfth-century Western Europe: The Hebrew

and Latin Sources of Herbert of Bosham's Commentary on the Psalms' (PhD Leeds, 2003).

39 Gilbert Dahan, *Les Intellectuels Chrétiens et les Juifs au Moyen Âge* (Paris, 1990), 239–41, 253–5, 267, 284; Herbert Loewe, 'Alexander Neckam's Knowledge of Hebrew', *Mediaeval and Renaissance Studies* 4 (1958), 17–34.

40 *CSJMA*, 227; Solomon Grünbaum, *Sefer Vikuah R. Yehiel mi-Paris* (Thorn, 1873), 2.

Further reading

The footnotes to each chapter refer to the studies consulted in writing this book, including specialised works in languages other than English. The purpose of what follows is to provide a select bibliography of mainly English works covering the history of the Jews in Latin Christendom, 1000–1300, organised according to the topics of this book.

General reading
Accessible collections of primary source material in English translation include:

Robert Chazan, *Church, State and Jew in the Middle Ages*, New York, 1980 (henceforth: *CSJMA*) contains a good selection of translations of key Latin and Hebrew documents, as does Jacob R. Marcus, *The Jew in the Medieval World. A Source Book: 315–1791*, rev. edn with an introduction and updated bibliographies by Marc Saperstein, Cincinnati, OH, 1999 (original: 1938).

Lawrence Fine (ed.), *Judaism in Practice from the Middle Ages through the Early Modern Period*, Princeton, NJ, 2001 provides a translation of a rich selection of Hebrew sources.

Solomon Grayzel, *The Church and the Jews in the XIIIth Century. A Study of Their Relations During the Years 1198–1254, Based on the Papal Letters and the Conciliar Decrees of the Period*, rev. edn, New York, 1966, and his *The Church and the Jews in the XIIIth Century*. Volume 2: *1254–1314*, ed. Kenneth R. Stow, Detroit, MI, 1989, provide papal bulls and conciliar material concerning the Jews in Latin and in translation. Shlomo Simonsohn, *The Apostolic See and the Jews: Documents, 492–1404*. Pontifical Institute of Mediaeval Studies: Studies and Texts, 94, Toronto, 1988, provides only the Latin.

Amnon Linder's two collections of legal documents: *The Jews in the Legal Sources of the Early Middle Ages*, Detroit, MI, 1997 (*JLSEMA*) and *The*

Jews in Roman Imperial Legislation, Detroit, MI, 1987 (*JRIL*) are
invaluable for analysing Christian legislative measures vis-à-vis Jews.

Secondary works:

A new overview of the history of the Jews in the medieval West is Robert
Chazan, *The Jews of Medieval Western Christendom, 1000–1500*,
Cambridge, 2006. See also his *Medieval Stereotypes and Modern
Antisemitism*, Berkeley, CA, 1997. Jonathan Elukin's *Living Together
Living Apart. Rethinking Jewish–Christian Relations in the Middle Ages*,
Princeton, NJ, 2007, offers a very positive re-appraisal of medieval
Christian–Jewish relations, suggesting that Christian–Jewish interaction in
northern Europe should be characterised as '*convivencia* in a minor key'
(p. 136). Another new overview is Theodore L. Steinberg, *Jews and
Judaism in the Middle Ages*, Westport, CT, 2008.

Overviews are also provided in *The New Cambridge Medieval History* by
Michael Toch, 'The Jews in Europe, 500–1050', vol. 1, ed. Paul Fouracre,
2005, 547–70; Robert Chazan, 'The Jews in Europe and the
Mediterranean Basin', vol. 4.1, ed. David Luscombe and Jonathan Riley-
Smith, 2004, 623–57; Kenneth R. Stow, 'The Church and the Jews',
vol. 5, ed. David Abulafia, 1999, 204–19.

Christoph Cluse (ed.), *The Jews of Europe in the Middle Ages (Tenth to
Fifteenth Centuries). Proceedings of the International Symposium held at
Speyer, 20–25 October 2002*, Turnhout, 2004 (Cluse) is invaluable for the
many excellent articles on different parts of Europe. Especially useful are
the contributions on Germany which make some of the newest German
research on Jewish history accessible to an English audience.

Jeremy Cohen (ed.), *Essential Papers on Judaism and Christianity in Conflict.
From Late Antiquity to the Reformation*, New York, 1991, brings together
some excellent articles covering a broad selection of topics.

Mark R. Cohen, *Under Crescent and Cross. The Jews in the Middle Ages*,
Princeton, NJ, 1994 explores the different experiences of Jews in the
Christian and Muslim world. A new edition with fresh material appeared in
2008.

Gavin Langmuir, *Toward a Definition of Antisemitism*, Berkeley, CA, 1990,
is a collection of Langmuir's articles on a wide range of topics, including
an assessment of how medieval historians in the past have dealt with
the history of the Jews and the relationship between anti-Judaism and
anti-Semitism.

Ivan G. Marcus, 'A Jewish–Christian Symbiosis: The Culture of Early Ashkenaz', in David Biale (ed.), *Cultures of the Jews. A New History*, New York, 2002, 449–516, gives an interesting assessment of the multiple ambiguities of Jewish–Christian interaction in northern Europe.

Michael A. Signer and John Van Engen (eds), *Jews and Christians in Twelfth-century Europe*, Notre Dame, IN, 2001, contains the papers of an important conference on Jewish–Christian relations which was held in Notre Dame in 1996.

Kenneth R. Stow, *Alienated Minority. The Jews of Medieval Latin Europe*, Cambridge, MA, 1992, gives a useful overview of Jewish life in the Middle Ages.

Diana Wood (ed.), *Christianity and Judaism*. Studies in Church History, 29, Oxford, 1992, publishes many interesting papers which were delivered at the 1991 summer and 1992 winter meetings of the Ecclesiastical History Society.

Israel J. Yuval, *Two Nations in Your Womb: Perceptions of Jews and Christians in Late Antiquity and the Middle Ages*, trans. Barbara Harshav and Jonathan Chipman, Berkeley, CA, 2006, provided the long awaited English translation of Yuval's provocative ideas about the reciprocal engagement of medieval Jews and Christians with each other in all manner of social and religious encounters.

A new study on Jewish women and families is Elisheva Baumgarten, *Mothers and Children. Jewish Family Life in Medieval Europe*, Princeton, NJ, 2004. Jonathan Chipman provides an English translation of Avraham Grossman, *Pious and Rebellious. Jewish Women in Medieval Europe*, Waltham, MA, 2004. See also Ivan G. Marcus, *Rituals of Childhood. Jewish Acculturation in Medieval Europe*, New Haven, CT, 1984.

Specific topics
Antecedents: developments before 1000

Bernard S. Bachrach, *Early Medieval Jewish Policy in Western Europe*, Minneapolis, MN, 1977, is a determined attempt to assess the position of the Jews in the early Middle Ages as positively as possible.

Jeremy Cohen, *Living Letters of the Law. Ideas of the Jew in Medieval Christianity*, Berkeley, CA, 1999, examines the genesis and reception of Augustine's witness theory throughout the Middle Ages.

Wolfram Drews, *The Unknown Neighbour. The Jew in the Thought of Isidore of Seville*, Leiden, 2006, is useful for the Visigothic period.

Paula Fredriksen, *Augustine and the Jews. A Christian Defense of Jews and Judaism*, New York, 2008, draws together her earlier articles on the special contribution by Augustine to the preservation of Jews and Judaism in Christendom.

John Gilchrist, 'The Canonistic Treatment of Jews in the Latin West in the Eleventh and Early Twelfth Centuries', *Zeitschrift der Savigny-Stiftung für Rechtsgeschichte Kanonistische Abteilung* 106 (1989), 70–106 and 'The Perception of Jews in the Canon Law in the Period of the First Two Crusades', *Jewish History* 3 (1988), 9–24 are an essential guide to understanding the development of canon-law measures concerning the Jews. They need to be studied in conjunction with the texts in Linder's *JRIL* and *JLSEMA*. John Watt continues the story in his 'Jews and Christians in the Gregorian *Decretals*', in Wood, *Christianity and Judaism*, 93–105.

Martin Goodman, *Rome and Jerusalem. The Clash of Ancient Civilisations*, London, 2007, is the best recent book on the relationship between Rome and the Jews.

Yuval's *Two Nations* (see under General reading) explores the many intricacies of the early rivalry between nascent Christianity and rabbinic Judaism. On this topic see also Peter Schäfer, *Jesus in the Talmud*, Princeton, NJ, 2007.

Germany

Michael Toch, *Die Juden im Mittelalterichen Reich*, Munich, 1998, gives a comprehensive bibliography of primary and secondary sources on the history of the Jews of medieval Germany which includes some items in English.

English translations of *Responsa* material include Irving A. Agus, *Urban Civilization in Pre-Crusade Europe. A Study of Organized Town-life in Northwestern Europe During the Tenth and Eleventh Centuries Based on the* Responsa *Literature*, 2 volumes, Leiden, 1965 and Agus, *Rabbi Meir of Rothenburg. His Life and His Works as Sources for the Religious, Legal, and Social History of the Jews of Germany in the Thirteenth Century*, two volumes, Philadelphia, PA, 1947; an abridged translation of the *Sefer Hasidim* can be found in Sholom A. Singer, *Medieval Jewish Mysticism. Book of the Pious*, Wheeling, IL, 1971; the vast literature on the Pietist Movement includes Peter Schäfer's contribution in Cluse as well as Ivan

Marcus's seminal study, *Piety and Society: The Jewish Pietists in Medieval Germany*, Leiden, 1981 and Haym Soloveitchik, 'Piety, Pietism and German Pietism: *Sefer Hasidim I* and the Influence of *Haside Ashkenaz*', *Jewish Quarterly Review* 92 (2002), 455–93 and 'Three Themes in the *Sefer Hasidim*', *Association for Jewish Studies Review* 1 (1976), 311–57; numerous references to the *Sefer Hasidim* occur in Baumgarten's *Mothers and Children*, Grossman's *Pious and Rebellious* and Fine's *Judaism in Practice from the Middle Ages* (see under General reading). On Jewish families see also Kenneth Stow, 'The Jewish Family in the Rhineland in the High Middle Ages: Form and Function', *American Historical Review* 92 (1987), 1085–1110; see also relevant sections of his *Alienated Minority*. Haym Soloveitchik's numerous articles shed light on how medieval Jews engaged with Jewish law, see his contribution to the Cluse volume on Jewish views on wine in Ashkenaz, and also 'Catastrophe and Halakhic Creativity: Ashkenaz – 1096, 1242, 1306 and 1298', *Jewish History* 12 (1998), 71–85 and 'Religious Law and Change: The Medieval Ashkenazic Example', *Association for Jewish Studies Review* 12 (1987) 205–21. Avraham Grossman, 'The Cultural and Social Background of Jewish Martyrdom in Germany in 1096', in A. Haverkamp (ed.), *Juden und Christen zur Zeit der Kreuzzüge*, Sigmaringen, 1999, 73–86 is also very useful.

Guido Kisch, *The Jews of Medieval Germany. A Study of Their Legal and Social Status*, 2nd edn, New York, 1970 should now be used alongside the new research by Professor Alfred Haverkamp and his many pupils throughout Germany. An example of the quality of this research is the exquisite annotated atlas edited by Haverkamp, *Geschichte der Juden im mittelalter von der Nordsee bis zu den Südalpen. Kommentiertes Kartenwerk*, 3 volumes [maps in vol. 3], Hanover, 2002. Most of this research is only accessible in German, but the Cluse volume contains some excellent articles on Speyer, Worms, Regensburg, Cologne and Würzburg.

Friedrich Lotter, 'Scope and Effectiveness of Imperial Jewry Law in the High Middle Ages', *Jewish History* 4 (1989), 31–58 should be studied in conjunction with Linder's *JLSEMA* to gain some understanding of imperial legislation concerning the Jews. See also Alexander Patschovsky, 'The Relationship between the Jews of Germany and the King (11th–14th Centuries). A European Comparison', in Alfred Haverkamp and Hanna Vollrath (eds), *England and Germany in the High Middle Ages*, London, 1996, 193–218.

Michael Toch 'The Formation of a Diaspora: The Settlement of Jews in the Medieval German *Reich*', *Aschkenas* 7 (1997), 55–78 is essential for understanding Jewish demography in Germany.

Useful for the Carolingian background to this legislation is Bat-Sheva Albert, '*Adversus Iudaeos* in the Carolingian Empire', in Ora Limor and Guy G. Stroumsa (eds), *Contra Iudaeos. Ancient and Medieval Polemics between Christians and Jews*, Tübingen, 1996, 119–42.

France

William C. Jordan, *The French Monarchy and the Jews. From Philip Augustus to the Last Capetians*, Philadelphia, PA, 1989 is the essential study for France. See also various papers in his volume of collected articles, *Ideology and Royal Power in Medieval France. Kingship, Crusades and the Jews*, Aldershot, 2001.

English versions of much of the legislation analysed by Jordan can be found in Chazan's *CSJMA*; Chazan's views are further explored in his *Medieval Jewry in Northern France. A Political and Social History*, Baltimore, MD, 1973; Paul Hyams's 1998 English translation of Rigord is available through the internet: http://web.search.cornell.edu/search?q= cache:qAcV3tt6LaYJ:falcon.arts.cornell.edu/prh3/408/texts/ Rigindex.html+rigord&access=p&output=xml_no_dtd&ie= UTF-8&client=default_frontend&proxystylesheet= default_frontend&oe=ISO-8859-1.

The vast literature on Rashi and the *Tosafists* includes Michael A. Signer, 'God's Love for Israel: Apologetic and Hermeneutical Strategies in Twelfth-century Biblical Exegesis', in Signer and Van Engen's *Jews and Christians in Twelfth-century Europe*, 123–49, relevant sections in Stow's *Alienated Minority*, relevant chapters in Jane Dammen McAuliffe, Barry D. Walfish and Joseph W. Goering, *With Reverence for the Word. Medieval Scriptural Exegesis in Judaism, Christianity, and Islam*, Oxford, 2003; Erwin J. Rosenthal, 'The Study of the Bible in Medieval Judaism', *The Cambridge History of the Bible*, vol. 2, Cambridge, 1969, 252–79 and the relevant chapters in *The New Cambridge History of the Bible*, vol. 2, ed. Richard Marsden and E. Ann Matter, forthcoming. See also Haym Soloveitchik's, 'Catastrophe and Halakhic Creativity: Ashkenaz – 1096, 1242, 1306 and 1298', *Jewish History* 12 (1998), 71–85 and 'Religious Law and Change: The Medieval Ashkenazic Example', *Association for Jewish Studies Review* 12 (1987) 205–21.

Many of the conclusions presented by Norman Golb in his *The Jews in Medieval Normandy. A Social and Intellectual History*, Cambridge, 1998 have received a sceptical response.

Gérard Nahon's articles on Zarfat in Cluse's volume and in Signer and Van Engen's *Jews and Christians* offer useful perspectives.

Kenneth R. Stow, *Jewish dogs. An Image and Its Importance*, Stanford, CA, 2006, offers valuable insights into the writings of Rigord and William the Breton.

England

Joseph Jacobs (ed.), *The Jews of Angevin England*, New York, 1893; repr. New York, 1977 is very dated, but it provides a wealth of source material concerning the Jews of England. Some of the material can now be found in Chazan's *CSJMA* and the Marcus collection. Jacobs includes some of the rabbinical material; a collection of English *Responsa* material is available in a German translation by Hans-Georg von Mutius, *Rechtsentscheide Mittelalterlicher Englischer Rabbinen*, Judentum und Umwelt, 60, Frankfurt am Main, 1995. M.D. Davis, *Hebrew Deeds of English Jews before 1290*, London, 1888, provides useful English summaries of the deeds (the so-called *shetaroth*) issued by the Jewish courts. For Jewish cultural activities see also Cecil Roth, *The Intellectual Activities of Medieval English Jewry*, The British Academy, Supplemental Papers, 8, London, [1950] and Susan L. Einbinder, 'Meir b. Elijah of Norwich: Persecution and Poetry among Medieval Jews', *Journal of Medieval History* 26 (2000), 145–62.

The standard book on English Jewry remains H.G. Richardson, *The English Jewry under Angevin Kings*, London, 1960 but this needs to be supplemented by the very useful collection by Patricia Skinner (ed.), *Jews in Medieval Britain*, Woodbridge, 2003 and the many excellent articles by Robert Stacey, including:

Robert Stacey, 'The Conversion of Jews to Christianity in Thirteenth-century England', *Speculum* 67 (1992), 263–83; 'The English Jews under Henry III', in Skinner, *Jews in Medieval Britain*, 41–54; 'Jewish Lending and the Medieval Economy', in R.H. Britnell and B.M.S. Campbell (eds), *A Commercialising Economy. England 1086 to c. 1300*, Manchester, 1995, 78–101; 'Jews and Christians in Twelfth-century England: Some Dynamics of a Changing Relationship', in Signer and Van Engen, *Jews and Christians in Twelfth-century Europe*, 340–54; 'Recent Work on

Medieval English Jewish History', *Jewish History* 2 (1987), 61–72; 'Royal Taxation and the Social Structure of Medieval Anglo-Jewry: The Tallages of 1239–1242', *Hebrew Union College Annual* 56 (1985), 175–249; '1240–1260: A Watershed in Anglo-Jewish Relations?', *Bulletin of the Institute of Historical Research* 61 (1988), 135–50.

R.B. Dobson, *The Jews of Medieval York and the Massacre of March 1190*, Borthwick Papers, 45, York, 1974, gives a full account of the massacre in York in 1190; Michael J. Kennedy, ' "Faith in One God Flowed over You from the Jews, the Sons of the Patriarchs and the Prophets": William of Newburgh's Writings on Anti-Jewish Violence', *Anglo-Norman Studies* 25 (2003), 139–52 is illuminating on William of Newburgh's position on the affair.

Sophia Menache, 'Matthew Paris's Attitude toward Anglo-Jewry', *Journal of Medieval History* 23 (1997), 139–62.

Robin R. Mundill, *England's Jewish Solution. Experiment and Expulsion, 1262–1290*, Cambridge, 1998, is essential reading for the final years of the presence of Jews in medieval England. New is Richard Huscroft, *Expulsion, England's Jewish Solution: Edward I and the Jews*, Stroud, 2006.

Zefira E. Rokeah, 'Money and the Hangman in late-thirteenth-century England: Jews, Christians and Coinage Offenses Alleged and Real', *Jewish Historical Studies* 31 (1988–90), 83–109; 32 (1990–2), 159–218 is essential reading on the coin-clipping episode.

John A. Watt, 'The Jews, the Law, and the Church: The Concept of Jewish Serfdom in Thirteenth-century England', in D. Wood (ed.), *The Church and Sovereignty*, Studies in Church History, subsidia, 9, 1992, 153–72, is important for understanding the nature of Jewish service.

The Latin Mediterranean

The literature is vast on the Jews of Christian Iberia. Yitzhak Baer, *A History of the Jews in Christian Spain*. Volume 1: *From the Age of Reconquest to the Fourteenth Century*, trans. Louis Schoffman with introduction by Benjamin R. Gampel, Philadelphia, PA, 1992, remains a classic.

Particularly useful recent publications for understanding the interaction between Jews and their new Christian framework are: Lucy K. Pick, *Conflict and Co-existence: Archbishop Rodrigo and the Muslims and Jews of Medieval Spain*, Ann Arbor, MI, 2004 and Jonathan Ray, *The Sephardic Frontier. The Reconquista and the Jewish Community in Medieval Iberia*,

Ithaca, NY, 2006. See also the relevant contributions to the Cluse volume and Elka Klein, *Jews, Christian Society and Royal Power in Medieval Barcelona*, Ann Arbor, MI, 2006.

An English translation of Alfonso X's *Siete Partidas* can be found in Samuel Parsons Scott (trans.) and Robert I. Burns (ed.), *Las Siete Partidas*, five volumes, Philadelphia, PA, 2001; see also Dwayne E. Carpenter, *Alfonso X and the Jews: An Edition of and Commentary on* Siete Partidas 7.24 '*De los judíos*', Berkeley, CA, 1986. James F. Powers provides an English translation of the code of Cuenca: *The Code of Cuenca. Municipal Law on the Twelfth-century Castilian Frontier*, Philadelphia, PA, 2000.

For southern France see Jordan, *The French Monarchy and the Jews* as well as Danièle Iancu-Agou's contribution to the Cluse volume on Provence. See also Richard W. Emery, *The Jews of Perpignan in the Thirteenth Century*, New York, 1959 and the interesting slant on moneylending given in Joseph Shatzmiller, *Shylock Reconsidered. Jews, Moneylending, and Medieval Society*, Berkeley, CA, 1990.

On Sicily much of the secondary material is in Italian, but see the classic work by Cecil Roth, *The History of the Jews of Italy*, Philadelphia, PA, 1946. See also David Abulafia, 'The Jews of Sicily and Southern Italy: Economic Activity', in Michael Toch (ed.), *Wirtschaftsgeschichte der mittelalterlichen Juden*, Oldenbourg, 2008, 49–62 and 'Ethnic Variety and Its Implications: Frederick II's Relations with Jews and Muslims', in W. Tronzo (ed.), *Intellectual Life at the Court of Frederick II Hohenstaufen*, Studies in the History of Art, 44, Center for Advanced Study in the Visual Arts, Symposium Papers xxiv, National Gallery of Art, Washington, DC, 1994, 213–24, the relevant chapters in B.D. Cooperman and B. Garvin, *The Jews of Italy: Memory and Identity*, College Park, MD, 2001 and Shlomo Simonsohn's contribution in the Cluse volume.

On Jewish culture in the Latin Mediterranean, see relevant chapters in Daniel H. Frank and Oliver Leamon (eds), *The Cambridge Companion to Medieval Jewish Philosophy*, Cambridge, 2003 and Colette Sirat, *A History of Jewish Philosophy in the Middle Ages*, Cambridge, 1985. See Bernard Septimus, *Hispano-Jewish Culture in Transition. The Career and Controversies of Ramah*, Cambridge, MA, 1982 and Harvey J. Hames, *Like Angels on Jacob's Ladder. Abraham Abulafia, the Franciscans and Joachimism*, Albany, NY, 2007 for more information on Meir ha-Levi Abulafia and Abraham Abulafia and their respective milieux. On Jewish responses to Christianity, see Robert Chazan, *Fashioning Jewish Identity in*

Medieval Western Christendom, Cambridge, 2004 and Hanne Trautner-Kromann, *Shield and Sword. Jewish Polemics against Christians in France and Spain from 1100–1500*, Tübingen, 1993. Examples of Jewish poetry of Muslim and Christian Spain can be found in T. Carmi, *The Penguin Book of Hebrew Verse*, Harmondsworth, 1981 and David Goldstein (trans.) *The Jewish Poets of Spain, 900–1250*, Harmondsworth, 1971.

Jewish experience of the crusades

A brief overview is offered by Anna Sapir Abulafia, 'Hebrew Sources' and 'Jews and the Crusades' in A.V. Murray (ed.), *Crusades, An Encyclopedia*, vol. 2, Santa Barbara, CA, 2006, 561–3 and 679–83. Her edited volume, *Religious Violence between Christians and Jews. Medieval Roots, Modern Perspectives*, Basingstoke, 2002, contains useful articles on many aspects of the crusades, as does Alfred Haverkamp (ed.), *Juden und Christen zur Zeit der Kreuzzüge*, Sigmaringen, 1999. See Christopher Tyerman, *God's War. A New History of the Crusades*, London, 2006 for a new general history of the crusades.

The most accessible translation of the Hebrew chronicles of the First and Second Crusades remains Shlomo Eidelberg (ed.), *The Jews and the Crusaders. The Hebrew Chronicles of the First and Second Crusades*, Madison, WI, 1977; translations of two of the three chronicles of the First Crusade appear in Robert Chazan, *European Jewry and the First Crusade*, Berkeley, CA, 1987; see also source material for these and other crusades in *CSJMA* and the Marcus source collection and Cecil Roth, 'A Hebrew Elegy on the York Martyrs of 1190', *Transactions of the Jewish Historical Society of England*, vol. 16 (1945–1951), 213–20. The definitive edition of the Hebrew chronicles of the First Crusade is *Hebräische Berichte über die Judenverfolgungen während des Ersten Kreuzzugs*, ed. Eva Haverkamp. Monumenta Germaniae Historica, Hebräische Texte aus dem Mittelalterlichen Deutschland, 1, Hanover, 2005, which includes a German translation of the texts.

The electronic translation of William of Newburgh, which includes the sections on the attacks of 1189–90, by Joseph Stevenson (*The Church Historians of England*, vol. 4.2, London, 1856), ed. Scott McLetchie (1999) can be found on http://www.fordham.edu/halsall/basis/williamofnewburgh-intro.html.

The vast literature includes:

Anna Sapir Abulafia, 'The Interrelationship between the Hebrew Chronicles on the First Crusade', and 'Invectives against Christianity in the Hebrew Chronicles of the First Crusade', in idem, *Christians and Jews in Dispute. Disputational Literature and the Rise of Anti-Judaism in the West (c. 1000–1150)*, Aldershot, 1998, XVII and XVIII.

Robert Chazan, *European Jewry and the First Crusade*, Berkeley, CA, 1987 and *God, Humanity and History. The Hebrew First Crusade Narratives*, Berkeley, CA, 2000.

Jeremy Cohen, *Sanctifying the Name of God. Jewish Martyrs and Jewish Memories of the First Crusade*, Philadelphia, PA, 2004 and ' "Witness of Our Redemption": The Jews in the Crusading Theology of Bernard of Clairvaux', in B.-S. Albert *et al.*, (eds), *Medieval Studies in Honour of Avrom Saltman*, Ramat-Gan, 1995, 67–81.

Susan Einbinder, 'Signs of Romance: Hebrew Prose and the Twelfth-century Renaissance', in Signer and Van Engen (eds), *Jews and Christians in Twelfth-century Europe*, Notre Dame, IN, 2001, 221–33.

Simha Goldin, *The Ways of Jewish Martyrdom*, trans. Yigdal Levin, translation ed. C. Michael Copeland, Turnhout, 2008.

Ivan G. Marcus, 'From Politics to Martyrdom: Shifting Paradigms in the Hebrew Narratives of the 1096 Crusade Riots', in J. Cohen (ed.), *Essential Papers on Judaism and Christianity in Conflict. From Late Antiquity to the Reformation*, New York, 1991, 469–83.

Jonathan Riley-Smith, 'The First Crusade and Persecution of the Jews', in W.J. Sheils (ed.), *Persecution and Toleration*, Studies in Church History, 21, Oxford, 1984, 51–72.

Shmuel Shepkaru, *Jewish Martyrs in the Pagan and Christian Worlds*, Cambridge, 2006.

Robert C. Stacey, 'Crusades, Martyrdoms and the Jews of Norman England, 1096–1190', in A. Haverkamp (ed.), *Juden und Christen zur Zeit der Kreuzzüge*, 233–51.

Kenneth Stow, 'Conversion, Apostasy, and Apprehensiveness: Emicho of Flonheim and the Fear of Jews in the Twelfth Century', *Speculum* 76 (2001), 911–33.

Israel J. Yuval's ideas on the impact of Jewish self-martyrdom on the emergence of blood libels can be found in his, *Two Nations* (see under General works) and in his 'Vengeance and Damnation, Blood and

Defamation: From Jewish Martyrdom to Blood-libel Accusations', *Zion* 58 (1993), 33–90 [Hebrew with English summary] and his follow-up article and the many responses to this thesis in *Zion* 59 (1994) [Hebrew with English summaries].

Anti-Jewish libels

Sources can be found in Chazan's *CSJMA*, Marcus's collection and Susan Einbinder, 'The Jewish Martyrs of Blois', in Thomas Head (ed.), *Medieval Hagiography. An Anthology*, New York, 2000, 537–60, 'The Troyes Laments: Jewish Martyrology in Hebrew and Old French', *Viator* 30 (1999), 201–30 and her book listed below. See also August Jessopp and Montague Rhodes James (ed. and trans.), *The Life and Miracles of St. William of Norwich*, Cambridge, 1896.

The vast literature includes:

Anthony Bale, 'Fictions of Judaism in England before 1290', in Patricia Skinner (ed.), *Jews in Medieval Britain*, Woodbridge, 2003, 129–44 is very useful for the English context. See also his *The Jew in the Medieval Book. English Antisemitism, 1350–1500*, Cambridge, 2006, which provides useful information for the earlier period.

Jeffrey Cohen, 'The Flow of Blood in Medieval Norwich', *Speculum* 79 (2004), 26–65 offers new ideas on the context of the ritual-murder allegation in Norwich.

Susan Einbinder, *Beautiful Death. Jewish Poetry and Martyrdom in Medieval France*, Princeton, NJ, 2002, is essential reading for gauging Jewish responses to the libels. The book contains numerous source extracts in translation.

Elliott Horowitz, *Reckless Rites. Purim and the Legacy of Jewish Violence*, Princeton, NJ, 2006, focuses on the festival of Purim.

Gavin Langmuir's 'Thomas of Monmouth: Detector of Ritual Murder', 'The Knight's Tale of Young Hugh of Lincoln', 'Ritual Cannibalism', 'Historiographic Crucifixion', in his collection *Toward a Definition of Antisemitism*, Berkeley, CA, 1990, 209–98 remain essential reading.

John M. McCulloh, 'Jewish Ritual Murder: William of Norwich, Thomas of Monmouth and the Early Disseminations of the Myth', *Speculum* 72 (1997), 698–740 is a seminal re-interpretation of Langmuir's idea that Thomas of Monmouth 'invented' ritual murder.

Miri Rubin, *Gentile Tales. The Narrative Assault on Late Medieval Jews*, Philadelphia, PA, 1999 is essential reading for host-desecration libels.

Jennifer Shea, 'Adgar's *Gracial*', *Journal of Medieval History* 33 (2007), 181–96 looks at the impact of vernacular versions of the Marian miracle tales.

The intriguing re-assessments of the evidence concerning Blois by Kenneth R. Stow, *Jewish Dogs. An Image and Its Importance*, Stanford, CA, 2006, are as interesting as they are problematic.

For Israel Yuval's essential works see those listed in the crusade section. See also his ' "They Tell Lies: You Ate the Man": Jewish Reactions to Ritual-Murder Accusations', in Anna Sapir Abulafia (ed.), *Religious Violence between Christians and Jews. Medieval Roots, Modern Perspectives*, London, 2002, 86–106.

Encounters between Christians and Jews
Primary source material

David Berger (ed. and trans.), *The Jewish–Christian Debate in the High Middle Ages. A Critical Edition of the* Nizzahon Vetus, Philadelphia, PA, 1979 translates the *Nizzahon Vetus*, which provides a wealth of material concerning Jewish views of Christianity. Berger also provides copious references to all relevant medieval Christian–Jewish and Jewish–Christian disputations. Hanne Trautner-Kromann, *Shield and Sword. Jewish Polemics against Christians in France and Spain from 1100–1500*, Tübingen, 1993, contains many useful extracts of Hebrew polemical material of Sefarad, including some material from Zarfat. See also Joseph Kimhi, *Book of the Covenant*, trans. Frank Talmage, Toronto, 1972. Other useful material can be found in Chazan's *CSJMA* and Marcus's collection. The translation of Abelard's *Dialogue between a Christian and a Jew and a Philosopher*, in Peter Abelard, *Collationes*, ed. and trans. John Marenbon and Giovanni Orlandi, Oxford, 2001, gives interesting insights into Abelard's view of Jews and Judaism, including Jewish moneylending. Odo of Tournai, *On Original Sin, and A Disputation with the Jew, Leo, Concerning the Advent of Christ, Son of God: Two Theological Treatises*, trans. Irvin M. Resnick, Philadelphia, PA, 1994, is an example of an early twelfth-century Christian polemic against Judaism. Hyam Maccoby (ed. and trans.), *Judaism on Trial. Jewish–Christian Disputations in the Middle Ages*, London, 1982, produces translations of Latin and Hebrew reports of the Talmud trials in

Paris (1240) and Barcelona (1263). See also source material cited in other sections.

For art-historical material see Sara Lipton, *Images of Intolerance. The Representation of Jews and Judaism in the* Bible moralisée, Berkeley, CA, 1999, Ruth Mellinkoff, *Outcasts: Signs of Otherness in Northern European Art of the Later Middle Ages*, two volumes, Berkeley, CA, 1993, Debra H. Strickland, *Saracens, Demons, and Jews. Making Monsters in Medieval Art*, Princeton, NJ, 2003 and Heinz Schreckenberg, *The Jews in Christian Art*, London, 1996. The companion volume to Cluse's *Jews of Europe* (see General reading) catalogue of the exhibition 'The Jews of Europe in the Middle Ages', 19 November 2004 to 20 March 2005 in Speyer and 23–28 April 2005 in Berlin, ed. Historisches Museum der Pfalz, Speyer, provides excellent pictorial material with a very useful running commentary.

Secondary source material

Anna Sapir Abulafia, *Christians and Jews in Dispute. Disputational Literature and the Rise of Anti-Judaism in the West (c. 1000–1150)*, Aldershot, 1998, contains articles on Christian–Jewish polemics and the Hebrew chronicles of the First Crusade. Her *Christians and Jews in the Twelfth-century Renaissance*, London, 1995, investigates how Christian scholars of the Twelfth-century Renaissance used reason as a weapon against Jews. Her 'The Bible in Jewish–Christian Dialogue', in Richard Marsden and E. Ann Matter (eds), *The New Cambridge History of the Bible*, forthcoming, explores the encounter between Christians and Jews in biblical exegesis, disputations and liturgy. Other relevant articles include: 'The Conquest of Jerusalem: Joachim of Fiore and the Jews', in M. Bull and N. Housley (eds), *The Experience of Crusading*, vol. 1: *Western Approaches*, Cambridge and New York, 2003, 127–46, 'Twelfth-century Christian Expectations of Jewish Conversion: A Case Study of Peter of Blois', *Aschkenas* 8 (1998), 45–70 and 'Walter of Châtillon: A Twelfth-century Poet's Engagement with Jews', *Journal of Medieval History* 31 (2005), 265–86.

Robert Chazan, *Barcelona and Beyond. The Disputation of 1263 and Its Aftermath*, Berkeley, CA, 1992 and *Daggers of Faith. Thirteenth-century Christian Missionizing and Jewish Response*, Berkeley, CA, 1989, concern the Barcelona disputation. His *Fashioning Jewish Identity in Medieval Western Christendom*, Cambridge, 2004, explores the responses of a number of key Jewish scholars of late-twelfth- and thirteenth-century Sefarad to the challenges posed by Christian scholasticism.

Jeremy Cohen, *The Friars and the Jews. The Evolution of Medieval Anti-Judaism*, 1982, argues that the major shift in Christian attitudes towards Jews should be sought in the thirteenth century when Christians discovered the Talmud. His, 'The Jews as the Killers of Christ in the Latin Tradition, from Augustine to the Friars', *Traditio* 39 (1983), 1–27 and his *Christ Killers. The Jews and the Passion from the Bible to the Screen*, Oxford, 2007, discuss the evolution of the accusation against the Jews of killing Christ.

Lawrence E. Frizzell and J. Frank Henderson, 'Jews and Judaism in the Medieval Latin Liturgy', in Thomas J. Heffermann and E. Ann Matter (eds), *The Liturgy of the Medieval Church*, Kalamazoo, MI, 2001, 187–211 provides an overview of references to Jews and Judaism in Christian liturgy.

Amos Funkenstein, 'Basic Types of Christian Anti-Jewish Polemics in the Late Middle Ages', *Viator* 2 (1971), 373–82, is a seminal article on the development of Christian–Jewish polemics.

Deborah Goodwin, *'Take Hold of the Robe of a Jew'. Herbert of Bosham's Christian Hebraism*, Leiden, 2006, is important for the study of twelfth-century Christian Hebraism.

Harvey J. Hames, *The Art of Conversion. Christianity and Kabbalah in the Thirteenth Century*, Leiden, 2000, is a perceptive study of Ramon Llull and his relations with Jews.

Dominique Iogna-Prat, *Order and Exclusion. Cluny and Christendom Face Heresy, Judaism and Islam*, trans. Graham R. Edwards, Ithaca, NY, 2002, explores the increasing exclusivity of Christian culture in the eleventh and twelfth centuries.

Jacob Katz, *Exclusiveness and Tolerance. Jewish–Gentile Relations in Medieval and Modern Times*, Oxford, 1961, remains a classic.

Steven F. Kruger, *The Spectral Jew. Conversion and Embodiment in Medieval Europe*, Minneapolis, MN, 2006, re-interprets the works of central figures of the Christian–Jewish debate through the prism of sexuality.

Lester K. Little, *Religious Poverty and the Profit Economy in Medieval Europe*, London, 1978, gives an interesting analysis of ideas about usury within the developing economies of medieval Europe and its impact on Christian attitudes towards Jews.

Ivan G. Marcus, 'A Jewish–Christian Symbiosis: The Culture of Early Ashkenaz, in David Biale (ed.), *Cultures of the Jews. A New History*, New York, 2002, 461–72 offers perceptive insights into medieval Jewish–Christian interactions.

David Nirenberg, *Communities of Violence. Persecution of Minorities in the Middle Ages*, Princeton, NJ, 1996, offers an interesting perspective on the role of violence in Christian–Jewish relations.

Jay Rubenstein, *Guibert of Nogent. Portrait of a Medieval Mind*, London, 2002, also explores Guibert's fraught relationship to Jews and Judaism.

Beryl Smalley, *The Study of the Bible in the Middle Ages*, 3rd edn, Oxford, 1983, stimulated the study of Christian Hebraism.

Michael Signer, 'Thirteenth-century Christian Hebraism: The *Expositio* on Canticles in MS. VAT. Lat. 1053', in D. Blumenthal (ed.), *Approaches to Judaism in Medieval Times*, vol. 3, Atlanta, GA, 1988, 89–100 sheds light on Christian Hebraism.

Haym Soloveitchik, 'Pawnbroking: A Study in *Ribbit* and of the Halakah in Exile', *Proceedings of the American Academy for Jewish Research* 38–9 (1970–1), 203–68 is essential reading for Jewish ideas on moneylending.

Kenneth R. Stow, 'Papal and Royal Attitudes toward Jewish Lending in the Thirteenth Century', *Association for Jewish Studies Review* 6 (1981), 161–83 is essential reading on papal views on Jewish usury.

John Tolan, *Petrus Alfonsi and His Medieval Readers*, Gainesville, FL, 1993 gives a good overview of Alfonsi's role in the Christian–Jewish debate and his role in transmitting the knowledge of Sefarad to northern Europe.

John A. Watt, 'Grosseteste and the Jews: A Commentary on Letter V', in M. O'Carroll (ed.), *Robert Grosseteste and the Beginnings of a British Theological Tradition. Papers Delivered at the* Grosseteste Colloquium *Held at Greyfriars, Oxford on 3rd July 2002*, Rome, 2003, 201–16, is very useful to understanding Christian ideas on usury. His 'Parisian Theologians and the Jews: Peter Lombard and Peter Cantor', in P. Biller and B. Dobson (eds), *The Medieval Church: Universities, Heresy, and the Religious Life. Essays in Honour of Gordon Leff*, Woodbridge, 1999, 55–76 offers interesting perspectives on ideas concerning Jewish service and guilt.

Israel J. Yuval, *Two Nations in Your Womb: perceptions of Jews and Christians in Late Antiquity and the Middle Ages*, trans. Barbara Harshav and Jonathan Chipman, Berkeley, CA, 2006, [trans. from Hebrew], explores Jewish–Christian interaction in many different spheres.

Index

biblical, xiii, 3, 220, 11, 75, 76, 151,
153, 154, 181, 200, 202, 208, 209,
213, 218, 219; see also post-biblical
Black Death, 45, 46, 50
Blanche of Castile, 71, 77, 79, 81
Blanche, Countess of Champagne, 66,
67, 73, 74
blaspheme, blasphemous, blasphemy, 28,
74, 81, 93, 127, 150, 173, 210, 211
Blois, 62, 63, 103, 160, 182–4, 201
blood, 67, 69, 91, 94, 140, 146, 151,
152, 154, 167, 170, 172, 176, 178,
179, 182, 185, 186, 188, 195, 198,
218; see also blood libel
blood libel(s), 37, 45, 52, 57, 167, 170,
179, 182, 185, 186, 217
Blumenkranz, Bernhard, 66
Bohemund of Taranto, 138
Bologna, 26, 204, 205
bond(s), 95, 97, 98, 101, 160
Boniface VIII, Pope, 84, 188
Bonn, 38, 156
Boppard, 184
Bourges, 63
Bouvines, Battle of, 68
boy(s), see child, children
boycotting of Jews, 99
Bray-sur-Seine, 180–2
Brie-Comte-Robert, 180–2
Bristol, 90, 101, 104
Brittany, 78, 82
Bronisch, Alexander, 27, 29
Brunhild, Queen of the Franks, 22, 29
Bungay, 89
Burchard of Worms, 26, 51, 204,
Decretum, 26, 29, 51
Burgos, 125
Burgundy, 65, 73, 74, 136
Bury St Edmunds, 89, 90, 91, 92, 93, 95,
99, 159, 170, 175, 176, 178, 189
butchers, 39, 96, 113, 123
Byzantium, 12, 19, 129,

Cahors, Cahorsins, 102, 216
Cain, 6, 7,

Calixtus II, Pope, 50
call, 122, 123, 124; see also Jewish
quarter
Callinicum, 11, 13
Cambridge, 89, 104
cannibalism, 178, 179, 184, 185
canon(s) (Augustinian), 93, 172, 219
canon(s), canonical, 25, 26, 27, 28, 29,
30, 38, 41, 50, 51, 52, 55, 99, 100,
120, 215, 223
canon law, lawyer(s), xi, 19, 25, 51, 64,
77, 119, 121, 177, 198, 204, 205
canonists, 64, 204, 215
Canterbury, 19, 90, 99, 101, 102, 151,
176, 189, 214
Cantigas de Santa Maria, 121, 172, 173,
174
Capetian(s), 61, 71, 72, 77, 80, 83, 84,
128
Carolingian, 197, 205
Carpenter, Dwayne, 121
Castile, Castilian, 109, 110, 112, 113,
114, 115, 116, 118, 119, 122, 124,
127, 222
castle(s), 72, 89, 92, 95, 159, 160, 169
Catalonia, Catalan, 83, 110, 122, 126,
127, 129, 211
Cathar(s), 71, 128
cathedral, 41, 44, 46, 49, 63, 92, 116,
173, 194
Cerdagne, 83, 84, 127
Châlons, 72
Champagne, 62, 63, 65, 66, 67, 70,
72–4, 75, 76, 78, 82, 83, 138, 180,
184, 187; fairs, 72
Charlemagne, 128
Charles I of Anjou, 77, 78, 81, 129
Charles II of Anjou, 81, 82, 83, 129
Charles IV, King of France, 84
Charles VI, King of France, 84
Charles IV, Emperor, 46
charoset, 97
charter(s), 38, 41, 42, 43, 45, 49, 51, 52,
53, 54, 55, 62, 66, 91, 95, 118, 148,
185

Mishna(ic), 13
monasticism, monastic, 19, 62, 67, 84,
135, 136, 138, 205
moneychangers, moneychanging, 72,
88–9
moneyers, 89, 90
moneylender(s), moneylending, 40, 49,
51, 62, 63, 66, 67, 68, 69, 70, 72, 73,
74, 78, 79, 81, 82, 88, 89, 90–3, 94,
96, 97, 98, 99, 102, 113, 117, 119,
128, 129, 158, 159, 160, 161, 173,
176, 178, 180, 183, 213, 214, 215,
216, 221; see also usury
Montpellier, 83, 127, 206
Morella, 112
Moses of Coucy, 76, 81
Moses of York, 160
Mundill, Robin, 102
Murcia, 110
Muslim(s), xi, 28, 51, 84, 109, 110, 111,
112, 114, 115, 116, 117, 118, 122,
126, 127, 128, 129, 135, 139, 142,
150, 156, 211, 222; see also Islam,
Saracen(s)

Nachmanides, 126, 127, 128, 211
Nahon, Gérard, 66
Naples, 20
Narbonne, 79, 80, 83, 128, 129, 170,
210, 215, 223
Navarre, 82, 83, 84, 109, 110
Ne Iudei administratorio, 25
Nebuchadnezzar, 9, 194, 195, 200
Neuss, 38, 184
Nevers, 67, 73, 82
Newcastle upon Tyne, 100
Nicholas III, Pope, 127
Ninth of Av, 23
Nirenberg, David, 190n. 10, 197,
201
Nizzahon Vetus ('Old Polemic'), 182,
202
Noah, 196
non-retention of Jews, agreement on, 67,
70, 73, 80

Norman, 89, 92, 129, 169, 171, 175
Normandy, 61, 62, 65, 66, 69, 76, 91,
92, 97, 137, 138, 158, 200
Northampton, 89, 101
Norwich, 89, 90, 92, 93, 95, 97, 103,
104, 159, 169–70, 171, 175, 178,
182
Notre Dame, 63, 64, 65
Nottingham, 98, 101
Nuremberg, 40

O'Callaghan, Joseph, 119
Oberwesel, 186
Odo, Ysagoge in Theologiam, 219
Odo of Cambrai, Disputation with a Jew,
209
Oral Law, 13
Original Sin, 5
Orléanais, 138
Orléans, 63, 76
Ospringe, 159
Otto I, Emperor, 37, 41
Otto II, Emperor, 41
Otto of Brunswick, 68
Oxford, 89, 98, 99, 206

Pagan(s), xi, 5, 6, 8, 12, 15, 20, 40, 42,
194
Palatinate, 39
Palermo, 21
Palestina, 11
Papacy, see Pope(s), papal
Paris, Parisian, 56, 61, 63, 64, 65, 70,
74, 76, 77, 80, 81, 82, 98, 179,
188, 195, 205, 206, 207, 211,
219, 223
Parkes, James, 168
Passion, 93, 94, 144, 152, 156, 157, 167,
176, 195, 197, 214
Passion Sunday, 176
Passover, 7, 16, 97, 169, 170, 177, 178,
179, 182, 187, 188, 200, 214
Paul Christian, 127, 211
Paul, St, Pauline, 7, 8, 15, 16, 22, 25, 26,
28, 30, 140, 172, 208

Soissons, 72
Solomon bar Simson, 142, 143, 146, see also Hebrew crusade chronicles
Solomon ben Isaac, see Rashi
Soloveitchik, Haym, 40, 47, 57, 72, 215
Song of Songs, 93, 94, 97, 217–9
Southern France, 62, 109, 110, 127, 128–9, 140
Spain, 28, 29, 37, 57, 109, 110, 111, 115, 116, 120, 124, 125, 128, 139, 140, 143, 189, 197, 201, 205; see also Iberia and Mediterranean, Latin
Speyer, 38, 41, 42, 43–5, 46, 48, 49, 51, 52, 53, 142, 148, 184
spirituality, 136, 138, 145
St Edmund, 91, 175
St Emmeram monastery, Regensburg, 49
St Peter's Gloucester, 176–7
St Victor, school of, see school(s)
Stacey, Robert, 89, 1001, 101, 102, 103, 190n. 10
Stamford, 90, 93, 95, 159
Statute of the Jewry, 100, 101–2
Stephen, King of England, 89, 90, 92, 96, 169
Stephen Harding, 219
Stephen Langton, 99, 100
Stephen, St, 11
stigmata, 156
Stow, Kenneth, 166 n. 47, 215
Swabia, 39
Schwabenspiegel, 55
synagogue(s), 11, 12, 13, 14, 20, 21, 25, 43, 44, 45, 46, 47, 48, 49, 62, 63, 64, 66, 74, 94, 96, 97, 98, 99, 100, 101, 113, 114, 118, 121, 123, 124, 140, 148, 151, 173, 211
Synod of Vienna, 48, 202

tabula, 98, 99, 100, 102, see also Jewish badge
Tagus, 109
taifas, 109, 110
tallage(s), 66, 73, 95, 97, 98, 100, 101

Talmud, Talmudic, 24, 47, 56, 57, 75, 76, 80, 81, 96, 125, 127, 146, 185, 188, 210–2, 223
Tam, see Jacob ben Meir
tax(es), taxation paid by Jews, xi, 10, 35, 41, 42, 49, 53, 54, 56, 61, 62, 66, 68, 73, 82, 90, 94, 95, 97, 98, 102, 104, 111, 112, 114, 115, 118, 120, 123, 125, 128, 214, 215, paid by others, 82, 83, 97, 111, 112
temple(s), 9, 10, 12; Jewish Temple, 3, 147, 154, 157, 183, 208; First Temple, 9, 200; Second Temple, 3, 8–12, 24, 146, 168; Temple of Jupiter, 10
Terracina, 21
Teruel, 116, 117, 118
Testimonium veritatis, see Witness, 5
Tetragrammaton, 208
Theobald, Count of Blois, 63, 182–4
Theobald, III, Count of Champagne, 65
Theobald IV, Count of Champagne, 73, 78
Theodosius I, the Great, 11, 13
Theodosius II, 12, 14, 168; Theodosian Code, 12, 13, 24, 25, 27, 205
theologian(s), 4, 11, 24, 64, 151, 198, 206, 207, 213, 215
theology, theological, xii, xiii, 20, 21, 22, 24, 26, 27, 31, 94, 98, 100, 111, 122, 123, 124, 129, 140, 144, 145, 161, 167, 176, 197, 202, 203, 205, 206, 209, 212, 219, 221, 222
Theophilus, 173
Thetford, 89, 159
Thomas Aquinas, 126, 206, 214, *Summa Theologica*, 206
Thomas Becket, 219
Thomas Chobham, 98, 100, 195
Thomas of Cantimpré, 186
Thomas of Monmouth, 103, 169–70, 175; *Life of William of Norwich*, 103, 169, 170, 175
Thuringia, 39

CPSIA information can be obtained
at www.ICGtesting.com
Printed in the USA
FSOW02n0604161216
28585FS